ISBN: 9781313454001

Published by:
HardPress Publishing
8345 NW 66TH ST #2561
MIAMI FL 33166-2626

Email: info@hardpress.net
Web: http://www.hardpress.net

HISTORICAL SKETCH

OF

SALEM.

1626. 1879.

BY

CHAS. S. OSGOOD AND H. M. BATCHELDER.

SALEM:
ESSEX INSTITUTE.
1879.

A. 80728

WRIGHT & POTTER PRINTING COMPANY, 79 MILK STREET, BOSTON.

To the Memory

OF

EDWARD AUGUSTUS HOLYOKE, M.D., LL.D.,

AND HIS ASSOCIATES

IN THE

ORGANIZATION OF THE ESSEX HISTORICAL SOCIETY,

This Volume

IS GRATEFULLY INSCRIBED.

PREFACE.

That there is no elaborate and exhaustive history of Salem seems strange, when we see the accumulated material that lies ready to take shape and form under the hand of the master. It is not because there have been none among her citizens competent to perform the arduous and responsible task, for the published portion of her history relating to the witchcraft delusion, shows what the same hand might have wrought in the wider field. Let us hope, that ere long some chronicler may be found, whose love for the old city may induce him to devote the years necessary to prepare a thorough and complete narrative, and, while giving us a standard history, make for himself a lasting monument.

The future historian will find in the two editions of Felt's "Annals of Salem" a valuable collection of facts and dates relating to the history of the city from its first settlement to about the year 1845, and the publications of the Essex Institute, which are especially devoted to the preservation of documents, memoirs, and facts having reference to such history, will be of invaluable assistance to him in his labors.

The sketch contained in this volume presents the salient points in the city's history, and brings that history down connectedly to the present day. The facts are gleaned from authentic sources, and many of them are stated for the first time in these pages. While this little volume does not claim to present more than an outline of the events connected with the history of Salem, yet it is believed that the reader will find much herein of interest, and will gain a good general knowledge of the subjects treated of in the various chapters.

The essentially new feature in this sketch is the chapter devoted to commerce. No attempt has heretofore been made to present a connected account of this most brilliant episode in the history of Salem. Probably no port in this country can point to such a wonderful record. The houses of Salem to-day are full of unique and curious articles gathered in former years from all quarters of the globe, and the stories of the daring and venturesome voyages of the early mariners, are still repeated as family traditions in many of her households. In the preparation of this chapter, liberal use has been made of the original records of the custom-house, which contain a complete list of all vessels and their cargoes entered at Salem since 1789, and reference has also been had to the files of contemporaneous newspapers.

Thanks are due to many friends for advice and assistance, especially to Dr. Henry Wheatland, for general information and valuable aid, and to Augustus D. Small, Esq., for facts connected with the history of the public schools.

The volume is presented to the public with the hope and in the belief that it will meet, in a measure at least, the desire for a connected sketch of the history of Salem brought down to the present time, and will give a better insight into the interesting and remarkable story of the city's progress, than can be gained from the pages of any other single volume.

SALEM, May, 1879.

TABLE OF CONTENTS.

CORRIGENDA.

Wherever the words "St. Peter's Street" occur, read "St. Peter Street."

Page 59—The Hon. David Roberts, ex-mayor, died in Salem March 19, 1879.

Page 63—Charles S. Osgood, Esq., was appointed Register of Deeds for the southern district of Essex County, March 31, 1879, to fill the vacancy occasioned by the death of Ephraim Brown, Esq. He accepted the office April 1st, thereby vacating the seat he then held as a Representative from Salem in the Massachusetts House of Representatives.

Page 114—six lines from top. This exhibition of antique relics was under the auspices of the Ladies' Centennial Committee, and not of the Essex Institute, though held in Plummer Hall.

Page 116—twenty-one lines from top. For "1877" read "1876." In the next line, for "the following season" read "the two following seasons."

Page 141—sixteen lines from top. For "May" read "June."

Page 145—eighteen lines from top. For "Gibant" read "Gibaut." Thirty-three lines from top. For "were 115" read "was 115."

Page 174—twenty-eight lines from top. For "was eleven" read "were eleven." In the next line, for "was 58" read "were 58."

Page 270—first line. For "the readers" read "the reader." Nine lines from top. For "the students" read "the student."

SKETCH OF SALEM.

CHAPTER I.

HISTORICAL SKETCH OF SALEM FROM THE FIRST SETTLEMENT TO THE
TIME OF THE WITCHCRAFT DELUSION.

The history of ancient Salem forms one of the most interesting chapters in the history of the settlement of this continent. The early settlers came hither, not attracted by a mild and even climate, where with little exertion the various products of the earth could be obtained; not as to a land flowing with milk and honey, and rich in all those natural advantages that more favored climes offer to the sojourners within their borders; but with the knowledge that on the bleak and rock-bound shores of their newly chosen home they must endure hardship and privation and suffering, and a constant and never-ceasing contest and strife for their very existence. Driven from their home in England by religious persecution and oppression, these sturdy and courageous men sought to establish in a new world a haven of refuge for themselves, and for all others who, led by a desire to worship God according to the dictates of conscience, free from religious bigotry and intolerance, might come to join them. No desire to amass large fortunes, no expectation of a life of ease and comfort, no dreams of conquest, or of political power and renown, brought the founders of Salem across the ocean to establish on these shores the germ of a new State and nation; but, actuated by a nobler ambition, impelled by an inborn love of liberty and freedom, undaunted by perils and afflictions, and unflinching in the face of adversity, they sought in a foreign clime that relief from persecution which was denied them in their native land. Few communities can boast a nobler origin as to the motives and character of their founders.

Roger Conant, with his companions, came to Salem, then called Naumkeag, in 1626. They had previously settled at Cape Ann, and engaged in a planting, fishing, and trading enterprise, having received a charter or indenture for that place under date of Jan. 1, 1623, old style, or Jan. 12, 1624, new style. The original indenture, over the signature of Lord Sheffield, is now in the possession of the Essex Institute. Being unsuccessful in their venture they removed to Salem, and established here a plantation, receiving encouragement from friends in England who took measures to secure a patent.

Among those who came with Conant were John Lyford, John Woodbury, John Balch, Peter Palfray, Richard Norman and son, William Allen, and Walter Knight. The Rev. John White, of Dorchester, a famous Puritan divine, who was deeply interested in the settlement at Cape Ann, hoping to secure there a retreat for such of his countrymen as were subject to severe trials because, while adhering to the government of the national church, they could not approve of what they deemed its faults, and who "grieved in his spirit" when the Cape was abandoned, wrote to Conant urging him and his associates not to forsake Naumkeag, and encouraging them to expect a patent for their better protection. Many of them, however, became discontented with their new abode; and it required much reasoning and persuasion to prevent them from accompanying their pastor, Mr. Lyford, to Virginia. Mr. Conant says, writing of the settlement of Naumkeag, that "in the infancy thereof, it was in great hassard of being deserted. I was a meanes, through grace assisting me, to stop the flight of those few that then were heere with me, and that by my vtter deniall to goe away with them who would have gone either for England or mostly for Virginia, but thereupon stayed to the hassard of our lives." In spite of discouragement and discontent among his companions, and the fear of hostilities from the surrounding Indians, Conant and many of his followers remained "the sentinels of Puritanism on the Bay of Massachusetts."

An interest in this plantation having been aroused in England, it was deemed best to send one of their number across the sea, to explain their condition; and for this purpose John Woodbury was selected, and he went, and remained abroad some six months. As a consequence of the newly awakened interest, and the application of Mr. White for license and protection, a grant was obtained from the Council for New England, by a written document dated March 19, 1628, new style, which conveyed the soil then denominated Massachusetts Bay to Sir Henry Roswell, John Endicott, and others. The bounds of the colony so granted were "between three miles to the northward of Merrimac river and three miles to the southward of Charles river, and in length within the described breadth from the Atlantic ocean to the South sea." The grantees selected from among their number John Endicott — "a man of dauntless courage; benevolent though austere; firm though choleric; of a rugged nature which his stern principles of non conformity had not served to mellow" — as a "fit instrument to begin this wilderness work." He was appointed governor of the plantation, Matthew Cradock being governor of the Massachusetts Company in London; and in June, 1628, he set sail for Salem in the "Abigail," accompanied by his wife and a band of emigrants. They cast anchor in Salem harbor on the 6th of September, O. S. Conant and his companions were gathered on the shore to receive them, and the scene presented to the view of the voyagers must have been striking and impressive. Uniting with those already here, Endicott founded the oldest town in the Colony, soon to be called Salem; and extended some supervision over the waters of Boston harbor, then called Massachusetts Bay.

Until this time, the Massachusetts Company acted under the patent from the Council for New England; but this was a grant of property in the soil, rather than an authority to establish municipal government, and the company solicited, and on the 4th of March, 1629, Charles I. put the broad seal of England to the letters-patent for Massachusetts. This created a corporation under the name of the "Governor and Company of the Massachusetts Bay in New England," and was the instrument under which the Colony of Massachusetts continued to conduct its affairs for fifty-five years.

Among those named in this charter were Sir Henry Roswell, John Endicott, Richard Saltonstall, and Matthew Cradock. It gave power to the freemen of the company to elect annually from their own number a governor, deputy, and eighteen assistants, on the last Wednesday of Easter term, who were to meet once a month or oftener, "for dispatching such businesses as concerned the company or plantation." Four times a year, the governor, assistants, and all the freemen, were to be summoned to "one great, general, and solemn assembly," and these "great and general courts" were invested with full powers to choose and admit into the company so many as they should think fit to elect, and constitute all requisite subordinate officers, and to make laws and ordinances for the welfare of the company and for the government of the lands and inhabitants of the plantation, "so such laws are not repugnant to the laws and statutes of the realm of England." Matthew Cradock was the first home governor under this charter, and John Endicott the governor of the plantation. A duplicate of the charter was sent over to Endicott, and is now deposited in Plummer Hall, in the keeping of the Salem Athenæum, reposing in the very settlement where it was once the Magna Charta on which the council at Naumkeag made their laws and grounded their authority.

After the organization under the charter, the company made haste to send over colonists, and six vessels were despatched, containing eighty women, twenty-six children, and three hundred men, with "one hundred and forty head of cattle." The company were careful to make plentiful provision of "godly ministers." The Rev. Francis Higginson and the Rev. Samuel Skelton came over among the passengers in the "Talbot," and reached Salem June 29, 1629. In Mr. Higginson's journal, referring to their arrival, he says: "By God's blessing we passed the curious and difficult entrance into the spacious harbor of Naimkecke and as we passed along it was wonderful to behold so many islands replenished with thick woods and high trees and many fayre green pastures." In a letter written in 1629, by the same hand, we find, "that Naimkecke contained at that time about half a score of houses built and a fayre house newly built for the Governor," and that in all, about two hundred planters were settled there.

After the arrival of Higginson, Gov. Endicott set apart the 20th of July, 1629, "to be a solemn day of humiliation for the choyce of a pastor and teacher at Salem." The vote was taken by each one's writing in a note the name of his choice. Such is the origin of the use of the ballot on this continent. Skelton was chosen pastor, and Higginson teacher. Higginson lived but a short time after his arrival. He left his native land hoping to gain health and strength in a new country; but his hopes were all in vain, and he died at the early age of forty-three. He was greatly loved by his people, and his talents were of a high order. A primitive writer of New England describes him as "a man indued with grace, apt to teach, mighty in the Scriptures, learned in the Tongues, able to convince gainsayers."

All the freemen under the charter met in "Great and General Court till 1634," when deputies became a part of the Legislature; and it was ordered that the whole body of freemen be excused from attending the four annual General Courts, except that for election of magistrates in May. This continued till 1663, when a vote passed that the freemen should choose part of their number to assemble at the court of election, and choose a governor and other magistrates. This latter change was so unpopular that it was repealed the subsequent year. The people were apprehensive that they might lose their political heritage, so jealous were they, even then, of any encroachment on their political rights, which might be subversive of their liberty. The charter made provision for a common seal for the company, and such a seal in silver was sent to Endicott in 1629. The Indian which is to-day a part of the seal of our Commonwealth, was a principal figure on this colonial seal.

Shortly after Endicott's arrival at Salem, the colonists found themselves unprovided with suitable food and shelter, and sadly afflicted with sickness. Being destitute of regular medical attendance, word was sent to the Colony at Plymouth, and Dr. Samuel Fuller was sent to Salem. The visit of Dr. Fuller was not without results other than those which attended his ministrations to the needs of the sick. He was the means of strengthening the friendship between Gov. Bradford at Plymouth, and Gov. Endicott, and of interesting the colonists at Salem in the congregational form of worship followed by the people of Plymouth. The Massachusetts Company at London was still attached to the Church of England, its liturgy and forms, and gave no encouragement to Messrs. Higginson and Skelton, who adopted the congregational discipline of Plymouth. Some of the Salem colonists also clung to their old faith, and Messrs. John and Samuel Brown wrote letters of complaint to the company at London, whereupon they were charged by Gov. Endicott with factious conduct and sent back to London. Upon their arrival they made complaint of Endicott and his ministers, "concerning some rash innovations begun and practiced in the civil and ecclesiastical government."

The difficulties arising from having the government of the plantation in London now began to be apparent; and Gov. Cradock, at a meeting of the company proposed, "for weighty reasons to transfer the Gouernment of the Plantacon to those that shall inhabit there, and not to continue the same in subordination to the Company heere as now it is." This matter was fully discussed at several meetings of the company at London, until at the meeting of Aug. 29, 1629, it was decided " by erecon of hands that the Gouernment and Pattent should be settled in New England, and accordingly an order to be drawne vpp." Having decided to transfer the government to New England, Gov. Cradock resigned, and Messrs. John Winthrop, Richard Salton-stall, Isaac Johnson, and John Humphrey were put in nomination for the position, the first named being chosen " with full consent by erec-con of hands."

Winthrop was a man well fitted for the difficult task in which he was to engage. "An honest royalist, averse to pure democracy yet firm in his regard for existing popular liberties; in his native parish a conformist, yet wishing for 'gospel purity'; disinterested, brave, and conscientious, his character marks the transition of the reformation into virtual republicanism; when the sentiment of loyalty which it was intended to cherish, gradually yielded to the irresistible spirit of civic freedom." Winthrop, with a company of emigrants, arrived in Salem harbor, in the " Arbella," June 12, 1630, after a long and stormy passage, bringing with him the original charter, now deposited in the State archives at Boston.

After the long voyage, the shores of their new home must have been a welcome and attractive sight. Arriving in the month of June, when all Nature is at her best, before the heat of summer has scorched the foliage and robbed the fields of their freshness, it was a fair and attractive landscape that greeted the eyes of these weary and tempest-tossed travellers. Winthrop writes, that " most of our people went on Shore upon the land of Cape Ann, which lay very near us, and gathered store of fine strawberries." But while Nature had donned her choicest robes to welcome them, they were doomed to disappointment at the unexpected condition in which they found the colonists. More than eighty had died the winter before; that terror of our climate, consumption, had fastened upon Higgin-son, and he was slowly wasting away; others were weak and sick; and the corn and bread was scarcely sufficient for a fortnight's supply. To add to Winthrop's distress, his son Henry, who arrived in the harbor of Salem July 1st, in the ship "Talbot," was drowned while crossing the North River to visit the Indian settlement of wigwams.

With Winthrop came Isaac Johnson, and his wife, the Lady Arbella Johnson, a daughter of the Earl of Lincoln, who, with a woman's devòtion, left "a paradise of plenty and pleasure which she enjoyed in the family of a noble Earldom" for this "wilderness of wants," that she might accompany her husband in his voluntary exile. She died within a month of her arrival, and was buried in Salem.

After remaining at Salem about a week, Winthrop proceeded with a party in quest of some more attractive place of settlement. He traced Mystic River to its source, and, after an absence of three days, returned to Salem to spend the Sabbath. When ten or eleven vessels had arrived, the colonists kept the 8th of July as a day of thanksgiving. Winthrop selected Charlestown as the seat of government, and early in August, with much cost and labor, the removal was made from Salem. Ten weeks after the landing, the first Court of Assistants was held at Charlestown.

With the coming of Winthrop and the supersedure of Endicott, Salem ceased to be the capital town; but the record of her people during the first two years of the Colony will always remain as an example of fortitude in the face of danger and suffering, and of a supreme reliance on that overruling Power who guided their footsteps to this trackless wilderness. Neither death nor danger nor disaster could turn them from the path in which conscience told them they should walk; and we of to-day do well to pause, and, turning back the pages of history, contemplate the heroic virtues, the unflinching devotion to duty, the dauntless courage which endured through sorrow and suffering and death, which will make the names of the Puritan fathers of Salem respected so long as a free people shall enjoy the blessings of civil and religious liberty, and so long as the printed page shall endure to preserve the record of their acts.

The Commoners.—The territory of Salem was included in that held by the corporation of the Massachusetts Company, under their patent. Nearly all the early settlers were "freemen," and had an interest in the common lands. We find in the earliest records the "freemen" of the town exercising the power of granting land to individuals. With increasing population this method of holding the lands became unwieldy and cumbersome, and in 1713 the then owners of the common lands under the province laws became organized into a *quasi* corporation with the title of "commoners." In 1713 the "commoners" granted all the highways and burying-places and common lands lying within the town bridge and block-houses, to remain forever for the use of the town of Salem ; and the Common was then dedicated forever as a "training field." In 1714 the "commoners," at a meeting held at "ye meeting house of ye first parish in Salem," voted that Winter Island be wholly reserved and granted for "ye use of ye fishing," rights to use the same to be let by the selectmen of Salem ; and the same year the Neck lands were granted and reserved to the town of Salem for a pasture for "milch cows and riding horses," the same to be fenced at the town's charge.

In 1722–23, Feb. 26, the grand committee of the commoners who had charge of affairs reported the whole number of rights to be 1,132, and the number of acres held 3,733. Several distinct proprietaries were formed under an Act of the colonial Legislature ; and the commoners of the two lower parishes, having 790 rights and 2,500 acres of land lying between Spring Pond and Forest River, organized themselves into a corporation. This organization continued till 1855, when they were incorporated into the Great Pasture Company ; and by that company the last of the common lands, about 400 acres in extent, are now held.

House-lots and Town-ways.—After the arrival of Gov. Endicott, in 1628, the town was regularly laid out in house-lots ; and the first houses built in Salem appear to have been located in what is to-day the most central part of the city. Washington Street was the first street, and was laid out four rods wide, connecting the two rivers and the primitive highways which ran along their banks at the point where they approach nearest together. A fort was enclosed between this street on the east and North and Summer streets on the west, and was built near the western corner of Sewall and Lynde streets, on the highest land in that part of the town. The manner in which the house-lots in the central part of the town were originally laid out seems to indicate that the earliest settlement was made in the vicinity of Elm Street and Washington Street, upon the South River. Between these streets the lots were small, irregular, and not in conformity with the plan upon which the rest of the town was laid out. East of these, all along the South River to the Neck, house-lots were laid out running back from the river; and along the North River, west of North Street, were larger house-lots, also running back from that river. Essex Street was probably a way that came gradually into use along the ends of these lots; and, as they were all of the same depth from the river, this street acquired, and has retained, the same curves the river originally had. Among the earliest ways laid out in Salem was one along the shore eight feet wide, Essex Street, which, as just stated, ran along the end of the water-lots, and Daniels, Elm and Central streets, which probably led to promontories and town landings.

The Indians.—Before proceeding further with our narration, let us turn for a moment and consider the condition of the aboriginal inhabitants of this territory, found here on their arrival by the early settlers. A "great and grevous plague" had, a few years previously, swept away the larger portion of the Indian tribes living hereabouts, so that but a small remnant were found inhabiting the region about Salem. Tradition seems to point to an Indian settlement on the north side of the North River, and to another on Marblehead shore. Indian remains have been exhumed at the lower part of the city and on the Marblehead side of the harbor, and it is related that, down to 1725, a company of Indians paid an annual visit to Salem and encamped on the side of Gallows Hill. It is very likely that some, if not all of them, were descendants of those who once occupied this territory.

In 1686 the inhabitants of Salem fearing that, by a possible forfeiture of their charter, the land they held might be taken from them, endeavored to provide for such a contingency by obtaining from the Indians then residing around Salem, for the sum of £40, a deed of the territory within the town limits. Such a deed was drawn and formally executed on the eleventh day of October, 1686, and the original now hangs on the walls of the city hall.

Town Government.—In 1635 the township of Salem comprehended the present towns of Beverly, Danvers, Manchester, Marblehead, Middleton, Peabody, and a part of Topsfield, Wenham, and a part of Lynn. Marblehead was recognized as a distinct settlement in 1635, and was incorporated in 1649. Wenham was incorporated in 1643; Manchester in 1645; Topsfield in 1650; Beverly in 1668; and Danvers, which then included the present town of Peabody, in 1757. Salem cannot strictly be said to have been ever incorporated. Gov.

Winthrop, on his arrival, in 1630, found it the only settlement or town in the Colony, except, perhaps, Charlestown. It was recognized as a town by the government of the Colony, and indeed it had been established as such before the existence of any authority here superior to that of its own government. Upon the settlement of Boston and other places, town governments sprang up and were gradually moulded into the form in which they have continued until this time, and which constitutes one of the peculiar institutions of New England. Their origin was not derived from the authority of the General Court, but, like that of all governments, was from the necessity of the case. Their foundation was in the voluntary though tacit compact of the proprietors and settlers of the different towns.

It was necessary that some form of town government should be established, and as early as 1633 the inhabitants chose several of their principal proprietors, then styled "Townsmen," and not till some years afterwards "Selectmen," to whom were intrusted the principal concerns of the town. These held regular meetings, at which the important affairs of the town were transacted, and their proceedings were afterwards brought before general or town meetings for confirmation. The first records of the town of Salem bear date, the "Book of Grants," Oct. 1, 1634, and the "Town Records," Dec. 26, 1636, a portion of the record being in the handwriting of Gov. Endicott.

Town and Court Houses.—Town-meetings were held, prior to 1655, in the first meeting-house.

About 1677, a building for town purposes was erected in the middle of Washington Street, anciently called School Street, near what is now Lynde Street and facing Essex Street. Its upper part was fitted up for the accommodation of the court. In this building the innocent victims of delusion charged with the crime of witchcraft were tried, and here was anxiously agitated the question of submission to the Commissioners of Charles II.

In 1719, a building was erected, the lower story to be used for town purposes and the upper for the courts. This building stood on Washington Street, its northern wall nearly coinciding with the line upon which stands the southern parapet of the Eastern Railroad tunnel. Here for nearly half a century the freeholders held their town-meetings, and the selectmen consulted upon municipal affairs. In this building the session of the Provincial Congress was held October 5, 1774, which is referred to more at length hereafter.

In 1785, a building was erected for the joint use of the town and county. It stood in the middle of Washington Street, its west side facing the Tabernacle Church, and fronting Essex Street. The expense of its erection was divided between the town and county. Town-meetings were held here until the erection of the town hall in Derby Square in 1816, when the town sold its interest in the building to the county, and it was thereafter used exclusively to accommodate the courts and court records until the building of the Eastern Railroad tunnel, in 1839, compelled its removal. The present granite court-house was thereupon erected in 1841; and twenty years thereafter, in 1861, the brick court-house was built, in which to-day all the courts are held, save the probate court, which still holds its sessions in the granite building.

In 1816, the town hall and market-house now standing on Derby Square was built, and the lower part was opened as a market, Nov. 26, 1816. The town hall was first used on the occasion of President Monroe's visit to Salem, July 8, 1817, and from that time until the town was incorporated as a city it continued to be used for all town-meetings.

Modes of Punishment. — While speaking of the courts where sentence was passed on the offender, it may be well to note the ancient instruments of punishment by which that sentence was carried into effect. In 1638, Isaac Davis is paid for a pair of stocks, and in 1657, two persons "undertake to make stocks sufficientlie and to sett vp the whipping post." Both of these were formerly placed in Washington Street, near Essex Street. The county court orders, Nov. 27, 1666, that a cage shall be erected in Salem, in which to display wrong-doers, and in 1715, Miles Ward is paid by the county for making a pillory. It was erected in front of the court-house and near the whipping-post. On Sept. 28, 1630, the Court of Assistants order that two persons shall sit in the stocks here four hours for being accessories in crime; and June 14, 1631, Philip Ratclif is sentenced to be whipped, have his ear cropped, and be banished for hard speeches against Salem church as well as the government. On Dec. 4, 1638, the Assistants order a resident of Salem to sit in the stocks, on lecture day, for travelling on the Sabbath.

Mary Oliver seems to have given the magistrates much trouble. In January, 1642, she was presented for neglect of public worship. In February, 1644, she was sentenced to be publicly whipped for reproaching the magistrates, and in August, 1646, she had a cleft stick put on her tongue for half an hour, for slandering the elders. She was finally banished from the town. On May 14, 1714, an inhabitant of Salem is found guilty of passing counterfeit bills. He is sentenced to the pillory, to have his ear cropped, to be imprisoned twelve months, branded with F on his right cheek, and pay £30. The pillory, stocks, and whipping-post ceased to be used as a means of punishment in 1805; but it is still a question whether a certain class of offenders, especially those guilty of wife-beating or cruelty to children, could not be more effectually punished at the whipping-post than by our present system of punishment.

Salem Neck seems to have been the place for the execution of criminals. Jan. 16, 1772, Bryan Sheehan was hanged there in the presence of 12,000 people, the Rev. Mr. Diman preaching a sermon; and Dec. 21, 1786, Isaac Coombs, an Indian, suffered the same fate, his crime being the murder of his wife. Jan. 14, 1796, Henry Blackburn, an Englishman, and a chimney-sweeper in town, was hanged there for murder. In 1821, May 10, Stephen M. Clark, of Newburyport, aged seventeen, was hanged on Winter Island, for setting fire to a stable, by which a dwelling-house was consumed. Since then executions have taken place in the yard of the present jail on St. Peter's Street.

Prisons.—For the confinement of prisoners, provision was made June 30, 1668, for the building of a prison. It was located near the south-western end of the first meeting-house; and June 29, 1669, Benjamin Felton was appointed its keeper. In 1684, a new prison was built near the corner of Federal and St. Peter's streets, at the charge of the county, on common land given by Salem. Its dimensions were thirteen feet stud and twenty feet square. A curious custom prevailed for a long time, of allowing the keeper of the prison the perquisites of selling liquor to his prisoners. The county, in 1813, built the present stone jail which stands at the foot of St. Peter's Street.

Almshouses.—While providing accommodation for criminals, the town was also careful to provide for care of the poor; and, in 1698, authorized the selectmen to hire a house for their accommodation. In 1719, a building was finished for their occupancy, located on the site of the present State Normal School. This building was afterwards enlarged, and, in 1750, overseers of the poor were for the first time chosen. May 16, 1770, upon report made by Dr. E. A. Holyoke, the town votes to build an almshouse and workhouse upon the northeast part of the common, at a cost of £452 lawful money; and in 1772, upon the completion of the building, rules are adopted for the management of the inmates. The rooms in the old almshouse were rented by the town till 1807, when it was taken down to allow of the erection of a registry office. On the 30th of November, 1816, the present brick almshouse on the Neck was ready to receive the poor, and Paul Upton was its first master.

Roger Williams. — In February, 1631, Roger Williams arrived in Boston, and a few weeks afterwards the First Church at Salem invited him to succeed Higginson as their teacher. Mr. Williams, in the short time he had been in Boston, had made himself obnoxious to the government, and a letter was written from the Court to Mr. Endicott to this effect, "that whereas Mr. Williams had refused to join with the congregation at Boston because they would not make public declaration of their repentance for having communion with the churches of England while they lived there, therefore they marvelled they would choose him without advising with the Council." The Salem church, however, chose Williams their teacher, despite the remonstrance. He remained there but a short time, when he went to Plymouth, and became assistant to the pastor of the church there. He was invited back to Salem, and returned; but was not immediately called to the clerical office. When it was proposed to appoint him to the place lately vacated by the death of Mr. Skelton, the Massachusetts magistrates interfered, but he was, nevertheless, installed. The magistrates soon found additional cause for complaint; and when Salem applied to them for a grant of land, they replied that "because they had chosen Mr. Williams for their teacher and so offered contempt to the magistrates their petition was refused." The next General Court unseated the deputies from Salem, till their constituents should apologize for having "exceedingly reproached and vilified the magistrates and churches," and adopted the following resolution : —

"Whereas Mr. Roger Williams one of the elders of the church of

Salem hath broached and divulged divers new and dangerous opinions against the authority of magistrates as also writ letters of defamation both of the magistrates and churches here, and that before any conviction and yet maintaineth the same without retraction, it is therefore ordered that the said Mr. Williams shall depart out of this jurisdiction within six weeks now next ensuing; which if he neglect to perform it shall be lawful for the Governor and two of the magistrates to send him to some place out of this jurisdiction not to return any more without license from the Court."

The six weeks was extended to the next spring; but, in the meantime, the magistrates, thinking he was better out of the country, sent a vessel from Boston to take him to England. Williams, hearing of this, left Salem three days before the vessel's arrival, and made that memorable journey in midwinter through the deep snows of a New England forest, guided only by a rude compass through the pathless wilderness. This compass is preserved at Providence, among a people who look back with a just pride upon the history of this remarkable man, whose daring and heroism well fitted him to be the founder of a new State. The house in which he lived while in Salem is still standing, on the north-western corner of Essex and North streets.

John Endicott charged with Assault. — The methods of communication in these early days were rude and primitive, and journeys were made, whenever practicable, by water. In April, 1631, John Endicott, then one of the Court of Assistants under Gov. Winthrop, was charged with an assault upon Thomas Dexter, and being found guilty was fined 10s. In reference to this matter, Mr. Endicott writes to Gov. Winthrop a quaintly worded letter, which shows that human nature has not changed much since our early days, although it would be thought strange if one of our present governors should be found guilty of an assault, even under the provocation so naïvely stated in Endicott's letter, which is dated at Salem, April 12, 1631, and which proceeds as follows: —

RIGHT WORSHIPFUL — I did expect to have been with you in person at the Court and to that end I put to sea yesterday and was driven back again, the wind being stiff against us. And there being no canoe or boat at Saugus, I must have been constrained to go to Mystic and thence about to Charlestown, which at that time durst not be so bold, my body being at this present in an ill condition to wade or take cold

Jo. Endicott   Simon Bradstreet

Timothy Pickering   Leverett Saltonstall

and therefore I desire you to pardon me. The eel pots you sent for are made; which I had in my boat, hoping to have brought them with me. I caused him to make but two for the present; if you like them and his prices (for he worketh for himself), you shall have as many as you desire. He sells them for 4*s.* a piece. Sir, I desired the rather to be at Court, because I hear I am much complained of by goodman Dexter for striking him. I acknowledge I was too rash in striking him, understanding since it is not lawful for a justice of the peace to strike. But if you had seen the manner of his carriage with such daring of me with his arms akimbo, &c., it would have provoked a very patient man. But I will write no more of it, but leave it till we speak before face to face. Only thus far further that he hath given out if I had a purse he would make me empty it; and if he cannot have justice here he will do wonders in England, and if he cannot prevail there he will try it out with me here at blows. Sir, I desire that you will take all into consideration. If it were lawful to try it at blows, and he a fit man for me to deal with, you should not hear me complain; but I hope the Lord hath brought me off from that course. I thought good further to write what my judgment is for the dismissing the court till corn be set. It will hinder us that are far off exceedingly, and not further you there. Men's labour is precious here in corn setting time, the Plantations being yet so weak. I will be with you, the Lord assisting me, as soon as conveniently I can. In the meanwhile I commit you to his protection and safeguard, that never fails his children, and rest

Your unfeigned and loving friend to command,

Jo. ENDICOTT.

Cutting out the Red Cross.—A few years later, March 4, 1635, Endicott was again summoned before the court, on the charge of having mutilated the English ensign at Salem by cutting out the red cross. At that time a strong opposition was felt towards Popery, in all its signs as well as services, and the bold act of Endicott was secretly approved by the principal men of the Colony. Had it not been for fear of the consequences, for in England the act was construed as one of rebellion, no notice would have been taken of Endicott's act; but the General Court felt constrained to bring in some sentence against him, as a sign of their loyalty. They recommended that he should be admonished and left out of office for a year. In consequence of this he lost his election as assistant. One of Salem's distinguished authors, in speaking of this occurrence, says: "It is one of the boldest exploits which our history records. And forever honored be the name of Endicott! We look back through the mist of ages, and recognize in the rending of the Red Cross from New England's banner, the first omen of that deliverance which our fathers consummated after the bones of the stern Puritan had lain more than a century in the dust."

House of Representatives.—On the 14th of May, 1634, the General Court defined the powers of the Legislature, and provided that the whole body of freemen should be present at only one of the four General Courts to be held each year, and that their deputies should act fully for them in the three others. The addition of representatives to the assistants and governor was an imitation of the House of Commons in England. The House of Representatives in this Colony was the second in America. One had already been formed in Virginia. The Salem representatives were Messrs. John Holgrave, Roger Conant, and Francis Weston.

Sir Henry Vane.—On the 9th of July, 1636, Salem was visited by Sir Henry Vane, the new governor of the Colony, then only twenty-four years old. He came to this country in consequence of his non-conformity, and to escape the displeasure of the Bishop of London. After his return to England, and on the accession of Charles II., he was tried for high treason, and beheaded June 14, 1662.

Salem in 1634.—Wood, in " New England's Prospect," gives the following description of the town as it was during the year 1634 : " Salem stands on the middle of a necke of land very pleasantly, having a South river on one side and a North river on the other side. Upon this necke where most of the houses stand, is very bad and sandie ground, yet for seaven years together it hath brought forth exceeding good corne, by being fished but every third year. In some places is very good ground and good timber, and divers springs hard by the sea side. There likewise is store of fish, as Basses, Eels, Lobsters, Clammes &c. Although their land be none of the best, yet beyond these rivers is a very good soyle, where they have taken farms and get their hay and plant their corne ; there they cross these rivers with small Cannowes, which were made of whole pine trees, being about two foote and a halfe over and twenty foote long. In these likewise they goe a fowling, sometimes two leagues at sea. There be more cannowes in this towne than in all the whole Patent, every household having a water horse or two. This town wants an alewive river which is a great inconvenience. It hath two good harbors, the one being called winter and the other summer harbors, which lieth within Derbins Fort which place, if it were well fortified might keepe shippes from landing forces in any of those two places."

Town Records.—In January, 1644, "The seaven men chosen for the year ensuing" for the government of the town of Salem were John Endicott, William Hathorne, William Lord, Jeffrey Massey, Peter Palfray, Thomas Gardner, and Henry Bartholomew, and they agree that if either of them are absent from their meetings without good excuse he shall pay 4s. The town records about this time contain some curious and quaintly worded entries. In order to insure an attendance at church, it was ordered, on July 7, 1644, "that twoe be appointed every Lord's day to walk forth in time of God's worshippe, to take notice of such as either lye about the meeting house without attending to the word or ordinances, or that lye at home or in the fields without giving good account thereof, and to take the names of such persons and to present them to the magistrates whereby they may be accordingly proceeded against."

In 1676, "three constables are to be at the three great doors of the meeting-house, and allow none to go out till all the exercises are finished. All the boys are to sit on the three pair of stairs in the meeting-house, including those of the pulpit. One constable is to keep the dogs out of the meeting-house."

In a book entitled "Truth held forth and maintained," published in 1694, by Thomas Maule, it is stated that "In the church of Salem, the women in time of service have their faces covered with a veil, which practice did not many years continue; and when this practice was laid aside, they had for the more order in their church to keep people from sleeping, a man that wholly tended with a short clubbed stick, having at one end a knob, at the other a fox tail, with which he would stroke the women's faces that were drowsy, and with the other would knock unruly dogs and men that were asleep."

As showing the importance attached by our fathers, at that early day, to popular education, we find on the town records, under date of Sept. 30, 1644, an order "that a note be published on next Lecture day that such as have children to be kept at school would bring in their names and what they will give for one whole year, and also that if any poore body hath children or a childe to be put to schoole and not able to pay for their schooling, that the towne will pay it by a rate."

The General Court, at its session of October, 1647, orders "every town consisting of fifty householders to have a school for reading and writing, and of one hundred families to have a grammar school, so as to fit scholars for college"; and further enacts, no doubt much to the discomfiture of the younger portion of the community, "that if any young man attempt to address a young woman without the consent of her parents or, *in their absence, of the County Court*, he shall be fined £5, for the first offence, £10 for the second, and imprisonment for the third." Several instances of such fines being imposed appear on the records of the court.

In 1654, the persons chosen to conduct the business of the town having been called, for the most part, the "seven-men," began to have the title of "select-men," and on the 27th of May of that year an order was passed, "that any townsman duly warned, and declining to take part in public meeting, either in person or by proxy, should be fined 18*d*." On August 22d, the General Court appoints Samuel Archer, of Salem, to examine all persons going out of Massachusetts, to see that they carry no more than 20*s*. in coin to pay expenses.

Persecution of the Quakers.—Although the founders of Salem left country and friends that they might worship according to their own belief, they rigorously excluded from among their number all who held different religious views. The stern and uncompromising nature which had prompted them to separate from the church in their native land, and cross an ocean to establish a church where the gospel should be preached according to their understanding of its doctrines, would not brook interference on the part of any person or sect. The religious intolerance from which they had suffered did not deter them from being equally intolerant to others of a differing belief. They banished Roger Williams and Anne Hutchinson, and they fined and whipped and hanged the Quakers.

In 1658, Samuel Shattuck, Lawrence and Cassandra Southwick, Nicholas Phelps, Joshua Buffum, and Josiah Southwick, all of Salem, and all Quakers, were ordered to leave the Colony before the next election day. And on the 11th of May, 1659, Daniel and Provided Southwick, the two children of Lawrence and Cassandra Southwick, having no home to shelter them, and no one being allowed to harbor them under severe penalties, were arrested as vagabonds, and the treasurer was authorized to sell them to any of the English nation in Barbadoes or Virginia, as slaves. Provided Southwick was baptized at the First Church Dec. 6, 1639, and was therefore, at the date of this event, probably a little over twenty years of age. Christopher Holder and John Copeland, of the Friends denomination, being at Salem Sept. 21, 1657, the former attempted to address the people after the minister had done. They were both secured till the next day, and then sent to Boston, where they received thirty stripes each, and were imprisoned nine weeks.

William Robinson and Marmaduke Stevenson, Quaker ministers journeying from Virginia and Rhode Island, held open-air meetings in Salem in the year 1659, and were soon after both executed on Boston Common by the Puritan magistrates, being sentenced to death by Gov. Endicott.

On the 16th of November, 1662, the wife of Robert Wilson, for going through Salem without any clothes on, as a sign of spiritual nakedness in town and Colony, was sentenced to be tied to a cart's tail, uncovered to her waist, and be whipped from Mr. Gedney's gate to her own house, not exceeding thirty stripes. Her mother Buffum and sister Smith, being abettors of her conduct, were sentenced to be tied on each side of her, with nothing on to their waists but an under garb, and to accompany her the distance mentioned. Of this conduct there is no doubt the Friends in Salem disapproved. Edward Wharton, who was actively engaged in spreading the doctrines of the Friends, was apprehended in Boston, in May, 1664, and ordered by the governor to be whipped and carried to his house in Salem.

Thomas Maule, who in 1688 built the first Quaker meeting-house, was on the third day of May, 1669, sentenced to be whipped for saying that "Mr. Higginson preached lies and that his instruction was the doctrine of the devil." Maule was a remarkable man, and a merchant of no inconsiderable business. His house was on the south side of Essex Street, on the spot where the house of James B. Curwen now stands. The building was demolished in the year 1852. Here it was that the Quakers of Salem, in 1680 and for several years thereafter, held their meetings for worship and business.

In 1694, Maule published a book, entitled "Truth held forth and maintained," with a desire to explain and defend the views of the Quakers ; whereupon the governor and council directed the sheriff to search his house and burn all the obnoxious volumes he could find. Maule was arrested and indicted for publishing and putting forth a book "wherein is contained divers slanders against the churches and government of this province"; and for saying at the honorable court at

Ipswich, in May last, "that there were as great mistakes in the Scriptures as in his book." He was tried by a jury and acquitted, despite the adverse rulings of the presiding justice.

Sir Edmund Andros. — In 1689, Sir Edmund Andros passed through Salem on his way to Boston from Pemaquid, where he had been to suppress Indian hostilities. The Colony charter had been abrogated, and Andros was the appointed ruler of New England. During his stay in Salem, he had a conference with the Rev. Mr. Higginson, the aged minister of Salem, and, in the presence of a large company, asked him if all the lands in New England did not belong to the king. Higginson answered him in the negative, stating two reasons for his position : first, that the colonists held by right of just occupation ; and second, by right of purchase from the Indians ; therefore the lands in New England are the subjects' property and not the king's. After much discussion, Sir Edmund said at last, with much indignation, " Either you are subjects or you are rebels." The foregoing was a part of the testimony of Mr. Higginson after Sir Edmund was displaced. The latter part of the same year, Andros was arrested and imprisoned, and a provisional government was formed, which elected the venerable Simon Bradstreet, resident in Salem, to be its president, and Wait Winthrop to command the militia. The General Court again convened, and Salem sent her deputies, and, during the year 1690, raised troops to serve against the Eastern Indians.

CHAPTER II.

SKETCH OF THE WITCHCRAFT DELUSION, WITH AN ACCOUNT OF THE
TRIALS AND EXECUTIONS.

Salem is famous the world over as the scene of the witchcraft delusion of 1692. It was no new delusion that had taken root and sprung
up in the Colony, for executions for witchcraft, and charges of "com-
muning with the Devil" had been recorded from the earliest days of
history; but the Salem witchcraft was regarded as a deep plot to
destroy the Christian church in New England and set up the kingdom
of Satan, whose individual efforts were supposed to be directed towards this object. It was religious fanaticism and ignorance, always
the strongest incentive to action, that led to the deplorable results
hereafter recorded, and made the year 1692 a memorable one in the
annals of Salem.

There were isolated cases of accusations before the general outbreak. In September, 1652, the grand jury presented John Bradstreet, of Rowley, "for suspicion of having familiarity with the
Devil." On the 28th of that month he was convicted in court, at
Ipswich, of lying; and this being a second offence, he was fined to
pay twenty shillings, or else be whipped. In 1658, John Godfrey,
of Andover, was accused of causing losses in the estates of several
people, and "some affliction in their bodies also." No sentence was
ever imposed on Godfrey, though the case was several times in court;
and about 1659, he sued his accusers for defamation. He is reputed
to have challenged, and even courted, the imputation of witchcraft.
In November, 1669, "Goody Burt," a widow, was prosecuted, a physician testifying that "no natural cause" could have led to such effects
as were wrought by her. Her operations were mainly in Lynn, Marblehead, and Salem. Philip Reed, the physician, preferred similar
charges against Margaret Gifford, "a witch," in 1680: but no record
of action against her appears. In 1679, Caleb Powell was arrested
for bewitching, or, as the warrant specified, "for suspicion of work-

ing with the Devil to the molesting of William Morse and his family." This man was not found guilty, but "so much suspicion" was proved, that he was ordered to pay the costs of court. The arrest of Mr. Morse's mother was next demanded, on charge of causing the trouble; and as Essex County courts could not be relied on for convictions in these cases, she was tried in Boston before the highest court in the Colony. She was found guilty, and the death sentence was imposed on her; but she was twice reprieved. A new trial was granted by the House of Deputies, but was refused by the magistrates; and, finally, she was released. The "witchery" in this case was caused by the mischievous son of Mr. Morse. Margaret Jones and Ann Hibbins were also sentenced as witches. These, and similar instances, wrought up the public mind to that pitch of anxiety, that the people were in condition to succumb to the far greater excitement of 1692.

Briefly traced, the history of the Salem witchcraft is here narrated. During the winter of 1691–92, a company of young girls were in the habit of assembling at the residence of the Rev. Samuel Parris, the clergyman of Salem Village, then including what is now Danvers Centre, Danversport, Tapleyville, Putnamville, and a part of Danvers Plains. At the social parties held at the minister's house, the arts of fortune-telling, palmistry, necromancy and magic were practised, till considerable skill in this direction was attained. After a little time, these people began to ascribe their peculiar actions to supernatural agencies, and the whole neighborhood became intensely interested, then alarmed, and an examination by the village physician, resulting in pronouncing them "bewitched," capped the whole, and the witchcraft delusion had taken root, to grow apace, and to lead to the terrible tragedies that the page of history records.

The persons who were of the party that met at the house of Mr. Parris, and who acted in the opening scenes, are thus named and described by the late Hon. Charles W. Upham of Salem, in his valuable and exhaustive volumes entitled "Salem Witchcraft": Elizabeth, daughter of Mr. Parris, was nine years of age; she performed a leading part in the first stages of the affair. Abigail Williams, a niece of Mr. Parris, was eleven years old; she acted conspicuously from the inception to the end of the excitement. Ann Putnam, a daughter of the parish clerk, was twelve years old; this girl was in many respects the leading agent in the mischief that followed. Mary Walcot, seventeen years of age, was a daughter of Jonathan Walcot. Mercy Lewis was also seventeen; she lived as a servant in the house of Thomas Putnam; she was responsible for much of the crime and horror connected with the affair. Elizabeth Hubbard, aged seventeen, was a niece of Mrs. Dr. Griggs, and lived in her family. Elizabeth Booth and Susannah Sheldon, each eighteen years old, belonged to families in the neighborhood. Mary Warren, twenty years of age, and Sarah Churchill, of the same age, were servants in the families of John Procter and George Jacobs, Sr. These last two acted prominently in the tragedy, actuated, it is reputed, by malicious feelings towards their employers. Mrs. Ann Putnam, mother of the girl mentioned above, Mrs. Pope, and Mrs. Bibber, living in Wenham, acted with the "afflicted" children.

Matters went from bad to worse. The bewitched at first had exhibited their afflictions, by such strange actions as creeping under benches and chairs, making wild gestures, and uttering strange exclamations. They would be seized with spasms, and apparently suffer dreadful tortures. The next feature was the extension of these actions to the time of the church services. The minister would be interrupted in his services; and Ann Putnam is mentioned as having such severe attacks, that she had to be held to prevent her breaking up the meeting. Mr. Parris invited neighboring ministers to assemble at his house, and unite in a day of prayer, invoking the aid of God for rescue from the terrible visitation. The same feats were performed in their presence, and the clergy corroborated the opinion of the doctor, that the Evil One had taken possession of the spirits of these people. This expression was the last straw. Public opinion all turned in one direction now, and the belief that these people were bewitched became almost universal. It was demanded of the "afflicted ones" who it was that bewitched them, for it was the accepted doctrine in those days, that the devil acted, not directly, but through some human agent, or witch. Tituba, an Indian servant of Mr. Parris, Sarah Osburn, who was bedridden, and Sarah Good, a woman of ill-repute, were accused, and on the 29th of February, 1692, warrants were issued for their arrest, the complainants being Joseph Hutchinson, Edward Putnam, Thomas Putnam, and Thomas Preston.

On March 1st, an examination of the accused was held before John

Hathorne and Jonathan Corwin, the two leading magistrates in the vicinity. These magistrates "entered the village in imposing array, escorted by the marshal, constables and their aids, with all the trappings of their offices," and a great crowd gathered to hear the testimony taken. The examination was held in the meeting-house, Sarah Good being arraigned first. Her bad name in the community made the people all the more ready to receive the charge against her. She stoutly denied all the charges preferred, as did also Sarah Osburn; but Tituba, the Indian, admitted that she had pinched, and otherwise hurt the children, and declared that she was inspired to do it by the devil, who had bid her serve him. She also accused Sarah Good and Sarah Osburn of participation in the bewitching of the afflicted ones. This woman was perfectly familiar with the whole affair; and evidently she had been used as an instrument to give effect to the delusion; perhaps, says Mr. Upham, being frightened into confessing what she never did, and accusing the others of what she was instructed to; or, perhaps, being promised immunity from punishment if she acknowledged her own guilt, and fixed a greater responsibility on the other women. Under date of March 7, the court records show that all three were sent to the jail in Boston, the magistrates having held them for trial. All that is known of them after this is very indefinite. The jailer's bill seems to indicate that Sarah Osburn died May 10. Tituba is recorded as being "sold for her fees" about a year later.

Martha, or "Goody" Corey, the third wife of Giles Corey, was the next person accused. She was examined March 21st, and the records appear in the handwriting of Mr. Parris. She was committed to Salem jail. Rebecca Nurse was arrested on the 24th, and was examined, and she, too, was cast into jail. Martha Corey was a church-member, and was evidently a person perfectly free from the terrible delusion. Rebecca Nurse was a person of acknowledged worth. She was of infirm health and advanced in years. Each of these two women declared and protested their entire innocence, but the result of any examination was a foregone conclusion, and each new person accused was fully committed for trial, the flimsiest evidence being admitted as conclusive. Dorcas, a little daughter of Sarah Good, between four and five years old, was arraigned and committed with her mother to Boston jail.

Mr. Upham, in his work on this dark delusion, says: — "There was no longer any doubt in the mass of the community that the devil had effected a lodgment at Salem Village. Church-members, persons of all social positions, of the highest repute and profession of piety, eminent for visible manifestations of devotion, and of every age, had joined his standard, and become his active allies and confederates." "The public mind was worked to red heat, and now was the moment to strike the blow that would fix an impression deep and irremovable upon it." Deodat Lawson preached a sermon that "re-enforced the powers that had begun their work. It justified and commended everything that had been done, and everything that remained to be done." It was printed and endorsed by several of the most eminent divines in the country.

One week passed before any further action was taken; but on April 8th, complaints against Sarah Cloyse and Elizabeth Procter, "for high suspicion of sundry acts of witchcraft," having been preferred, warrants for their arrest were procured. Their examination was before a representation of the government of the Colony, headed by the deputy-governor, Thomas Danforth, and took place in the meeting-house of the First Parish. A number of witnesses were examined, and all testified that the accused had "hurt" them, — choked and pinched them, and "tormented" them. Mr. Upham, after a careful examination of all the records and papers relating to those terrible days of evil doing, concludes that nothing was worse than this examination before the deputy-governor and members of the council. As a result of the examination, Sarah Cloyse, John Procter and his wife Elizabeth Procter, were held for trial, and were confined in the jail at Boston, with Rebecca Nurse, Martha Corey, and Dorcas Good. On April 18th, warrants were issued against Giles Corey and Mary Warren, of Salem, Abigail Hobbs, of Topsfield, and Bridget Bishop, of Salem, the second mentioned being one of those who had before been an accuser. She was cast into prison, and was several times examined by the judges, till she appeared to the magistrates and the people to have been delivered from the devil's clutches, and was then released. Mr. Upham expresses the opinion that she played an important part as one of the party of conspirators to develop and carry on a deep-laid plot — for such he considers the whole phenomena. After her discharge from jail, she appeared as a witness in ten prosecutions. Giles Corey was examined in the village meeting-house

4

April 19th.   Abigail Hobbs " confessed," and, secured immunity from
heavy punishment, though she was imprisoned, as was the custom to
do with those who confessed, that they might be held in subjection.
Bridget Bishop was examined at the same session of court before
which Mary Warren was arraigned, and all of the four mentioned
were incarcerated in jail.

On the 22d of April, William Hobbs, his wife Deliverance, Nehemiah Abbot, Jr., Mary Easty, and Sarah Wilds, all of Topsfield or
Ipswich, Edward Bishop, Sarah his wife, Mary Black, a negro, and
Mary English, wife of Philip English, all of Salem, were arraigned
at the house of Lieutenant Nathaniel Ingersoll.   The first-named of
these was committed, but was bailed out and the bail forfeited, the
parties not deeming it expedient to have him come into court.   At
the May term the next spring, the fine was remitted, and he was discharged by proclamation.   Abbot was dismissed, — the only one
reported to have been after an examination, — and it is not quite certain that he was not re-arrested, for a man by the name of Abbot is
recorded to have been, though the Christian name is not given in the
records.   The other seven were all committed, as was the rule.
Records of their trials exist only in the cases of Edward Bishop and
his wife.

The judges — Hathorne and Corwin — showed signs of relaxing
their stern methods of conducting the trials, and Thomas Putnam
wrote a letter to them immediately, in which he urged them to be a
terror to evil-doers, and assured them that, though the people would
never be able to make them recompense, a full reward would be given
them of the Lord God of Israel, whose cause and interest they had
espoused.

On April 30th, warrants were granted against Philip English, of
Salem, Sarah Morrel and Dorcas Hoar, of Beverly.   Marshal Herrick,
the officer entrusted with the serving of the warrants, returned that
for English with the indorsement, "Mr. Philip English not to be
found.   G. H."   The others were duly taken into custody.   On the
6th of May, English was arrested in Boston, examined, and committed
to jail, from which he and his wife escaped, and fled to New York.
After the delusion had run its race, they returned to Salem, and continued to reside there.   He was one of the leading men of the town,
a merchant, owning twenty-one vessels, beside much real estate.

Just what became of Sarah Morrel is not known. She did not suffer the death penalty, and was probably one of those long imprisoned, but finally discharged. Dorcas Hoar was a widow, and among other accusations brought against her in court was the killing of her husband. She protested her innocence of all charges, and reproached her accusers by crying out in court, "Oh, you are liars, and God will stop the mouths of liars." She suffered the common fate of imprisonment. Susanna Martin, of Amesbury, was arrested on a warrant bearing date April 30, and was examined on May 2d, and her name was added to the list of the imprisoned.

In the letter, previously referred to, written by Sergeant Thomas Putnam to Judges Corwin and Hathorne, reference was made to "high and dreadful" things to be disclosed, that would make "ears tingle." This proved to be the arrest, probably planned long before it was made, of the Rev. George Burroughs, who was settled in Salem in the fall of 1680, but who was at this time preaching in the frontier settlements of Maine. He was a graduate of Harvard College in the class of 1670, and is known to have been a man of great ability and of sterling worth. The plans looking to his arrest go to show what a deep and firm hold the superstition had taken among the people, else the arrest of a former pastor would not have been tolerated. The order for his arrest was issued in Boston by Elisha Hutchinson, a magistrate in that place, and was addressed to John Partridge, of Portsmouth, field-marshal of the provinces of New Hampshire and Maine. It bore date April 30, 1692, and commanded his arrest on suspicion of "confederacy with the devil." The "afflicted children" became as if influenced by him, and various charges of bewitching were brought against him. One deposition, that of Ann Putnam, taken by her father, and sworn to, is as follows: —

"The Deposition of Ann Putnam, who testifieth and saith, on the 20th day of April, 1692, at evening, she saw the apparition of a minister, at which she was grievously affrighted, and cried out, 'Oh, dreadful, dreadful! here is the minister come! What! are ministers witches too? Whence came you, and what is your name? for I will complain of you, though you be a minister, if you be a wizard.' Immediately I was tortured by him, being racked and almost choked by him. And he tempted me to write in his book, which I refused with loud outcries, and said I would not write in his book though he tore me all to pieces, but told him that it was a dreadful thing, that he, which was a minister that should teach children to fear God, should come to persuade poor creatures to give their souls to the devil. 'Oh, dreadful, dreadful! tell me your name that I may know who you are.' Then again he tortured me, and urged me to write in his book, which I refused. And then, presently, he told me that his name was George Burroughs, and that he had had three wives, and that he had bewitched the two first of them to death; and that he killed Mrs. Lawson because she was so unwilling to go from the village, and also killed Mr. Lawson's child because he went to the eastward with Sir Edmon and preached so to the soldiers; and that he had bewitched a great many soldiers to death at the eastward when Sir Edmon was there; and that he had made Abigail Hobbs a witch, and several witches more. And he has continued ever since, by times, tempting me to write in his book, and grievously torturing me by beating, pinching, and almost choking me several times a day. He also told me that he was above a witch. He was a conjurer.

[Signed]   ANN PUTNAM."

Burroughs was brought to Salem, May 4. On the 9th, his examination was held before a special sitting of the magistrates, Judges William Stoughton, of Dorchester, Samuel Sewall, of Boston, and Hathorne and Corwin, of Salem, being on the bench, the former acting as chief justice. A private examination was first held before the magistrates and ministers alone, and then he was taken into the public court; and, as he entered, "many, if not all the bewitched, were grievously tortured," according to the records. As a matter of course, he was committed. George Jacobs, Sr., and his grand-daughter, Margaret Jacobs, were the next victims, and were arrested May 10. They were examined at the house of Thomas Beadle. On the same day of their examination, a warrant was issued for John Willard; but he had fled from the town, and was subsequently arrested in Groton. About the same time, Alice Parker and Ann Pudeator, of Salem, were taken into custody. They were examined July 2, the same sort of evidence — in fact, no evidence at all — being offered.

On May 14, the following parties were subjects of warrants: Daniel Andrew, George Jacobs, Jr., his wife Rebecca Jacobs, Sarah Buckley, and Mary Whittredge, of Salem; Elizabeth Hart and Thomas Farrar, Sr., of Lynn; Elizabeth Colson, of Reading, and Bethiah Carter, of Woburn. Andrew, with Jacobs, Jr., heard of warrants for their arrest, and fled from the country. Sarah Buckley and her daughter, Mary Whittredge, were not tried till January, 1693, when they were acquitted. Mary Easty, who had been arrested April 22, and discharged May 18, was again arrested, May 20, as one Mercy Lewis asserted that she was "afflicted," and could not be delivered from her tortures till Mary Easty was again in irons. Testimony was given that Mercy Lewis's afflictions ceased the same afternoon that her "witch" was incarcerated.

The following parties were next "charged" and arrested : On May 21, the wife of William Basset, of Lynn, Susanna Roots, of Beverly, Sarah Procter, of Salem. A few days later, Benjamin Procter and Mary Derich, of Lynn, and wife of Robert Pease, of Salem. On the 28th, Martha Carrier, of Andover, Elizabeth Fosdick, of Malden, Wilmot Read, of Marblehead, Sarah Rice, of Reading, Elizabeth How, of Topsfield, Capt. John Alden, of Boston, William Procter, of Salem, Capt. John Flood, of Rumney Marsh (now Chelsea), Mrs. Toothaker and her daughter, of Billerica, and —— Abbot, of Topsfield or Wenham. On the 30th, Elizabeth Paine, of Charlestown. On June 4, Mary Ireson, of Lynn. Many others were complained of, and warrants for them issued ; among them Mary Bradbury, of Salisbury, Lydia and Sarah Dustin, of Reading, Ann Sears, of Woburn, Job Tookey, of Beverly, Abigail Somes, of Gloucester, Elizabeth Carey, of Charlestown, and Candy, a negro woman.

In commenting on the trials, Mr. Upham calls special attention to the fact that "every idle rumor ; everything that the gossip of the credulous, or the fertile imaginations of the malignant could produce ; everything gleaned from the memory or the fancy that could have an unfavorable bearing upon an accused person, however foreign or irrelevant it might be to the charge, was allowed to be brought in evidence before the magistrates, and received at the trials." ·That " children were not only permitted but induced to become witnesses against their parents, and parents against their children. Husbands and wives were made to criminate each other as witnesses in court." The Rev. Cotton Mather, a clergyman of Boston ; a man who, according to his own declaration, believed that " no place has got such a spell upon it as will always keep the devil out," gave an account of the proceedings of the courts. In the conclusion of his report of the trial of Martha Carrier, he wrote as follows ¿ " This rampaut hag was the person of whom the confessions of the witches, and of her own children among the rest, agreed that the devil had promised her that she should be queen of hell.") John Alden, mentioned above, was a son of John Alden, of Plymouth, one of the founders of the Colony there. He made his escape from jail in September of the eventful year, and fled to Duxbury, telling his relatives there that he was fleeing from the devil.

An Andover woman, who was sick with a fever, became the cause of a terrible outbreak in that town. Her husband was informed by the "afflicted girls" at Salem that she was suffering from witchery, and, once alarmed, Andover became the scene of another act in the sad tragedy. More than fifty people were imprisoned, and several of them were hanged. Dudley Bradstreet, the local magistrate, committed forty or thereabouts, and then refused to act further, which so exasperated the people that they threatened the judge and his family with punishment for his refusal to assist in banishing the evil ones, and they were obliged to flee from the vicinity. The prisons at Salem, Ipswich, Boston, and Cambridge were full of parties awaiting trial for the crime of witchcraft.

About this time Sir William Phipps became governor under the royal charter, and a special court of oyer and terminer was created for witchcraft trials. William Stoughton, of Dorchester, was chief justice, and Nathaniel Saltonstall, of Haverhill, Maj. John Richards, of Boston, Maj. Bartholemew Gedney, of Salem, Wait Winthrop, Capt. Samuel Sewall, and Peter Sargent, of Boston, his associates on the bench. Saltonstall resigned, and Jonathan Corwin, of Salem, succeeded him. Before this court the final trials and convictions occurred, though a doubt has been raised as to the legality of the court, it being a question whether the governor and council under the charter had power to create it without the concurrence of the General Court. The new government did away with the office of marshal, held by George Herrick, and created that of sheriff, to which George Corwin, of Salem, was appointed.

The jail at Salem, where many of the victims were lodged, was located on "Prison Lane," now St. Peter's Street, and the courthouse, where the trials took place, was on "Town-house Lane," now Washington Street. The meeting-house, where examinations had been held, was at what is now the south-east corner of Essex and Washington streets, the present site of the "First Church." The old "witch-house," the residence of Judge Corwin, which every stranger visiting Salem asks to see, was used for conferences and sessions of the grand jurors, and is not entitled to the prominence in connection with the witchcraft trials that many have given it. The house is still standing at the corner of Essex and North streets.

The trials opened in June, 1692. The attorney-general, Thomas Newton, had located at Salem to conduct the trials in behalf of the government. He addressed a letter to the secretary of the Province, in which he expressed the idea that progress would probably be slow, "as the afflicted cannot readily give their testimonies, being struck dumb and senseless for a season at the name of the accused." No complete records of the doings of this special court are in existence, but several depositions are on file in the county records. At the first session of the court, Bridget Bishop was the only "witch" tried. She was dragged before the assembled crowds through Prison Lane, up Essex Street, into Town-house Lane, to the court-house. Cotton Mather relates that "there was one strange thing with which the court was newly entertained. As this woman was, under a guard, passing by the great and spacious meeting-house, she gave a look towards the house, and immediately a demon invisibly entering the meeting-house, tore down a part of it, so that though there was no person to be seen there, yet the people, at the noise, running in, found a board which was strongly fastened with several nails, transported into another quarter of the house."

Owing to the lack of records of the testimony in this and other cases tried before this special court, no exact account of the trial can be given. By diligent research on the subject, our best authority, Mr. Upham, collected many interesting facts from various documents of the day now preserved in the archives of Essex County. The Rev. John Hale, of Beverly, appeared in court, and testified that he had examined the body of the woman whose death was attributed to the influenced acts of Bridget Bishop, and that, in his judgment, it was "impossible for her, with so short a pair of scissors, to mangle herself so without some extraordinary work of the devil, or witchcraft." The "bewitched" woman evidently committed suicide. She was known to have been an insane person. Samuel Shattuck and his wife swore to a deposition, which asserted the belief that a child of theirs was bewitched through this woman. They testified that the child, a young boy, had been afflicted with fits; had acted strangely, as if controlled by an evil spirit, and had lost power over himself, so that he fell into fire or water, or lay as if dead. These things occurred and strengthened as the Bishop woman "came oftener to the house," according to the testimony offered. A son of Mr. John Cook, who lived on the same street with Shattuck, testified, that "about five or six years ago, one morning, before sun-rising, as I was iu bed, before I rose, I saw goodwife Bishop, *alias* Oliver, stand in the chamber, by the window; and she looked on me and grinned on me, and presently struck me on the side of the head, which did very much hurt me; and then I saw her go out under the end window at a little crevice, about so big as I could thrust my hand into. I saw her again the same day, — which was the Sabbath day, — about noon, walk across the room; and having at the time an apple in my hand, it flew out of my hand into my mother's lap, who sat six or eight foot distance from me, and then she disappeared. And though my mother and several others were in the same room, yet they affirmed they saw her not."

. John Bly, who had purchased a hog of Bridget Bishop, testified to strange actions of that animal, and to his belief "that said Bishop had bewitched the sow." William Stacy swore that on his way to mill, "being gone about six rods from her, the said Bishop, with a small load in his cart, suddenly the off-wheel slumped, or sunk down into a hole upon plain ground; that this deponent was forced to get one to help him to get the wheel out. Afterwards, this deponent went back to look for said hole, where his wheel sunk in, but could not find any hole." He also testified that on another occasion, "after he had passed by her, this deponent's horse stood still with a small load going up the hill; so that the horse striving to draw, all his gears and tacklings flew to pieces, and the cart fell down."

John Louder, who lived with John Gedney, Sr., as a servant, gave lengthy testimony, including the following absurd declarations: "I, going to bed about the dead of night, felt a great weight upon my breast, and, awakening, looked, and, it being bright moonlight, did clearly see Bridget Bishop, or her likeness, sitting upon my stomach, and, putting my arms off of the bed to free myself from the great oppression, she presently laid hold of my throat, and almost choked me, and I had no strength or power in my hands to resist or help myself; and in this condition she held me to almost day. Some time after that, I, being not very well, stayed at home on a Lord's Day; and on the afternoon of said day, the doors being shut, I did see a black pig in the room coming towards me; so I went towards it to kick it, and it vanished away." He also claimed that a "black thing" appeared to him, and assured him that if he would "be ruled by him he should want for nothing in this world." He brings Bridget

Bishop into connection with this apparition, by affirming that just after its appearance to him he saw her, and, "seeing her, had no power to set one foot forward." John Bly, Sr., and William Bly, a lad of fifteen, testified that in working in the removal of a cellar-wall of the house where Bridget Bishop lived, they found "several puppets made up of rags and hogs' bristles, with headless pins in them, with the points outward." Such is a fair sample of the loose and utterly unconvincing testimony on which this poor woman was convicted and executed in those dark days of 1692.

It is but natural in these later days, to condemn, at first thought, all the actors in those terrible tragedies ; but more deliberate reflection, after a careful examination of the history of the affair as it comes down to us, tends to more charitable thoughts. We of to-day can form no definite idea of the feelings of the people who lived amidst those scenes. They were of Puritan stock, with the deepest reverence for their Maker, and a holy horror of neglecting to do all they were able to drive out any emissaries of the dark power that might oppose the right. Let us have only pity for those who were drawn into the whirlpool of public sentiment and public action of the day, and charitable thoughts and free forgiveness for those who, evidently from some unexplained reason, sought to establish and perpetuate such horrible delusions.

Bridget Bishop was executed the week after her trial, and her death-warrant is the only one preserved. The original document is framed, and hangs in the office of the clerk of the courts, at Salem. The court re-assembled June 29, and tried and sentenced Sarah Good, Sarah Wildes, Elizabeth How, Susanna Martin, and Rebecca Nurse, and these were hanged July 19. Quite a general opposition occurred to the execution of the last named. Nathaniel Putnam, Sr., at the solicitation of Francis Nurse, husband of the condemned, wrote a defence of her character, and a similar document was drawn up for public approval. This was signed by thirty-nine of the townspeople.

It was customary, under order of the court, to cause an examination to be made of the entire bodies of the accused, that any "witch mark" on them might be found. Marshal Herrick, after examining George Jacobs, reported that he found a "witch teat about a quarter of an inch long or better, with a sharp point drooping downwards,

5

so that I took a pin, and run it through the said teat, but there was neither water, blood or corruption, nor any other matter." This was regarded as the "devil's mark," but it may readily be supposed that some infirmity of the flesh would be found on a man advanced in years as Jacobs was. These declarations were received in court as evidence.

On August 5, George Burroughs, John Procter, Elizabeth Procter his wife, George Jacobs, Sr., John Willard, and Martha Carrier were tried and condemned. With the exception of Elizabeth Procter, they were executed August 19. Thirty-two inhabitants of Ipswich addressed a petition to the Court of Assistants, at Boston, in behalf of John Procter. This petition was headed by the Rev. John Wise, and the list of signers contained the names of many of the best people of that town. Another document in his favor was presented, and in court, evidence was offered to prove that one of the witnesses against him had sworn contrary to what she had stated outside. These facts furnish evidence that the persecutions did not receive universal sanction and approval. A tradition exists to the effect that the body of George Jacobs was buried on his own farm, about a mile from the present city of Salem. Remains, undoubtedly his, were exhumed in 1864, and were re-interred in the same place.

The court sat again, the last time, on the 9th of September. On that day * Martha Corey, * Mary Easty, * Alice Parker, *Ann Pudeator, Dorcas Hoar, and Mary Bradbury were condemned and sentenced; and on the 17th,* Margaret Scott, * Wilmot Reed, * Samuel Wardwell, * Mary Parker, Abigail Faulkner, Rebecca Eames, Mary Lacy, Ann Foster, and Abigail Hobbs were also sentenced. [Those whose names are indicated by a star were executed on the 22d.] By order of the governor, Sir William Phipps, Abigail Faulkner, daughter of the Rev. Francis Dane, of Andover, was pardoned, having laid in jail under sentence of death for thirteen weeks. The reason assigned for the pardon, the only one granted during the proceedings, was "insufficient evidence." The nineteen, who have been chronicled in the above brief narrative as suffering the death penalty, were the only ones who were executed; for, though it was some time before the excitement died away, there was an abatement in its violence that saved the other con-demned persons from suffering the sad fate of their neighbors and fellows. Without a single exception the executed protested their innocence to the very last, most of them making dying declarations on the scaffold. The hangings took place on a slight eminence, just removed from the town, and now known as Gallows Hill, from the sad tragedies whose final acts were enacted there.

One of the most remarkable cases on record, of heroic perseverance and unbroken persistence, is that of Giles Corey, husband of one of the executed, himself in jail at Ipswich, charged with witchcraft. He determined that his lips should remain sealed when arraigned in court, and that he would not answer to the inquiry, " guilty or not guilty." There are no records of the proceedings taken by the court when the prisoner failed to answer, but tradition has it that he was *crushed to death*. In a field somewhere between Howard Street Cemetery and Brown Street, Salem, is the locality designated by Mr. Upham. It is related that Corey urged that the weight might be increased, for his death was the only way to end the matter, as he should not answer ; and he did not. Not a word bordering on an acknowledgment of guilt, or an attestation of innocence, escaped his lips. He knew that death was the penalty, if he pleaded not guilty, and he would not confess to a crime of which he was innocent. This man was eighty-one years old ; and the barbarous death penalty inflicted on him by the officers of the law, tended to awaken the people to a realization of the grave responsibility resting on them as a Christian community. Doubts began to be felt in the public mind as to the justice of the prosecutions, and the inevitable sentence and execution. But the delusion had not reached its end.

The leaders in the prosecutions did not delay a new method of attempting to sustain the popular opinion in the course it had been running. The day after the death of Giles Corey, Thomas Putnam addressed a letter to Judge Sewall, reading as follows : " Last night, my daughter Ann was grievously tormented by witches, threatening that she should be pressed to death before Giles Corey ; but through the goodness of a gracious God she has had, at last, a little respite. Whereupon there appeared unto her (she said) a man in a winding-sheet, who told her that Giles Corey had murdered him by pressing him to death with his feet ; but that the devil there appeared unto him, and covenanted with him, and promised him that he should not be hanged. The apparition said God hardened his heart, that he should not hearken to the advice of the court, and so die an easy death ; because, as it said, it must be done to him as he has done to me. The apparition also said that Giles Corey was carried to the Court for this, and that the jury had found the murder ;. and that her father knew the man, and that the thing was done before she was born."

This "revelation" had some effect ; but the tide had turned, and the delusion was destined to die away as suddenly as it had appeared. The court adjourned the latter part of September, never to meet again. Though public opinion cannot be proved to have been the direct agent in causing the cessation of the prosecutions, yet it doubtless exerted a telling influence. Mr. Upham says that the sudden quieting down has been generally attributed to the fact that the "afflicted children" became over-confident of their power, and struck too high. When it was hinted that the Rev. Samuel Willard, and that two ladies of high social standing, one the wife of Gov. Phipps, and the other of the Rev. Mr. Hale, of Beverly, were to be accused, it brought to the excited people a realizing sense of the errors into which they had fallen, and with returning reason came a reaction which stopped the spread of the delusion, and opened the prison doors to the accused. The Rev. Mr. Hale had acted with the accusers, but when his wife was cried out against he stood up nobly in her defence. The community soon began to feel that the girls at Dr. Parris's had perjured themselves, and as this feeling gathered strength the storm which had raged so fiercely subsided.

It is a wonder, perhaps, that the reaction did not lead to the prosecution, or at least to the moral arraignment of the " afflicted children," but it did not, no doubt fortunately, for the reign of blood had been full terrible enough. Sir William Phipps, by his executive authority, divested the court of its power, and that tribunal was stricken from the lists of Courts in the Colony. It was superseded by a new court, known as the Superior Court of Judicature. Its judges were William Stoughton, chief justice, Thomas Danforth, John Richards, Wait Winthrop, and Samuel Sewall, associates. This court sat at Salem in January, 1693, and acquitted Rebecca Jacobs, Margaret Jacobs, Sarah Buckley, Job Tookey, Hannah Tyler, Candy, a negro woman, Mary Marston, Elizabeth Johnson, Abigail Barker, Mary Tyler, Sarah Hawkes, Mary Wardwell, Mary Bridges, Hannah Post, Sarah Bridges, Mary Osgood, Mary Lacy, Jr., and condemned Sarah Wardwell, Elizabeth Johnson, Jr., and Mary Post. These three were not executed, however, being discharged by order of the governor in the following May. After this many others were tried, but all were acquitted, and the number released in May, 1693, was about one hundred and fifty. Ann Foster and Sarah Osburn died in jail, and it is probable that others shared the same fate. Several had escaped from prison, and the whole number arrested and committed must have been several hundred. Those acquitted, or released by the governor, were obliged to pay all charges.

Such, briefly told, is the history of the " Salem witchcraft,"—a sad, sad tale; one not likely to be repeated in any nation. It has not been without its moral lessons. Let us hope that the memory of those who suffered death as condemned " witches," may remain green in history. The courage that faces the scaffold or the press, rather than confess to an uncommitted crime, is worthy of an epitaph engraven on the hearts of all who follow in the Christian world.

CHAPTER III.

While the witchcraft delusion was at its height, Sir William Phipps arrived in Boston, bringing the new charter from William and Mary. This charter constituted Massachusetts, Plymouth, Maine, and Nova Scotia one province, of which William Phipps was appointed governor by their majesties. The people hoped for a restoration of their former chartered rights. In this they were doomed to disappointment, but were still greatly rejoiced at obtaining so many concessions in their favor. Gov. Phipps arrived in Boston May 14, 1692, and superseded Bradstreet, who was then the acting governor of the Colony.

Simon Bradstreet.—The venerable Simon Bradstreet, who had been the last governor under the colonial charter, died in Salem March 27, 1697. He was born in England in 1603, and came to Massachusetts in 1630, as one of the Assistants. Mr. Bradstreet was deputy-governor in 1673, and so continued to 1679, when he was elected governor. He served in that office till the charter of Massachusetts was made void, in 1686. When Sir Edmund Andros was deposed by the people, in 1689, Mr. Bradstreet was again chosen governor, continuing in office until 1692, when Sir William Phipps, appointed by their majesties, came and took his place. "He was a man of deep discernment, whom neither wealth nor honor could allure from duty. He poised with an equal balance the authority of the king and the liberty of the people. Sincere in religion and pure in his life, he overcame and left the world." His house in Salem occupied the site on Essex Street, next west of Plummer Hall, and was taken down in 1750.

Ferries and Bridges.—At a very early period in the history of the settlement of Salem, ferries were established as a means of communi-

Elias Hasket Derby House.

Roger Williams House.

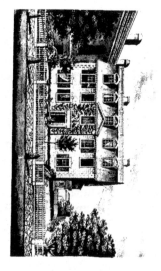

Pickman House.

Bradstreet House.

cation with the surrounding country. It is agreed by the town, Dec. 26, 1636, that John Stone shall keep a ferry betwixt his house on the neck and Cape Ann side, during the space of three years, and shall charge twopence from a stranger, and one penny from an inhabitant. This was the ferry to Beverly. Sept. 25, 1637, George Wright is granted certain land on the neck to build on, and five acres on the forest side for planting and " to keep a ferry between Butt point and Darby fort." This ferry was from the point of rocks on the southern side of the neck to Naugus Head. There ₊was at that time quite a settlement in the immediate vicinity of Butt point. Some time subsequently, possibly as late as 1725, when Timothy Day of Gloucester contracted to find materials, except iron, and make a causeway for the passengers "on yᵉ flatts by Coll. Turners," the location of the Salem end of the ferry was changed to the foot of Turner Street. When Marblehead was incorporated, in 1649, Salem reserved to itself the right of the ferry, and the appointment of the ferrymen. The Beverly ferry was continued, with numerous changes of rates and ferrymen, until the opening of Essex Bridge, Sept. 24, 1788. The ferry to Naugus Head was used till about 1785, when it was abandoned altogether.

The Mill Bridge, over South River, was built about 1664. The bridge over North River was built in 1744, and, in 1789, became the property of the town. The proposition to build a bridge from Salem to Beverly, in 1787, met with violent and determined opposition on the part of the Salem people. They assembled in town-meeting and instructed their representatives to oppose the granting of a charter, alleging as a reason that the navigation of North River would be destroyed ; and they invited the adjoining towns to join in the remonstrance, and to use their utmost endeavors to prevent the accomplishment of the project. In spite of the opposition, however, a charter was granted, and, Sept. 24, 1788, the bridge was opened to the public as a toll-bridge. The tolls were removed in 1868. A bridge was built over South River, in a line with Central and Lafayette streets, in 1805. It was built at the expense of Ezekiel Hersey Derby and others, and was accepted by the town in 1810.

The General Court at Salem.—In 1728, a dispute having arisen between Gov. Burnet and the General Court, in reference to his salary, the governor orders the General Court to meet at Salem

October 31st. And to accommodate them, the town has "the new town and court house fitted up." Salutes are fired as the governor arrives. He informs the House that he removed them from Boston because the people there endeavored to influence representatives from other places against granting him a salary. The House hold that they should not be moved from Boston, and desire the governor to order them back again, and they prepare a memorial to His Majesty " setting forth the reasons why the House cannot settle a salary on the Governor for the time being." The House having refused to do any business in Salem, holding that they should sit only in Boston, the governor, on December 12th, adjourns them to the Ship Tavern, and, on the 20th, prorogues them. April 2, 1729, the General Court again meets in Salem, and Gov. Burnet renews his call for fixing his salary, and again the question is put " whether the House will come into any further consideration of settling a salary on the Governor at this session," and decided in the negative ; and, on the 18th of the same month, the governor dissolves the Legislature, after informing the members that he had not ordered them any pay, because they had refused to do business one-third of their sessions, and to compensate him as the king required. The town of Salem votes to pay its representatives out of the town treasury.

On May 28th, the Legislature meets again in the court-house, which the town has had newly painted for its reception. Immediately after the Council is formed, the governor prorogues them to June 25th, without delivering a message, at which time they again assemble, and July 7th, without transacting any business, are adjourned to meet at Cambridge, August 21st. In the midst of his controversy with the representatives, Gov. Burnet dies September 7th. He was a son of the celebrated Bishop Burnet.

Jonathan Belcher is appointed governor in his stead, and reaches Boston in August, 1730, and, like his predecessor, has a dispute with the Legislature about his salary, and May 31, 1733, in his speech to the House, says : "In obedience to His Majesty I must inform you he still expects, that you make provision for the support of his government according to his Royal instructions "; but the House still refuses to grant the governor a fixed salary. Finally the House votes to supply the treasury with £76,500 in bills of credit, and in this manner the matter is adjusted. A misunderstanding arises soon after in regard to raising money to supply the treasury, and the governor complains bitterly of the action of the representatives in not following his instructions in relation to taxation. The Legislature agrees to supply the treasury with £100,000 in bills, and £900 is granted for fortifications at Salem. May 27, 1741, the General Court met, but was dissolved by Gov. Belcher, on the 28th, because they encouraged the formation of the Land Bank, which he says will injure unwary persons who will take the notes for money "which have no honest or solid foundation." A part of the proprietors of this bank lived in Salem.

Earthquakes. — Salem was visited by an earthquake, Nov. 18, 1755. Dr. E. A. Holyoke says in his diary, that "about 4 h. 15 m. we were awakened by a greater earthquake than has ever been known in this country. Tops of chimnies and stone walls were thrown down, and clocks stopped by the shake. I thought of nothing less than being buried instantly in the ruins of the house"; and on March 8, 1756, town-meeting was opened with prayer, by the Rev. Mr. Barnard, and several Province laws were read against profaneness and other immoralities, to the inhabitants, this seriousness being occasioned by the recent earthquake. March 12, 1761, another severe earthquake was felt in Salem, described as much the same as the one of five years before.

Stamp Act. — On the 13th of June, 1764, the House accepted a draft of a letter to their agent in London against the Sugar Act and the Stamp Act, though the latter had not gone into effect. In this letter, the House maintains that Parliament has no right to tax this Province, because it is not represented in the House of Commons. The inhabitants of Salem at once took firm and decided ground in regard to what they considered an encroachment of their rights and liberties, and at a town-meeting held Oct. 21, 1765, it was voted " that instructions be given to our representatives with regard to a late act of Parliament commonly called the Stamp Act." Benjamin Pickman, Joseph Bowditch, Edward A. Holyoke, William Pynchon, and John Higginson are appointed to draft such instructions.

On their report, the town sent instructions to Andrew Oliver and William Brown, their representatives, stating "that the Inhabitants of Salem being fully convinced that the Act, lately passed by the Parliament of Great Britain, commonly called the Stamp Act, would if carried into

6

execution be excessively grevious and burthensome to the inhabitants of this his Majesty's loyal Province ; and productive of the most fatal consequences to our trade, as it must soon drain us of the medium necessary for carrying it on, and be very injurious to Liberty, since we are therein taxed without our consent, having no Representative in Parliament. But if in any sense we are supposed to be represented, most certainly it is by such only as have an interest in laying burthens upon us for their own relief, and further as we are thereby deprived of another most valuable right, that of trial by juries and instead of it have the power of the Courts of Admiralty further extended, which must be unfavorable to Liberty. As these are some of our sentiments of this act and as we would give a public testimony of our disapprobation thereof — we do hereby request you to do everything you legally can towards obtaining a repeal of the Stamp Act."

Town Records. — Several curious entries are found on the town records about this time. It was voted in 1768, at town-meeting, that the selectmen be desired to petition the General Court in behalf of the town for an act for a lottery to raise a sum of money to be applied towards paving Main Street in said Salem ; and the same year the following vote appears on the town records : " Voted, that it is the mind of the town that proper means be used for preventing slaves especially on election days (so called) from wearing swords, beating drums and making use of powder." The townsmen, however, did not approve of slavery ; for we find that they voted, May 18, 1773, that the representatives of the town be instructed to use their utmost endeavors to prevent the future importation of negroes, "their slavery being a thing repugnant to the natural rights of mankind and highly prejudicial to the Province." But as late as Jan. 24, 1769, there appears in the "Gazette," of Salem, an announcement that a very strong, healthy negro boy is to be sold, and buyers are asked to " inquire of the printer."

Duty on Tea. — Hardly had the rejoicings ceased over the repeal of the Stamp Act, which, March 18, 1767, was "joyfully commemorated through the Colonies," when the imposition of new duties on paper, glass, and teas caused great dissatisfaction among the people. On the 13th of February, 1768, the House directs a letter to the "several Houses and Burgesses of the British Colonies on the Continent, setting forth their sentiments with regard to the great difficulties that must accrue by the operation of divers Acts of Parliament for laying taxes and duties on the Colonies with the sole and express purpose of raising a revenue. June 21st the Governor lays before the House a letter which expresses his Majesty's displeasure for their resolve for writing to other Colonies on the subject of their intended representations against some late Acts of Parliament and that it was the King's pleasure that the House rescind their vote." The House voted, ninety-two to seventeen, not to rescind. The Salem representatives, William Brown and Peter Frye, voted with the minority, and were exposed to much reproach therefor.

That the people of Salem did not sympathize with the views of their representatives is shown by their vote in town-meeting, July 18, approving the late vote of the House not to rescind, and thanking them "for their firmness in maintaining our just rights and liberties," a protest against such approbation being signed by only thirty of the inhabitants. Sept. 6, the merchants and traders of Salem meet at the King's Arms Tavern and unanimously vote "not to send any further orders for goods, and that from Jan. 1, 1769, to Jan. 1, 1770, they will not import, nor purchase of others any kind of merchandise from Great Britain except coal, salt and some articles necessary to carry on the fishery," and that they will not import any tea, glass, or paper until the Acts imposing duties on these articles are repealed.

On September 7th, one Row, for giving information that a vessel in the harbor was about to elude the payment of duties, was carried to the Common, tarred and feathered, set upon a cart, with the word "Informer," in large letters, on his breast and back, and carried through Main Street, preceded by a crowd, and bidden to flee out of town. He went to Boston, and was rewarded by the Crown officers for his sufferings.

The inhabitants of Salem, in town-meeting, held May 27, 1769, vote, after discussion, "that Messrs. Richard Derby, Jr., and John Pickering, Jr., the Representatives in General Court, be instructed to endeavor that inquiry be made into the conduct of the troops stationed among us, and that his Majesty's loyal subjects of this Province may be protected and secured against any violence or oppression; that, with regard to the revenue laws lately enacted, we esteem them our greatest grievance, as well as the unhappy cause of most others we now labor under; our obtaining full and effective relief from them you will, therefore, consider as the most weighty charge lying upon you. We earnestly recommend to you to use every means that may tend to restore the harmony and affection not long since subsisting between Great Britain and the Colonies, but which the late measures have, unhappily for both, greatly interrupted, and, if persisted in, may, in the end, totally destroy : but, at the same time, you are to keep the strictest watch over our essential constitutional rights and privileges, that none of them be in the least infringed upon."

On the first day of May, 1770, Samuel Flagg, Richard Derby, Jr., Warwick Palfray, Jonathan Ropes, Jr., John Gardner, Richard Manning, Thomas Mason, James King, and David Northey, are chosen, in town-meeting, a committee of inspection and correspondence ; said committee to offer to the inhabitants of the town a paper to sign against using tea or foreign goods ; and at the same meeting it is voted "that we do further agree to and with each other that we will not suffer any foreign tea to be used in our families, and that we will not buy any kind of goods whatever of those persons who shall sell said tea after the first day of the present month ; and further, that we will not employ any person that shall use it themselves, or shall suffer it to be used in their families."

On September 27th, "considering the memorial of the Committee on Inspection respecting the infamous conduct of John Appleton, Peter Frye, Abigail Eppes, and Elizabeth Higginson, who, in breach of a solemn agreement, took their imported goods by violence out of the hands of the committee, it was voted that a memorandum, setting forth their conduct, be read at every annual town-meeting, in March, for the space of seven years next ensuing, immediately before the choice of town officers," and that an account of their "base and infamous behaviour" be published in the "Essex Gazette" for the space of one year.

Meeting of the Provincial Assembly. — The action of the town just narrated was but a prelude to what was soon to follow ; and it was the fortune of Salem to be the theatre of the opening scenes in the great struggle that was to end in the independence of the Colonies. There is no year in the annals of Salem so memorable, and crowded so full of historic events, as the year which began on the first day of June, 1774. Here, during that time, were convened the last Provincial Assembly and first Provincial Congress ; here were chosen the first delegates to the Continental Congress ; here the assembled Province first formally renounced allegiance to the Imperial Legislature ; here was made the first attempt to enforce the last oppressive Acts of Parliament, and here that attempt was resisted ; and here, though no mortal wound was given, was shed the first blood of the American Revolution. If Salem had no history save that contained in the record of this eventful year, she would still be entitled to a high place among the historic cities of this country.

On the 13th of May, 1774, Gen. Thomas Gage arrived in Boston. He was the first British soldier appointed to the office of governor. On the 25th of the same month the General Court met at Boston, and a week later Gov. Gage adjourned them, to meet in Salem on the 7th of June. The governor proceeded to Salem on the Thursday before the Assembly met, and the next Saturday he was received with great parade, ending with a brilliant ball at the old Assembly Hall on Cambridge Street.

The Assembly met on the 7th of June, but the session lasted only eleven days. The House passed five Resolutions, protesting against the removal to Salem. No further political measure transpired in either branch until the 17th, when the House passed a Resolve, appointing as delegates to the Congress at Philadelphia, James Bowdoin, Thomas Cushing, Samuel Adams, John Adams, and Robert Treat Paine, the purpose of the Congress, as indicated by the Resolve, being "to consult upon measures for the restoration of harmony between Great Britain and the Colonies." The expenses of the delegates were also provided for. This action displeased Gov. Gage, and he ordered a proclamation for dissolving the General Court to be prepared by Thomas Flucker, the secretary of the Province. The proclamation was dated June 17, 1774, and with it the secretary proceeded to the town house, where the General Court was in session.

On arriving he found the door locked and the messenger on guard. He "directed the messenger to go in and acquaint the speaker that the secretary had a message from his Excellency to the honorable House, and desired he might be admitted to deliver it." The messenger returned, and said he had informed the speaker, as requested, "who mentioned it to the House, and their orders were to keep the door fast." Thereupon the secretary proceeded to read the paper upon the stairs, in the presence of the assembled multitude, and afterwards in the council chamber. Thus ended the last General Court held in Massachusetts under a provincial governor, and such, too, were the dramatic incidents attending the choice of the first five delegates to that congress which, by successive elections, continued throughout the war.

Governor Gage had taken up his residence at Danvers, in the mansion of Robert Hooper, now known as the " Collins House ; " and two companies of soldiers, from Castle William, land in Salem, march through the town, and encamp near the governor's abode. On the 12th of August, a Halifax regiment land, and are quartered on the neck. On September 10th, they march from the neck through the town, are joined at Danvers South Parish, now Peabody, by the guards from the governor's headquarters, and together they proceed to Boston.

On Thursday the 1st of September, writs for calling a new General Court, to be held at Salem, on the fifth of the next month, were issued by the governor's order ; but a week before the first day of the session, he published a proclamation, excusing the representatives elect from appearing at, or holding, a General Court.

Notwithstanding this proclamation, when the 5th of October arrived ninety of the representatives assembled. Among them were men of tried courage and determination, who were bent on executing the purpose they had in view, whether the governor appeared or not. We can imagine with what eager expectation the people watched their proceedings, and how earnestly the throng about the old town-house discussed the momentous questions of the day. That they might not be charged with unseemly haste, the assembly did no formal business on the first day. At three o'clock the next morning there was an alarm of fire, and when the representatives assembled they found twenty-four buildings, including the Rev. Dr. Whitaker's meeting-house, destroyed, and the town-house itself scorched and blistered.

The assembly now organized, and John Hancock was chosen chairman, and Benjamin Lincoln, clerk. A committee was appointed to consider the governor's proclamation, and the assembly adjourned. On Friday, the 7th of October, the committee reported four resolutions, declaring that the grievances which they set forth were such as " in all good governments " had " been considered among the greatest reasons for convening a parliament or assembly," and that the proclamation was further proof of the necessity of " most vigorous and

View on Essex Street.

View on Washington Street.

Heliotype Printing Co., Boston.

immediate exertions for preserving the freedom and constitution" of the province. The resolutions were adopted, and thereupon the following vote was passed : "*Voted*, That the members aforesaid do now resolve themselves into a Provincial Congress, to be joined by such other persons as have been or shall be chosen for that purpose, to take into consideration the dangerous and alarming situation of public affairs in this province, and to consult and determine on such measures as they shall judge will tend to promote the true interest of His Majesty, and the peace, welfare and prosperity of the province."

Having thus solemnly renounced the authority of parliament, and affirmed the fundamental right of the people to institute a government, when in their judgment the regular administration had overstepped the limits of the constitution, they adjourned to more comfortable quarters at Concord, to meet on the following Tuesday. Here they organized the Congress, by raising Hancock to the presidency, and electing Lincoln secretary. They continued their sittings at Concord and Cambridge, and by midsummer three sessions had been held, had transacted business, and finally dissolved. On the day of their dissolution, they again assembled, by the recommendation of the Continental Congress, as an independent government under the charter. The vote of the assembly at Salem, on the 7th of October, 1774, was the legitimate act of the Province, in the only way in which the Province could express its pleasure. From this fact the movement in Salem derives a peculiar significance, and it can be justly claimed as the first official act of the Province by which she put herself in open, actual opposition to the home government.[*]

Leslie's Retreat. — The winter of 1774–75 came on, and found the breach between the Colonies and the mother country growing wider and wider. Military stores had already been seized, in various places, by the British troops, under orders from Gen. Gage, when, on a Sabbath afternoon in midwinter, a detachment of about three hundred British soldiers, under Col. Leslie, land at Marblehead, and march through the town towards Salem, with the purpose of seizing cer-

---

[*] In preparing this brief account of the meeting of the Provincial Congress, liberal use has been made of an address delivered by Abner C. Goodell, Jr., Esq., before the Essex Institute, Oct. 5, 1874, in which the subject is elaborately and exhaustively treated. (See *Hist. Coll. Essex Institute*, vol. xiii., page 1.)

tain cannon loaned to the Provincial Congress. Maj. John Pedrick hastened to Salem to give the alarm, and, as the troops marched along through the " South fields," they were obliged to stop and repair the bridge at the South Mills, which the inhabitants had torn up to delay their passage. Hastily repairing it they cross, and the advance guard march towards Union Wharf as a decoy, while the main body advance towards the North Bridge, halting a few minutes at the court-house. It was about four o'clock on the afternoon of Sunday, Feb. 26, 1775. The inhabitants of Salem were already aroused. Pastors dismissed their congregations, and repaired with them to the scene of action. Capt. Mason, living near the old North Church, shouted the alarm cry at the door : " The regulars are coming ! " and then hastened to the bridge. Leslie and his men arrived at North Bridge, attended by a concourse of people, and found the draw raised to prevent their further progress. He requested Richard Derby, who owned part of the cannon,* to exert his influence for their surrender, and received the reply : " Find them if you can ; take them if you can ; they will never be surrendered."

On the other side of the river was Timothy Pickering, who had just been chosen colonel of the First Regiment, with forty armed militia ready to dispute Leslie's passage across the stream. Leslie threatened to fire on the people, when Capt. John Felt, who had " kept close to Leslie every step from the court-house," said to him : " You had better not fire, for there," pointing to the other side of the river, " is a multitude, every man of whom is ready to die in this strife."

On the top of the raised leaf of the draw, on the opposite side of the stream, the more adventurous spirits had clambered. They called to the soldiers in strong and defiant language, and received in reply a threat that if they did not desist they would be fired upon. " Fire and be d—d ! " calls out Capt. Joshua Ward, in language more forci-

---

* Mr. Gideon Tucker, who died in 1861, aged eighty-three, related that when a boy six or seven years old, being with his father, at his wharf, in North Salem, there was pointed out to him the place where the cannon were piled. They were owned, he was told, by various persons, and had been landed from merchant vessels, a general peace making them unnecessary. When the alarm came that Leslie was on the road from Marblehead, these cannon were carried off by the farmers, and were placed on land owned by Col. Mason, near the present head of School Street. There they remained till about 1793.

ble than elegant.   Three gondolas lay on the west side of the bridge, and Jonathan Felt, a shipmaster, Frank Benson, and Joseph Whicher, the foreman in Maj. Sprague's distillery, fearful that the enemy might use them to cross in, set about scuttling them to render them useless. A scuffle ensued between the soldiers and those in the gondolas, and Whicher received a wound from a bayonet, drawing blood, and of which he was afterwards exceedingly proud.   Others were somewhat scratched, and a bloody struggle seemed imminent.

While matters were fast tending to a disastrous conflict, the Rev. Thomas Barnard of the North Church appeared as a mediator between Leslie and the people.   " You cannot," said he, " commit this viola-tion against innocent men, here, on this holy day, without sinning against God and humanity.   Let me entreat you to return."   " And who are you, sir? " answered Leslie to this remonstrance.   The young minister replied, " I am Thomas Barnard, a minister of the gospel, and my mission is peace."   He suggests the compromise by which honor is to be saved, on one side, and no guns lost on the other. Leslie agrees that if the draw is lowered, and he permitted to lead his men thirty rods beyond, he would then countermarch and leave the town.   Col. Pickering consents, a line is drawn and guarded by Pickering's men, and the haughty Briton crosses, turns in the face of the enemy, and proceeds expeditiously back to Marblehead, and from thence to Boston.

For the first time in the history of the Colony, the military author-ity of Great Britain had received a check; for the first time, blood had been spilt in a strife between the Colony and the mother country ; and that the struggle was not as bloody and memorable as that at Lexington, which took place soon after, was due to the prudence and caution and forbearance of Col. Leslie.   A single shot, and the brave and determined men of Salem who stood at North Bridge, under the lead of the gallant Felt, would have left few of the British soldiers to report to Gen. Gage the result of their expedition.   A flag-staff now marks the spot on which the townspeople stood, in their opposition to the encroachment of the British troops on that eventful winter Sab-bath in 1775.

Salem Militia. — Leslie's expedition roused the people of Salem to a sense of their danger ; and on the 14th of March following, all persons on the alarm-list receive warning to meet in " School Street,"

7

and on the 25th, the town votes to raise two companies of minute-men " whose attachment to their country can be relied on." On the 19th of April, Benjamin Pierce, of Salem, is killed at the battle of Lexington. Col. Pickering, with three hundred soldiers, march as fast as they can from Salem towards Lexington, but do not arrive in sight of the enemy till the last of them are retreating through Charlestown. For the failure to arrive in season, the Salem troops are greatly censured ; the inhabitants are highly indignant at this unjust censure of their soldiers, and call a town-meeting, Aug. 10, 1775, to make statement of the facts to the General Court.   This is done at length, the statement beginning as follows : " On the 19th of April, very soon after the barbarous deeds of the King's troops at Lexington, the inhabitants mustered in arms, and near three hundred marched off and directed their course according to the intelligence they were continually receiving on the road, of the situation of the troops.   Thousands of men nearer, much nearer the scene of action, either stayed at home, or arrived no sooner than the Salem militia."

This statement is sent to the General Court, which body thereupon votes : " In House of Representatives, August 17, 1775.   On a petition from the town of Salem complaining of many illiberal reflections being cast by some individuals respecting the conduct of said town, in the present dispute between Great Britain and the Colonies. — Resolved : — That notwithstanding many ungenerous aspersions have been cast on said town, there is nothing appears to this court, in the conduct thereof, inimical to the liberties and privileges of America, but on the contrary, in many instances, its exertions have been such as has done its inhabitants much honor, and been of great advantage to the colony."

Benedict Arnold. — On the 14th of September, 1775, a detachment of troops sent from the headquarters at Cambridge, by Gen. Washington, stop for dinner at Salem, on their way to attempt the capture of Quebec.   This remarkable expedition was commanded by Benedict Arnold, then high in favor with Washington ; and his indomitable courage and unfailing resources made the passage of the trackless woods of Maine by his troops a possibility.   Congress, for this service, made Arnold a brigadier-general ; and, while we execrate his subsequent treachery, this should be remembered to his credit.

Salem in the Revolution. — From 1775 till the news of the declaration of peace was received, April 3, 1783, Salem bore an honorable part in the contest that was waged for liberty and freedom. She furnished men to fill the ranks of the army, and money and clothing for its support. Her people were ready to sacrifice all, if need be, in the cause of independence and for the establishment of the rights of the Colonies.

At a town-meeting, held Wednesday, June 12, 1776, the following stirring and patriotic address to their representatives was adopted by men who knew the meaning of the brave words they used : — " To the Gentlemen who represent the inhabitants of Salem in the present General Court. Gentlemen : We the inhabitants of the town of Salem in town meeting legally assembled hereby advise you that if the Honorable Congress shall for the safety of the United American colonies declare them independent of the Kingdom of Great Britain we will solemnly engage with our lives and fortunes to support them in the measure."

After the Revolution. — The War of the Revolution having been brought to a successful termination, the inhabitants of Salem turned their attention to the avocations of peace. Commerce flourished here with unexampled prosperity, and the white sails of Salem's ships were unfurled in every port in the known world, and carried the fame and name of Salem to the uttermost parts of the earth. Salem was at the height of her commercial prosperity during the period from the close of the Revolutionary War to the time of the embargo, in 1808. She had eight hundred men on the ocean imperilled by the declaration of war in 1812.

Being so largely engaged in commerce, her people naturally looked with alarm upon the opening of a contest that might sweep their vessels from the seas and destroy millions of their property. They assembled in town meeting June 22, 1812, and chose a committee to draft a memorial to Congress praying that the country might be saved from an "unjust and ruinous war." The committee consisted of the most respected citizens of the town : Jacob Ashton, Joseph Peabody, William Orne, Willard Peele, Samuel Putnam, Benjamin Pierce, Samuel Upton, John Pickering, and Nathaniel Bowditch. Their memorial declared that war was unnecessary ; that it was impolitic, because an immense amount of property would be abandoned to the cruisers of Great Britain ; and that the inhabitants of Salem would individually sustain immense losses. But the remonstrance came too late. The official announcement of the declaration of war was received the next day.

After war had been formally declared, Salem stood ready to assist in bringing it to a successful issue. An instance of the patriotic feeling which pervaded the very class that at first thought the war unnecessary and impolitic, may be found in the alacrity with which they fitted out a vessel and sent for the remains of Lawrence and Ludlow, the dead heroes of the memorable fight between the "Chesapeake" and "Shannon." This celebrated naval contest was fought on the 1st of June, 1813, so near the shores of Salem that many of the citizens witnessed it from the heights in the vicinity, Legge's Hill being a very prominent point of view.

Lawrence was only in his thirty-second year, but had before distinguished himself for his bravery and skill. The famous expression of the dying hero will never be forgotten. After he had been mortally wounded, and carried below, he issued from the cock-pit his memorable orders, "Keep the guns going," "Fight her till she strikes or sinks;" and when he knew that the enemy had carried the spardeck, he sent the emphatic message to the gun-deck, "Don't give up the ship." No officer was left on the deck of the "Chesapeake" undisabled, higher in rank than a midshipman.

When the particulars of the fight were received from Halifax, whither the "Chesapeake" was taken, the patriotic merchants and navigators of Salem made arrangements to recover the remains of Capt. Lawrence. Capt. George Crowinshield, Jr., projected the undertaking, and fitted and provisioned the brig "Henry," entirely at his own expense, had her commissioned with a flag of truce, and sailed for Halifax for the purpose of soliciting the body. The "Henry" was manned by Salem shipmasters, who volunteered their services to perform the voyage. Capt. George Crowninsheld, Jr., was commander; Capt. Holten J. Breed, first officer; and Capt. Samuel Briggs, second officer. The brig sailed from Salem on Saturday, August 7, and returned on Wednesday, August 18, with the bodies of Capt. James Lawrence and Lieut. Augustus C. Ludlow, both victims of the sea-fight off the shores of Salem.

The funeral observances, which took place on Monday Aug. 23, 1813, were on a scale of unwonted and imposing magnitude. The

Vice-President of the United States, Elbridge Gerry, and a large number of distinguished officers of the army and navy were present. On the day of the funeral every vessel in the harbor and at the wharves, and all the flag-staffs in town, wore the American ensign at half-mast. The brig "Henry," clad in sable, lay at anchor in the harbor. At half-past twelve o'clock the remains were placed in barges, and, preceded by a long procession of boats, filled with seamen uniformed in blue jackets, with a blue ribbon on their hats, bearing the motto, "Free Trade and Sailors' Rights," were rowed by minute-strokes to the end of India (now Phillips) Wharf, where hearses were ready to receive them. From the time that the boats left the brig until the bodies were landed, the U. S. brig "Rattlesnake" and the brig "Henry," in which they were brought, alternately fired minute-guns. A procession was formed at the head of India Wharf, under the direction of Maj. John Saunders, which, escorted by the Salem Light Infantry, Capt. James C. King, moved through a part of Derby Street, Hardy, Essex, North, Lynde, Court, Church, and Brown streets, to the Howard Street Church, where the funeral oration was pronounced by the Hon. Joseph Story, and the rites of sepulture performed by the Rev. Mr. Henshaw, of Marblehead, Capt. Peabody's company of artillery firing minute-guns from Washington Square. The bodies were temporarily deposited in the tomb of Capt. George Crowninshield, in the Howard Street Cemetery.

Such were the honors that Salem paid to the two youthful heroes who lost their lives while defending the flag of their country. Lawrence was thirty-one ; Ludlow, twenty-one. Short as had been their lives, they had so conducted themselves as to gain the gratitude of their countrymen and the respect and admiration of their opponents.

During the war, details from the several military companies were employed in constructing defences at "Juniper" and Hospital point, and in guarding the most prominent positions on the Neck. A large, heavy-timbered observatory was built just inside the "great pasture" gate, which stood until demolished by the storm of Aug. 1, 1815. Salem sent out a large number of privateers during this war, of which some notice is given in a succeeding chapter.

From the close of the war until the adoption of the city charter, in 1836, no very notable event marked the history of Salem. The calm and placid stream flows quietly along unnoticed, while the brawling and dangerous rapids fix our attention. History is little else than the record of disasters. War and turmoil, rebellion and riot, and their results, fill the larger part of the pages of history. Happy is the town whose record is short, because it is a record of peace and prosperity.

City Government. — As early as the year 1805 the subject of a city form of government was seriously considered, but the project took no definite shape until Jan. 29, 1836, on which day a town-meeting was called, upon petition of Joseph Peabody and others, to ascertain the sense of the town in relation to a city charter, the Hon. Leverett Saltonstall presiding. A committee of three persons was chosen from each ward, on motion of E. H. Derby, who, together with the select-men, were to constitute a committee to consider and report upon the expediency of a change in the form of government.

On the 15th of February the committee reported in favor of the change, and the meeting adopted a resolve "that it is expedient to adopt a city form of government." The selectmen were instructed to petition the General Court in behalf of the town for an Act of incorporation as a city, and a committee was appointed to draft a city charter. This committee consisted of Messrs. Leverett Saltonstall, Nathaniel Silsbee, Jr., Perley Putnam, Nathaniel J. Lord, Benjamin Merrill, Nathaniel L. Rogers, and Joseph G. Waters; and fifteen hundred copies of their report were printed and distributed forthwith. At a meeting of the committee on February 20th, it was voted that a charter for the city be obtained as soon as may be.

The Act "to establish the city of Salem" was approved March 23, 1836, by Edward Everett, governor of the Commonwealth. Warrants were now issued for a town-meeting, to be held April 4, 1836. This meeting was held in the town hall, the Hon. Benjamin Merrill presiding; 802 votes were cast, of which 617 were for the charter, and 185 against it.

This action closed the history of the town of Salem,—a history extending over two centuries, and replete in its earlier years with stirring events and honorable actions, and making a record of which any town might be justly proud.

CHAPTER IV.

SKETCH OF SALEM SINCE THE ADOPTION OF A CITY CHARTER.

Salem was the second city incorporated in the Commonwealth, the Act granting a city charter being dated March 23, 1836. Boston was incorporated Feb. 22, 1822 ; and Lowell, April 1, 1836. The charter of Salem was modelled after that of Boston. It provided for a city government, to consist of a mayor, six aldermen, and twenty-four common councilmen. The only change in this respect that has since been made has been the addition of one member to the board of aldermen. This was done by statute of 1878. The city charter having been accepted April 4, 1836, the selectmen issued their warrants for an election of mayor and members of the city council on the twenty-fifth day of April, 1836. At this election 1,104 votes were cast for mayor, of which the Hon. Leverett Saltonstall received 752 votes, and was elected. Perley Putnam had 260 votes, George Peabody 56, and David Putnam 36. Samuel Holman, Jr., George Peabody, Henry Whipple, David Pingree, John Waters, and Oliver Parsons were chosen to constitute the board of aldermen.

The organization of the new city government took place on Monday, May 9, 1836, at ten o'clock, in the Tabernacle Church. Prayer was offered by the Rev. Dr. Brazer, and David Cummins administered the oath of office to the mayor-elect. Mayor Saltonstall delivered his inaugural address, and at its close the two boards retired to rooms in the court-house, formerly used as a town hall. John Glen King was chosen president, and Nathaniel Cleaves clerk of the common council. Joseph Cloutman was elected city clerk, and the new government was ready to commence its labors. The city council continued to hold its sessions at the court-house until the present city hall was ready for occupancy.

City Hall. — On the third day of April, 1837, Mayor Saltonstall, with Aldermen Peabody and Parsons, and Councilmen Putnam, Rogers, Shepard, and Russell, were appointed a committee to report what measures were expedient to be taken to provide suitable accommodations for the city council and officers of the city; and May 19, 1837, they reported that it was expedient to erect a city hall on Court, now Washington Street. A committee of five was appointed to superintend its erection; and on the 24th of May, 1838, the mayor, as chairman of the committee, reported that the city hall was ready to be occupied, and Thursday, May 31, the first meeting of the city council was held therein, Mayor Saltonstall delivering an address upon the occasion. The cost of the city hall, completed and furnished, together with the land, was $22,878.69, which sum was wholly paid from the surplus revenue hereafter referred to. The city hall was enlarged, in 1876, during the administration of Mayor Williams, who delivered a dedicatory address May 8, 1876. The cost of the improvement was about $24,000; and, as enlarged, it will doubtless supply the needs of the city for many years to come.

The city hall has this noteworthy fact connected with its history: It is the only building that has been, or probably ever will be, built in Salem with surplus revenue returned by the United States government, because the coffers of the nation were full to overflowing. The income from customs duties and the sales of public lands so far exceeded the estimates that the secretary of the treasury found his receipts to be $40,000,000 in excess of his needs; and that sum was, by Act of Congress, distributed among the States, which, in turn, made a distribution among the cities and towns. Salem's share of this surplus revenue was $33,843.49.

City Seal. — An abiding place having thus been provided for the city officials, attention was turned to procuring an appropriate municipal seal; and March 11, 1839, an ordinance was adopted, providing for the seal as at present used by the city. The design was adopted substantially as drawn by Mr. George Peabody, then a member of the board of aldermen; and the ordinance before-mentioned provided that the following be the device of the seal of the city, to wit: In the centre thereof a shield, bearing upon it a ship under full sail, approaching a coast designated by the costume of the person standing upon it, and by the trees near him, as a portion of the East Indies; beneath the shield, this motto: "*Divitis Indiæ usque ad ultimum sinum,*" signifying "To

Court House.

City Hall.

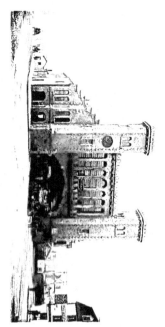

Eastern R. R. Station.

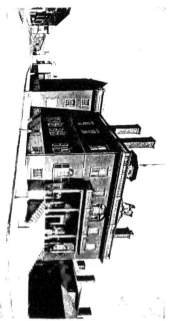

Custom House.

the farthest port of the rich East; " and above the shield, a dove, bearing an olive-branch in her mouth. In the circumference encircling the shield, the words "*Salem condita, A. D. 1626*," "*Civitatis regimine donata, A. D. 1836.*" The engraver, Mr. Stott, of Boston, substituted a female for the male figure intended by the ordinance, apparently without authority from any one. The seal of a city should be characteristic and unique, so that it could not fitly be borne by any other city; for it is an enduring link between the past and the future. It should bear upon its face an epitome of the city's history. The seal of Salem seems to meet the conditions of an historic work. It fitly typifies and commemorates that commercial enterprise that during the first half of this century gave Salem a peculiar distinction among the cities of the earth, and carried the fame of her merchants, as well as the flag of the country, into unknown seas.*

Mayors. — A brief notice of the men who have been assigned the position of mayor and of president of the lower branch of the city government will be of interest, as indicating the character of the municipal government of Salem.

Leverett Saltonstall was the first mayor, serving from May 9, 1836, to Dec. 5, 1838, when he resigned to take the seat in Congress to which he had been elected, and where he served until 1843. He was born in Haverhill, June 13, 1783, and graduated at Harvard in 1802. He was a member of both branches of the State Legislature, and President of the Senate in 1831. Harvard conferred upon him the degree of LL. D. in 1838. He was an active member of the American Academy of Arts and Sciences, and of the Massachusetts Historical Society. He was a distinguished lawyer, a graceful and pleasing orator, and a man universally respected and beloved. He died May 8, 1845.

Stephen C. Phillips was mayor from Dec. 5, 1838, to 1842. He was born in Salem, Nov. 4, 1801, and graduated at Harvard in 1819. From 1824 to 1829 he was a representative to the General Court; in 1830–31, a member of the State Senate; and 1832–33, again in the House. He was a representative to Congress from 1834 to 1838, and in 1848 and 1849 Free Soil candidate for governor. Mr. Phillips was

---

* For a full account of the proceedings on the adoption of the city seal, see an article by Robert S. Rantoul, Esq., in Historical Collections of Essex Institute, Vol. VIII., page 3.

8

deeply interested in the cause of education, and on his retirement from the office of mayor he gave the whole of his salary to the city for the benefit of the public schools. He was lost by the burning of the steamer "Montreal" on the St. Lawrence River, June 26, 1857.

Stephen P. Webb served as mayor in 1842, '43, and '44, and again in 1860, '61, and '62. He was born in Salem, March 20, 1804, and graduated at Harvard in 1824. He was mayor of San Francisco for one year from the autumn of 1854, which was during the stirring times of the vigilance committee. He was city clerk in Salem from 1863 to 1871.

Joseph S. Cabot was mayor four years, in 1845–46–47 and '48. He was born in Salem, Oct. 8, 1796, and died June 29, 1874. In 1829 he was chosen president of the Asiatic Bank, and continued in that office till his death, with brief intervals, when he was bank commissioner. He was greatly interested in horticulture, and was president of the Massachusetts Horticultural Society. He was also president of the Salem Savings Bank, and of the Harmony Grove Cemetery Corporation.

Nathaniel Silsbee, Jr., was mayor four years, — in 1849–50, and again in 1858–59. He was born in Salem, Dec. 28, 1804, and graduated at Harvard in 1824. He was for many years Treasurer of Harvard College.

David Pingree served as mayor in 1851. He was born in Georgetown, in 1795, and died in Salem, March 31, 1863. He was a prominent merchant, president of the Naumkeag Bank from its organization in 1831 ; and president of the Naumkeag Cotton Company from its establishment till his death.

Charles W. Upham was mayor in 1852. Born in St. John, N. B., May 4, 1802, he graduated at Harvard in 1821. He was settled over the First Church in Salem from 1824 to 1844. He was a member of the thirty-third Congress 1853–55, and a representative to the General Court in 1849, 1859, and 1860 ; a member of the State Senate in 1850, 1857, and 1858, — the last two years being president of that body. Mr. Upham is quite celebrated as an author, — the "History of Salem Witchcraft," and "Life of Timothy Pickering" being among his most recent productions. He was at various times editor of the "Christian Register" and "Christian Review." His death occurred June 15, 1875.

Asahel Huntington served as mayor in 1853. He was born in Topsfield, July 23, 1798, and graduated at Yale in 1819. He was county and district attorney, appointed first in 1830. In 1845 he resigned as district attorney; but in 1847 he was again elected to that office, and served till 1851, when he was appointed clerk of the courts for Essex County, which office he held till his death. He was twice a representative to the General Court, and was president of the Essex Institute. He was greatly interested in the cause of temperance. He died Sept. 5, 1870.

Joseph Andrews served as mayor in 1854–55. He was born in Salem Dec. 10, 1808, and died in Boston Feb. 8, 1869. He was captain of the Salem Light Infantry and brigadier-general of the State militia, which position he held in 1861, at the opening of the Rebellion. He commanded at Fort Warren, in Boston harbor, and had charge of the State troops sent to that station prior to their departure for the seat of war, and until it ceased to be used for that purpose. He was a bank official.

William S. Messervy was mayor in 1856–57. He was born in Salem Aug. 26, 1812. Appointed as territorial [secretary of New Mexico in 1853, he was at one time the acting-governor.

Stephen G. Wheatland served as mayor in 1863–64. He was born in Newton, Aug. 11, 1824, and graduated at Harvard in 1844. He served as representative to the General Court for several years, and is a lawyer by profession.

Joseph B. F. Osgood was mayor in 1865. He was born in Salem July 1, 1823, and graduated at Harvard in 1846. He has served in both branches of the State Legislature, and is the present judge of the first district court of Essex County, having been appointed on the establishment of the court in 1874.

David Roberts served as mayor in 1866–67, resigning on account of a disagreement with his board of aldermen, Sept. 26, 1867. He is a lawyer, has served in the lower branch of the State Legislature, and is the author of a book on Admiralty Law and Practice. He was born in Hamilton, April 5, 1804.

William Cogswell was elected mayor, Sept. 26, 1867, on the resignation of Mayor Roberts, and served in 1868–69, and again in 1873–74. He was born in Bradford, Aug. 23, 1838, and graduated at the Harvard Law School. He entered the War of the Rebellion as captain in the 2d Mass. Regiment, and rose to the rank of brevet brigadier-general. He was with Sherman during his memorable march through Georgia. In 1870–71 he was a representative to the General Court. A lawyer by profession, he now holds the office of State inspector of fish.

Nathaniel Brown was mayor in 1870–71. He was born in Salem, March 18, 1827, and was a captain in the merchant service for many years. He is president of the Salem Marine Society, and delivered the address on the centennial anniversary of the incorporation of that society in 1871.

Samuel Calley served as mayor in 1872. He was born in Salem, April 13, 1821, and is by trade a house-painter. He served as representative in the General Court in 1870 and 1871.

Henry L. Williams served as mayor in 1875–76. He was born in Salem, July 23, 1815. He is president of the National Exchange Bank, and of the Salem Five Cent Savings Bank, and was for a long time a director of the Eastern Railroad.

Henry K. Oliver was mayor in 1877, '78, and '79. He was born in Beverly, Nov. 24, 1800, and graduated at Harvard in 1818. He was adjutant-general from 1844 to 1848, and was State treasurer during the war, from 1861 to 1866. He has been interested in the labor question, and was chief of the State bureau of labor for several years. He served as mayor of Lawrence in 1859, and as agent of the State board of education in 1858 and '59. At the Philadelphia exhibition in 1876, he was one of the judges of musical instruments. He was a member of the first common council of Salem. Mr. Oliver was a teacher by profession, and taught many years in Salem, being the first teacher of the English High School. He was afterwards agent of the Atlantic Cotton Mills at Lawrence.

Presidents of the Common Council. — John Glen King was president of the common council in 1836–37. He was born in Salem, March 19, 1787, and died July 26, 1857. He graduated at Harvard in 1807, and was one of that corps of scholars who gave the type and character to the Essex bar. He was a member of both branches of the State Legislature, and one of the founders of the Essex Historical Society.

Richard S. Rogers was president in 1838. He was born in 1790, and was an active merchant in the firm of N. L. Rogers & Bros., who were pioneers in the United States of the Zanzibar and New Holland trades. For many years, down to 1842, they were engaged in foreign commerce with the East Indies, and were among the most distinguished merchants of Salem. He died at Salem, June 11, 1873.

John Russell was president in 1839–40–41. He was born in Boston in 1779, and was an apprentice in the office of the "Columbian Centinel." He served as colonel of the Salem Artillery Regiment; was president of the Salem Charitable Mechanic Association, a representative to the General Court, and cashier and president of the Bank of General Interest. He died in Salem, April 12, 1853.

Joshua H. Ward was president in 1842–43–44. He resigned Sept. 2, 1844, on his appointment as judge of the court of common pleas. He was born in Salem, July 8, 1808, and graduated at Harvard in 1829. He was the youngest judge upon the bench, being only thirty-six at the time of his appointment. He left a lucrative practice to take the seat, and won the respect and esteem of all who had occasion to attend the courts. He served repeatedly in the lower branch of the State Legislature, and died at Salem, June 5, 1848.

David Putnam was chosen president on the resignation of Judge Ward, Sept. 5, 1844, and served during the remainder of the year. He was born in Danvers, in 1780, was a dry-goods merchant, and brigadier-general in the State militia. He died in Salem, May 15, 1866.

Joseph G. Sprague was president in 1845–46–47. He was born in Danvers in 1786, and was for twenty years the cashier of the Naumkeag Bank. He died Dec. 1, 1852.

Jonathan C. Perkins was president in 1848. He was born at Ipswich, Nov. 21, 1809, and graduated at Amherst College in 1832. He was State senator in 1849, and was appointed a justice of the court of common pleas in 1848, which position he held till the abolition of the court in 1859. For several years he was the city solicitor. He was one of the trustees of Amherst College. He edited and annotated several valuable legal works. His death occurred at Salem, Dec. 12, 1877.

Benjamin Wheatland was president in 1849–50–51. He was born in Salem, May 27, 1801, and graduated at Harvard in 1819. He was agent of the Newmarket Manufacturing Company for many years, and died in Salem, Dec. 28, 1854.

John Whipple was president in 1852–53. He was born in Hamilton, and died Aug. 6, 1876, at the age of seventy-five years. He was a manufacturer of furniture, and represented Salem in the lower branch of the Legislature.

Daniel Potter was president in 1854–55. He was born in Ipswich, March 24, 1800, and was by trade a blacksmith. He has been a representative to the General Court, and for many years a deputy sheriff for Essex County, having served continuously in the latter office since 1855.

John Webster was president in 1856. He was born in Salem, Sept. 10, 1804, and was in early years a master mariner, making voyages to Zanzibar and other ports. He is now treasurer of the Newmarket Manufacturing Company.

William C. Endicott was president in 1857. He was born in Salem, Nov. 19, 1826, and graduated at Harvard in 1847. He was appointed one of the justices of the supreme judicial court in 1873, and is now upon the bench. He was for several years the city solicitor. He takes an active interest in science and literature, and is the present president of the Peabody Academy of Science.

Stephen B. Ives was president in 1858. He was born in Salem, April 12, 1801, and was a bookseller and publisher. He has served in the lower branch of the Legislature, and has always taken an active part in municipal affairs.

Henry L. Williams was president in 1859, and mayor during the years 1875–76.

James H. Battis was president in 1860. He was born in Salem, Dec. 10, 1819, and is a manufacturer of cigars. He has been storekeeper at the Salem custom-house.

Stephen G. Wheatland was president in 1861–62, and mayor during the years 1863–64.

William G. Choate was president in 1863–64. He was born in Salem, Aug. 30, 1830, and graduated at Harvard in 1852. He was assistant attorney-general of Massachusetts. He has practised law in New York City since 1865, and was appointed Judge of the United States Court for the Southern District of New York in 1878.

Gilbert L. Streeter was president in 1865, and again in 1870–71–72. He was born in Salem April 30, 1823, and is the editor of the Salem "Observer," and an officer in the First National Bank.

Charles S. Osgood was president in 1866–67–68 and '69. He was born in Salem March 13, 1839. He served in the board of aldermen two years, and in the common council seven years. He was deputy collector of the port of Salem from 1864 to 1873; and represented Salem in the Massachusetts House of Representatives for six years, from 1874 to 1879, inclusive.

William M. Hill was president from 1873 to Jan. 14, 1875, when he resigned to accept the position of city marshal, which office he held until 1877, when he was appointed on the State Detective Force. He was born in Salem Aug. 16, 1831, and is by trade a currier.

George W. Williams was chosen president on the resignation of Mr. Hill, Jan. 14, 1875, and held the position during the remainder of the year. He was born in Salem, Oct. 2, 1839.

George H. Hill was president in 1876. He was born in Salem July 14, 1842, and is in the drug business.

Arthur L. Huntington was president in 1877–78. He was born in Salem Aug. 12, 1848, and graduated at Harvard in 1870. He is a member of the Essex bar.

William A. Hill was president in 1879. He was born in Marblehead, June, 28, 1840, and is in the leather business.

Such is a brief history of the men who have been prominent in the government of Salem since its organization as a city. It includes the names of many who have attained great eminence in their different walks in life, and the name of no one appears there who has not striven to increase the prosperity and add to the material welfare of the city.

The years from the adoption of the city charter to the opening of the War of the Rebellion in 1861 were quiet and uneventful years in the history of Salem. During that period the commercial prosperity of the city, already declining, continued to decrease, and her ships engaged in foreign commerce were mostly entered and cleared at the great commercial cities. The opening of the Eastern Railroad to Boston Aug. 27, 1838, and the increased facilities for travel, have tended to concentrate business at the great centres of trade, and Salem no longer holds her place as one of the principal cities engaged in foreign commerce. Other avenues of business have been opened, however, which will be noticed more at length in a succeeding chapter.

Salem in the Civil War. — We have seen in the preceding chapter
that, during the War of the Revolution, the people of Salem, in town-
meeting assembled, declared themselves ready to support the cause
of freedom with "their lives and fortunes," and that upon her soil the
first blood of that contest was shed. When, nearly a century later,
civil war hung like a black and angry cloud over the nation, and
threatened to rend it asunder, Salem again took a prominent and
honorable part in defence of the national honor and life. The
complete history of Salem in the civil war would contain a record of
the movements of every regiment, battalion, and unattached company
from Massachusetts, and a description of the cruises of many of the
war vessels of the government. On the 16th of January, 1861, Gov.
John A. Andrew issued the order which caused the non-combatants to
leave the ranks of our militia organizations and their places to be filled
by those who were willing to enter upon active service in defence of
the country.

The Salem Light Infantry, on Monday evening, April 9, 1861, gave
an exhibition drill and ball at Mechanic Hall, at which Gov. Andrew
was present. At the close of the drill, he addressed the company,
expressing the pleasure he had derived from witnessing the brilliant
and beautiful exhibition. He closed by saying that he hoped there
would be no occasion for their services in the field ; but, if duty called,
he had no doubt that they would promptly rally to the defence of the
starry flag, under which their fathers had marched to battle. The
governor did not realize that the catastrophe he dreaded was so near
at hand. Within the week, on the morning of Friday, April 12, Fort
Sumter was fired on, and the loyal men in the North sprang to arms.
On the 15th of April, President Lincoln issued a proclamation calling
for 75,000 men to march to the defence of the country ; and on
Thursday, the 18th of April, but little more than a week from the
evening of the ball, the brave men who danced there to the soft and
melodious music of the waltz, followed the stirring and martial strains
of the band, to defend with their lives, if need be, the insult to the
national flag that floated from the battlements of Sumter.

The Salem Light Infantry, Capt. Devereux, was the first company
to leave Salem ; but the Mechanic Light Infantry, Capt. Pierson, and
the City Guards, Capt. Danforth, were not far behind, — both those
companies leaving Salem on Saturday morning, April 20. Eight

days after the first gun opened on Fort Sumter, three full companies had left Salem for the scene of action. The Salem Light Infantry, called also the Salem Zouaves, formed part of the 8th Regiment; and on their departure from Boston, Gov. Andrew closed his address to them as follows : " Mr. Commander, — Go forth with the blessing of your country and the confidence of your fellow-citizens. Under the blessing of God, in a good and holy cause, with stout hearts and stalwart arms, go forth to victory. On your shields be returned, or bring them with you. You are the advance-guard of Massachusetts soldiers. As such, I bid you God-speed and farewell."

The city council met on Friday evening, April 19th, and appropriated $15,000 " for the benefit of those of our fellow citizens who have so promptly and so nobly responded to the call of their country," and the private citizens did all in their power to encourage and assist them.

The noble record of the three months' volunteers, who so promptly obeyed the orders issued by Gov. Andrew in April, their valuable services rendered on land and water, the rescue of the frigate " Constitution," the brave deeds of the men of the 5th Regiment at Bull Run, the salvation to the Union of the city of Baltimore ; in all these historic events Salem volunteers bore an honorable part, and acquired in their short career an experience which fitted them for efficient service in the regiments which they found forming on their return. Out of the ranks of the Salem Light Infantry, known sometimes as the Salem Zouaves, twenty-six officers were commissioned.

When the call came for a response from the light batteries of the State, the old Salem Artillery, under Capt. Charles Manning, was one of the first in the field, with the title of the 4th Light Battery. In the heavy artillery regiments assigned to the defence of our border cities, but transformed later into infantry regiments, the city was so well represented that the First Heavy Artillery alone contained between two and three hundred Salem men. When Gen. Banks made his successful retreat down the Shenandoah Valley, the 2d Massachusetts Infantry performed the arduous and responsible duties of rear guard, and Company C of Salem, under command of Capt. William Cogswell, received especial mention for brave and meritorious conduct. This regiment was present at Antietam, at Gettysburg, at Averysborough, and on the march from Atlanta to the sea. In the brave

9

Irish regiment, the 9th Massachusetts, the city was ably represented by a full company, under Capt. Edward Fitzgerald, and they participated in the memorable battles of the Army of the Potomac.

Capt. Arthur F. Devereux, when he returned from the three months' campaign, accepted the position of lieutenant-colonel in the 19th Massachusetts Regiment. A large number of the officers of this regiment were Salem men, and a full company, recruited by Capt. Charles U. Devereux, was afterwards connected therewith. This command performed good service on the Peninsula, on the Potomac, and at Antietam, Gettysburg, Fredericksburg, Chancellorsville, and before Richmond. Capt. John F. Devereux recruited a company from this vicinity and joined the 11th Massachusetts Regiment. The organization of the 23d Regiment included two Salem companies: Company A, under Capt. E. A. P. Brewster; and Company F, under Capt. George M. Whipple. In this regiment were more than two hundred men connected with this city, and it participated in the battles of Newbern, Kingston, and Goldsborough, and saw active service in front of Petersburg. In the 40th Regiment there were twelve commissioned officers and forty-eight enlisted men from Salem. The colored regiments, the 54th and 55th Massachusetts, which performed such valiant service at Fort Wagner and the surrounding islands, contained Salem men in their ranks.

In the nine months' regiments, Salem furnished one full company, under command of Capt. George Wheatland, Jr., to the 48th, and one, under Capt. George D. Putnam, to the 50th Regiment. These regiments saw service in Louisiana and before Port Hudson. The Salem Cadets, under Maj. J. L. Marks, from whose ranks the three years' troops had drawn very freely, enlisted for 100 days, and were assigned to garrison duty in Boston harbor. The 13th Unattached Company, Capt. Robert W. Reeves, was stationed at New Bedford. The 1st Company of Sharpshooters, under Capt. John Saunders, and the 2d Company, under Capt. Lewis H. Wentworth, performed their especial work in a manner to reflect credit upon themselves and the city.

In the navy, the first enlistment was in April, 1861, and, between that date and the close of the war, nearly four hundred men represented Salem in the different squadrons and flotillas. We find them with Dupont, with Farragut, with Porter, on the "Kearsarge," and on the sinking "Cumberland."

In the early days of the war there were two funerals in Salem, which first brought home a full realization of the horrors of war. Brig. Gen. Frederick W. Lander was born in Salem, Dec. 17, 1822. He was a successful engineer and surveyor, and a valuable employee of the government. On the breaking out of the war he offered his services to Gen. Scott, and was appointed in July, 1861, a brigadier-general of volunteers. He distinguished himself at Ball's Bluff, where he was wounded, and March 2, 1862, he died of congestive fever, aggravated by his wounds. His funeral took place in Salem, March 8th, in the presence of a large assemblage of mourners.

Lieut. Col. Henry Merritt, of the 23d Massachusetts Regiment, was killed at the battle of Newbern, March 14, 1862. He was a brave and faithful officer, and his funeral occurring on Friday, March 21st, so soon after that of Gen. Lander, caused a general feeling of sadness in the community.

More than three thousand men entered the service from this city, and more than two hundred were killed. Fifty shared the suffering endured in the rebel prisons, and hundreds bear to-day the scars of honorable wounds. Such is briefly the record of Salem in the civil war, and it is a record of which she may be justly proud.

The members of the Salem High School Association have placed a marble tablet on the wall of their school-room, bearing the names of those scholars who entered the service of their country. Salem has as yet erected no monument or memorial hall to perpetuate the memories of her gallant sons; but their surviving comrades of the Grand Army, on each returning spring, strew flowers on their graves as a token that they are still held in affectionate remembrance.

Grand Army Post.—With the close of the civil war, there sprang up, all over the country, organizations composed of the soldiers and sailors who had been honorably discharged from the service of the country, and known as the Grand Army of the Republic. Salem has one of the largest Posts in the State. It is numbered 34, named the Phil. H. Sheridan, and was chartered Nov. 15, 1867, its charter members being George H. Pierson, George A. Fisher, George M. Whipple, Robert W. Reeves, E. H. Fletcher, John P. Tilton, John R. Lakeman, E. A. Phalen, and John P. Reynolds. Its commanders have been in the order named as follows: George H. Pierson, John R. Lakeman, Charles H. Chase, James G. Bovey, Gilman A. Andrews,

John W. Hart, J. Frank Dalton, William H. Eastman, and Charles J. Sadler, the latter commanding in 1878. Its present membership is 314; but it has reached the number of 525, which is believed to be the largest number ever attained by any Post in the State. It has furnished two members of the national staff, one member of the council of administration, one department commander, one member of the department council of administration, and three members of the department staff. It has raised and disbursed over $20,000 in charity. In 1874, Congress, by enactment, recognized this Post by a donation of four rebel cannon and thirty-six cannon-balls, which will, undoubtedly, be used to ornament the large and beautiful burial-lot given to the Post by the city, in the cemetery on Orne Street. The discriminating and conscientious disbursement of its charity fund, and its scrupulous observance of Memorial Day, early won for the Post the confidence of the Salem community, which it still fully enjoys.

Memorial Hall and Public Library.—There is as yet no memorial erected in Salem to the memory of her brave sons who died in the late civil war, but the failure to agree upon the particular form the memorial should assume seems to be the principal reason for the delay. The common council, in 1869, passed an order to a second reading appropriating $28,000 for a soldiers' monument; but the order failed of a final passage, many thinking that a memorial hall was the best form of testimonial.

In 1873 it was again discussed by the city council on a proposition to establish a memorial hall in connection with a free public library. A petition was received from R. S. Rantoul and others, asking for the establishment of a public library, which was referred to a committee consisting of Aldermen Oliver P. Ricker and William A. Brooks, and Councilmen Charles S. Osgood, George W. Williams, and John H. Conway. This committee gave public hearings, which were fully attended, and, on July 14th, a minority of the committee, Messrs. Osgood and Williams, reported in favor of making a proposition to the Salem Athenæum, Essex Institute, and Peabody Academy of Science, for the free use of their collections of books; the city agreeing to erect a fire-proof building in the rear of Plummer Hall, suitable for containing a memorial hall, to provide for the proper care and custody of the books, and keep the same forever as a free public library. The societies named were inclined to consider the proposition favorably, but a majority of the committee reported in favor of referring it to the next city government, which report was accepted by the city council, and no further action has as yet been taken regarding it.

City Water-Works.—The greatest public enterprise that Salem has ever engaged in was the introduction of water from Wenham Lake, and, before giving a history of it, it may be interesting to briefly notice the private companies that have, to a greater or less degree, supplied the city with water. From the settlement of the town until 1796, there is no record of any public association of citizens for the purpose of securing a supply of water. But in that year there was an organization of citizens "for the purpose of supplying the inhabitants generally of Salem and Danvers with pure spring water." On the 30th of December, 1796, a meeting was held at the Sun Tavern, with Jacob Ashton chairman, which appointed a committee of three to "procure an act of incorporation and to purchase the necessary logs, contract for boring the same, and do such other acts as were necessary to forward the business." This was the beginning of the Salem Aqueduct Company.

An Act of incorporation was obtained by the Salem and Danvers Aqueduct Company, March 9, 1797. The company organized April 7th, and William Gray, Jr., was president. In 1798, the corporation built a reservoir on Gallows Hill, ten feet deep, and about twenty-four feet square. In the spring of 1799, the corporation began to supply water from the present sources of the aqueduct to the inhabitants. Their operations were at first primitive and simple, consisting of a large-size fish hogshead for a fountain and a sapling of three-inch bore for the main pipe. A new fountain was built in 1802. In 1804 the three-inch bore gave out, and logs were substituted with a bore of five inches. The estimated cost was at least $20,000. In June, 1814, complaints began to be made of a failure of water, and, in 1816, the proprietors voted to discontinue all branches leading to manufactories, distilleries, stables, and similar establishments. In 1817, the corporation purchased a piece of land on Sewall Street, on which a reservoir of 22,000 gallons capacity was subsequently erected. In 1834, a charter was obtained for a new aqueduct company, but the old company voted to reduce its water rates, and the plan of building a new aqueduct was abandoned. In 1834, a six-inch iron pipe — the first used by this company — was laid down in Essex Street from North to Newbury Street. In 1839, a new main, without branches, was laid from the fountain to the reservoir at Gallows Hill.

In November, 1839, this new main was extended from Gallows Hill to the main iron pipe, near Summer Street. In 1849, an iron pipe was laid through Union Street to the Naumkeag Mills, which were authorized to draw water during the night. In May, 1850, leave was granted to lay a log to Spring Pond, and in 1851 a twelve-inch iron pipe was laid from the fountain to the head of Federal Street. A new reservoir was also built, capable of holding 652,000 gallons, and the company gradually laid iron pipes in the place of the wooden logs. Everything now went smoothly till 1858, when the tanners and curriers demanded a larger supply of water. They laid their complaints before the city government, and a conference was had with the aqueduct company. The effect of this complaint was the laying of an additional six-inch iron pipe from Federal through Boston and Essex streets to Summer, and the twelve-inch main was extended into Spring Pond. Complaints still continued of a short supply of water, and, in 1865, a connection was made with Brown's Pond, a sixteen-inch main was laid from the fountain to the head of Federal Street, and great expense was incurred in building dams. These last.expenses were incurred with the hope of deterring the city from building a system of city water works, but the supply was still insufficient, and the construction of the works to take water from Wenham Lake was vigorously pushed forward.

The history of this company shows how immensely the requirements of our city have increased in seventy years. Starting with a fish hogshead and saplings of three-inch bore in 1799, it had in 1865 absorbed the whole of Spring and Brown's ponds, and the aqueduct fountain, with a capacity of 600,000 gallons per day, and still the supply was inadequate to the demand. This company is now confined almost entirely to supplying the town of Peabody.

Salem Water-Works. — The first action of the city council upon the subject of a water supply was in July, 1858, when a committee was appointed to confer with the aqueduct company in regard to an increased supply. The result of this conference was the laying of an additional main by the aqueduct company. In 1863, the condition of our water supply became such that the citizens again invoked the aid of the city government, and, on the 12th of October, John Bertram and ninety-three others petitioned the city council "to take the necessary measures to procure from the Legislature power to establish city water works," which petition was referred to a committee consisting of Aldermen George R. Chapman and Francis W. Pickman, and Councilmen Rufus B. Gifford, Gilbert L. Streeter, and Charles Lamson. On their report, the mayor was requested to petition the Legislature to grant to the city such powers as will enable it to convey a sufficient supply of pure water for domestic and manufacturing purposes from Humphrey's, Brown's, and Spring ponds, and the springs in the land of the Salem and Danvers Aqueduct Company.

On the 23d of November, the city council chose in convention Stephen H. Phillips, James B. Curwen, and James Upton a committee, with authority to collect evidence, showing the necessity of a larger supply of water, and present the same to the Legislature. This committee examined the different sources of water supply, and on their suggestion a supplementary petition was presented to the Legislature, asking that Wenham Lake be included in the sources of supply for the city water-works. This petition was presented to the Legislature, and on the 29th of February, 1864, a hearing was had. This hearing was very protracted. The city was represented before the committee by Robert S. Rantoul, Esq., and the petition met with sharp opposition from the Aqueduct Company and others. An Act was approved, however, May 13, 1864, which provided that the city may take water either from Wenham Lake, or from Brown's and Spring ponds, and that the city council shall make careful investigation as to the sources mentioned, and determine by joint ballot, at least fourteen days before the first Monday of December, 1864, from which source the city will take the water, in the event of the acceptance of the Act by the citizens; the Act to be void, unless accepted by a majority of the voters, at a meeting to be held on the first Monday of December, 1864.

The committee of citizens reported to the city council May 23, 1864, and a committee of the city council, consisting of Aldermen John Webster, Peter Silver, and Nathaniel G. Symonds, and Councilmen Richard C. Manning, John C. Osgood, James F. Almy, Thomas Quinn, Rufus B. Gifford, and Charles S. Osgood were appointed to investigate the sources of supply, and report thereon to the city council. This committee examined both sources thoroughly and care-fully, and on the 11th of November reported, recommending "that the city council decide to take Wenham Lake as the source of sup-ply." On the 14th of November their report was accepted, and in joint convention it was decided by a vote of twenty-two to five to select Wenham Lake as the source of supply. On the fifth day of December next following, the citizens voted to accept the Act of May 13, 1864, by a vote of 1,623 yeas to 151 nays.

On the 22d of May, 1865, the city council passed an ordinance, providing "for the choice of three water commissioners, who shall, under the direction of the city council, commence .the work of con-struction," and Stephen H. Phillips, James B. Curwen, and James Upton were chosen; but Messrs. Curwen and Upton declining, on the 26th of June, Franklin T. Sanborn and Peter Silver were elected in their stead. The board met in July, and Mr. Phillips was chosen chairman. James Slade was appointed engineer; Charles H. Swan assistant engineer; and Daniel H. Johnson, Jr., clerk.

The commissioners were in favor of proceeding at once with the construction of the works, and asked the city council to place $40,000 at their disposal. A disagreement now arose between the water com-missioners and the city government, the former contending that they were authorized to proceed at once with the work, and bind the city for all expenses incurred; and Mayor J. B. F. Osgood taking the ground, in a communication sent by him to the city council, Sept. 11, 1865, that no money could be expended except that raised by a sale of the water-loan bonds, and stating that he had refused to sign the warrants to enable the commissioners to draw money from the city treasury. About this time two petitions were received by the city council, asking for delay in the construction of the water-works, and one asking that they be completed forthwith. These petitions were referred to a committee, before whom numerous public hearings took place; and Oct. 22, 1865, they made a lengthy report, signed by Abner C. Goodell, Jr., Charles S. Osgood, James F. Almy, and Thomas Nichols, Jr., favoring no unnecessary delay in the construction of the works. Alderman Chapman submitted a minority report, with an order directing the commissioners to suspend all work until the city council shall instruct them to commence. Both reports were widely circulated through the city.

The season of 1865 was very dry. The disagreement between the water commissioners and Mayor Osgood, and the consequent delay in pushing forward the work, caused much uneasiness among the citizens ; and prior to the municipal election of Jan. 1, 1866, public meetings were held, pamphlets were issued, and the matter was earnestly and warmly discussed. At the election it was the main issue before the people, and a city government favoring no delay was chosen by a large majority.

The new city government organized Jan. 22, 1866; and the Hon. David Roberts was qualified as mayor, and Charles S. Osgood, Esq., was elected president of the common council. Mayor Roberts, in his address, said that "the project so emphatically endorsed should, with all reasonable despatch, be pushed to its final completion." An ordinance establishing the Salem water loan, and authorizing its issue, was passed Feb. 12. On the same day, the commissioners advertised for proposals for the construction of a reservoir on Chipman's Hill in Beverly ; and on April 17, the proposal of Messrs. Collins & Boyle was accepted. On the 18th of May, work was commenced on the reservoir.

Caleb Foote and others petitioned the supreme court for an injunction, restraining the city from constructing works to cost over $500,000, and from payment of interest in coin. Their petition was dated May 30, 1866, and a hearing had June 16, on which day Judge Gray declined to issue an injunction. The matter was then carried before the full court, who, after hearing arguments, dismissed the petition, and decided that the city was not restricted by the Act to an expenditure of $500,000, and that the payment of the interest in coin was not illegal. On the 5th of July, the commissioners notified the city council that they had decided to purchase a Worthington pumping-engine for the sum of $40,000. One of the commissioners, Mr. Stephen H. Phillips, resigned July 9, and Mr. Willard P. Phillips was elected to fill the vacancy. The proposal of Messrs. J. W. & J. F. Starr to furnish 6,000 feet of thirty-inch and 25,000 feet of twenty-inch iron pipe was accepted Oct. 8. On April 15, 1867, the proposal of Boynton Brothers for building a pipe bridge and syphon at Bass River was accepted. Early in May, the laying of the supply-main was commenced ; and in July every portion of the work beyond the limits of the city was under contract. The total expenditure to July 1

10

had been $213,176.85. During the month of October the twenty-inch supply-main had been laid from the reservoir to Beverly Bridge, and from there nearly to the junction of Boston and Federal streets. Upon the 4th of November four of the iron pipes, furnished by the Messrs. Starr, were found to be deficient in weight, and the laying of pipe was at once discontinued. This resulted in a lawsuit, in which the city was successful in recovering damages against the Messrs. Starr. On Nov. 18, the syphon was lowered into place by the Messrs. Low of Boston. Up to Jan. 1, 1868, the total amount expended was $445,736.86.

In consequence of the great cost of the works, the amount being largely in excess of the estimates, there was another contest at the municipal election in January, 1868; but the friends of the water project again triumphed, although by a comparatively small majority. On the 3d of February, 1868, the commissioners contracted with George H. Norman, of Newport, R. I., to furnish and lay the iron and cement distribution-pipes, and to set hydrants and gates ; and on April 15 he commenced laying them. The Legislature, by an Act approved March 19, 1868, provided for a further loan of $500,000, making the whole amount of the water loan $1,000,000.

On the 12th of October, Mr. Norman commenced putting in service-pipes, and on the 31st of the same month he had laid in the streets of the city 127,000 feet of distribution-pipe, and set 196 hydrants and 228 gates. On Tuesday, November 24, the force-main was completed. The pumping-engine was put in order, and on November 25, at midnight, the pumping began, and at four o'clock on Thanksgiving morning, November 26, there was a foot of water in the reservoir. On the afternoon of November 29, water was let into the supply-main, and the section extending to the Gloucester Branch Railroad crossing was filled and tested, and November 30, the supply-main and syphon at the river were filled, and the first water from Wenham Lake reached Salem. On Wednesday, December 2, the filling of the distribution-pipes in the city was commenced, and on Christmas morning the water was let into the service-pipes, and the houses of the citizens were supplied. The total expenditures to Dec. 31, 1868, were $919,771.94.

On the first day of January, 1869, the city government made an inspection and examination of the works at Wenham, and after returning to the city hall the hydrants were tested, and seven of them, all in sight from the corner of Washington and Essex streets, were opened ; and to each of the seven, six lines of hose were attached, so that forty-two streams were playing at once, and the trial was entirely satisfactory. During 1869, the reservoir was sodded, fences were built, and the works completed, and on the 19th of November, 1869, Mr. W. P. Phillips, chairman of the water commissioners, formally transferred the charge of the Salem Water-Works to the city council, and delivered an address upon the occasion, from which most of the foregoing facts and figures are taken. The amount expended up to the date of transfer was about $1,060,000.

Wenham Lake, the source of supply, is situated partly in Beverly and partly in Wenham, and has an area of 320 acres. Its extreme depth is fifty-three feet, and its distance from the city hall by the pipe line is four and six-tenths miles. Its capacity is from two to three million gallons per day, and its level thirty-one feet above mean high tide. The reservoir, situated on Chipman's Hill, Beverly, is four hundred feet square, and has a capacity of twenty million gallons, and when filled the surface of the water is one hundred and forty-two feet above mean high tide. The supply-main can deliver five million gallons in twenty-four hours, and retain a head of eighty-eight feet, or three million gallons, with a head of one hundred and twenty-two feet. At first merely nominal rates were established for the use of water, but in 1873 regular water-rates were prescribed. In 1877, the number of Wenham water-takers was 6,895, and water was supplied to sixty-seven tanning and currying, besides numerous other manufacturing, establishments. The receipts from water-rates in 1877 were $35,646.

The history of the introduction of Wenham water has been recited somewhat at length, because it is the most extensive and important work that the city ever accomplished. The plan at the outset met with determined opposition from a portion of the citizens, and the municipal elections, when the water question was at issue, were hotly contested. The project has now stood the test of time. It is ten years since the water from Wenham Lake first flowed through the streets of Salem, and to-day those most bitterly opposed to the plan in the beginning are willing to acknowledge the benefit derived from the copious and bountiful supply of pure water which Salem now enjoys. The works are substantially built, and will compare favorably with any in the country.

The Fire Department.—The introduction of Wenham water worked an entire revolution in the methods employed for extinguishing fires. The fire department previous to this time had consisted of three steam fire-engines and five hand-engines, and there were between four and five hundred members of the department; now there are two steamers, six hose-carriages, and one hook-and-ladder carriage, with a total force of less than two hundred men, and no 'city is better protected or less liable to extensive fires. The first fire-engine used in Salem was bought by Richard Derby and others, March 20, 1749, and in the olden time most householders hung in the entries of their houses a number of leather buckets, to be ready to render prompt assistance in case of fire.

Great Fires.—Salem has suffered at different intervals from severe fires, the first of importance occurring Oct. 6, 1774, when the Rev. Dr. Whitaker's meeting-house, the custom-house, eight dwellings, and fourteen stores were burned. The town-house caught, but was saved. An aged lady was burnt to death in one of the houses. At four o'clock, on the morning of Aug. 22, 1816, a fire broke out on the corner of Liberty and Water (now Derby) streets, and sixteen buildings were burned and three badly damaged. No very destructive fire occurred again until Dec. 18, 1844, when, shortly before eleven o'clock at night, a fire was discovered which destroyed twenty buildings, including Concert Hall, seven being on Front, four on Lafayette, and nine on Fish (now Derby) streets. The loss was $100,000, the largest loss by fire that ever occurred in Salem. At one o'clock, on the morning of June 8, 1859, a fire broke out in the stable of the Mansion House, on Essex Street, and fourteen horses and the hostler, I. L. Hatch, perished in the flames. Twelve or fifteen buildings, including the Mansion House, were destroyed, the total loss being $68,400. The Franklin Building was consumed by fire, Oct. 21, 1860. The loss was $20,000, the insurance having expired the day previous to the fire. The last great fire occurred on May 14, 1866, when the Lynde Block, on Essex Street, and eight or nine other buildings, were destroyed, the total loss being about $70,000.

City Officials.—Since the adoption of a city charter, there have been but three city clerks. Joseph Cloutman served from 1836 to

1862; Stephen P. Webb from 1863 to November, 1871, when he resigned and Henry M. Meek, the present city clerk, was chosen in his stead.

There have been five city treasurers : Jonathan Hodges in 1836; Joseph Felt from 1837 to August, 1853, when he resigned and Henry B. Smith was elected to fill the vacancy. Mr. Smith served until 1859. Charles E. Symonds served from 1859 to March, 1865, when he resigned and Henry J. Cross, the present city treasurer, was elected in his place.

The only city official who has served continuously since the organization of the city is the present city messenger, William Mansfield. He was appointed constable and town messenger March 12, 1821, and has been in the employ of the town and city ever since; having received his appointment as city messenger in 1836.

Police Department.—With the government of a city or town there must always be connected a police department. John Woodbury was appointed constable at Salem in 1630, and, in early years, the inhabitants watched by turns. A contract was made, Nov. 10, 1676, with Arthur Hughes " to be bellman and to walk the streets from ten o'clock until day-break and to give notice of the time of night and what weather according to custom." About 1817, the custom of calling the hour and weather was abandoned. In 1666, the meeting-house was used for a watch-house, and afterwards a building, used for that purpose, stood in the middle of Washington Street, about as far north as the north end of the Stearns Building. It had a soldier in full uniform on the top of it. In 1725, it received a coat of paint,—a rare covering for those days. The bellman just mentioned, not only acted as a watchman, but it was his duty, by an order made in 1673, to ring the bell at five o'clock in the morning, and nine o'clock in the evening, "as an admonition to improve the light of day and keep good hours at night." After 1774, the bells of the North and East churches were rung at one and nine o'clock, P. M. The present police force consists of a marshal, assistant-marshal, captain, sergeant, and thirty-eight men.

Police Court.—The Salem Police Court was established June 23, 1831, and the Hon. Elisha Mack was appointed justice, which office he resigned four or five years afterwards, and was succeeded by the Hon. Joseph G. Waters, who held the office until the abolition of the court in 1874, at which time the First District Court of Essex County was created, and the Hon. J. B. F. Osgood was appointed justice. The new court includes in its jurisdiction, Salem, Danvers, Beverly, Hamilton, Middleton, Topsfield, and Wenham, and its sessions are held in the Flint Building on Washington Street.

Population.—Salem has gradually increased in population since the first settlement of the town. In 1638, there were about 900 inhabitants; in 1776, 5,337; in 1800, 9,457; in 1810, 12,617; in 1820, 12,731; in 1830, 13,886; in 1840, 15,082; in 1850, 20,264; in 1860, 22,252; in 1870, 24,117; and in 1875, 25,958. By the census of 1875, the valuation of Salem was $26,312,272, of which $11,988,627 was personal estate.

CHAPTER V.

HISTORY OF THE FORMATION OF THE CHURCHES OF SALEM.

The preceding chapters have briefly sketched the history of Salem, under its town and city government. It is the purpose of this chapter to give, as succinctly as possible, an account of the formation of the different churches, the history of some of them being a part of the history not only of Salem, but of the State and country.

The First Congregational Society of Salem dates its organization from the year 1629, and was the first Protestant church organized in America. There had previously been meetings for religious worship, but no attempt to form a regularly constituted church-organization. On the 20th of July, 1629, Samuel Skelton was chosen pastor, and Francis Higginson teacher. On the 6th of the following August, which day was observed as a day of fasting and prayer, they were duly ordained in their respective offices. Gov. Bradford, of Plymouth, and some others, "coming by sea were hindered by cross winds that they could not be there at the beginning of the day, but they came into the assembly afterward and gave them the right hand of fellowship wishing all prosperity and a blessed success unto such good beginnings."

The original covenant of the church is as follows : " We covenant with the Lord, and one with another and do bind ourselves in the presence of God to walk together in all his ways, according as he is pleased to reveal himself unto us in his blessed word of truth."

The original meeting-house, a small, single-story structure, stood on a portion of the site now occupied by the present church edifice, on the south-eastern corner of Washington and Essex streets. There is a tradition that the exact location of this building was on the corner of the lot at the opening of Higginson Square. The original building was erected in 1634. In 1639, it was enlarged by the addition of a second structure. The original building was discovered some years since on the premises of David Nichols, in the rear of the tanneries under the brow of Witch Hill, through the active agency of the late Francis Peabody. It is stated that it had been used at one time as an inn on the old "Boston Road." The subject was investigated by the Essex Institute, and all doubts as to its being the original church were subsequently removed. The original meeting-house was twenty feet long, seventeen wide, and twelve feet in the height of its posts. It consisted of a single room, with a gallery over the door. The frame of the church was carefully removed to the rear of Plummer Hall, and covered in, where it is preserved as an interesting relic.

The Rev. Francis Higginson was born in England in 1587. He was educated at Jesus College, Cambridge, and received his first degree in 1609. He was settled over one of the parish churches in Leicester, where he proved a very popular preacher. It is said of him, that "He was a good scholar, of a sweet and affable behaviour, and having a charming voice, was one of the most acceptable and popular preachers of the country." He was ejected from his living, and forbidden to preach in England, on his adoption of the doctrines of the Non-Conformists. He was well qualified to be a chief agent in the great enterprise for which he was sought; and, though his career was brief in the New World, he accomplished his work, and lived to secure the foundation of his church. He died Aug. 6, 1630, exactly one year after his ordination.

The Rev. Samuel Skelton, the first pastor, was born in England in 1584, and was educated at Clare Hall, Cambridge, taking his first degree in 1611. He survived his colleague about four years. He died Aug. 2, 1634. He received a grant of land at the "New Mills," near the "Orchard Farm," which was at one time known as "Skelton's Neck," and is now comprised in Danversport.

The Rev. Roger Williams was first settled as Mr. Skelton's colleague or "teacher," upon the death of Mr. Higginson. He was born in Wales, in 1599, and was educated at Oxford. He was a thorough Non-Conformist. He landed at Boston in February, 1631. He accepted an invitation extended to him by the Salem church to become its teacher, and was settled on the 12th of April, 1631. His settlement was so strongly opposed by the governor and magistrates that he was induced to leave Salem before the close of the summer, and to become the assistant of Mr. Ralph Smith, at Plymouth. In 1633 he returned to Salem and again became the assistant of Mr. Skelton. After the latter's death he was sole minister of the church, until November, 1635, when the renewed opposition of the magistrates drove him from Salem into exile, and he went forth into the wilderness to found the future State of Rhode Island upon the basis of civil and religious freedom. He died in that Colony in April, 1683. The cause of his offending was the divulging of obnoxious opinions, declaring that the ministers of Boston had conformed in a sinful degree to the English church, and ought to declare their repentance, and that the royal patent could give them no title to lands without a purchase from the natives; that the civil power could not rightly punish breaches of the Sabbath, nor in any way interfere with the rights of conscience.

The Rev. Hugh Peters was the successor of Mr. Williams. He was born at Fowey, in Cornwall, in 1599, and received the degree of A. M. from Trinity College, Cambridge, in 1622. He was afterwards lecturer at St. Sepulchre's, in London. In 1629, when Laud commenced his persecutions of the Puritans, he went to Holland, and was pastor of an independent church at Rotterdam. He came to this country from Holland, arriving Oct. 6, 1635. He was settled over the First Church in Salem, Dec. 21, 1636. He speedily took a prominent part in the town affairs, aiding in reforming the police, stimulating industry and encouraging the spirit of improvement. During his administration as pastor, a water-mill was erected, also a glass-house and salt-works. The planting of hemp was commenced and a market was established. Commerce received earnest attention. The pastor planned the mode of conducting the fishing business, the coasting and the foreign voyages, and the building of vessels. One of three hundred tons was undertaken under his influence. Mr. John Fisk, of King's College, Cambridge, assisted him in the ministry. Mr. Peters returned to England in 1641 to represent the Colony upon the matter of excise and trade. He was in high favor with Cromwell, and fell a martyr to his cause, after the Restoration, Oct. 16, 1660.

The Rev. Edward Norris was born in England in 1579; came to Salem in 1639, and joined the church in December of that year. He was ordained colleague to Mr. Peters, March 18, 1640. After the latter's departure, he was sole minister until his death, Dec. 23, 1659.

11

The Rev. John Higginson, the son of Francis, was born at Clay-brook, England, on the 6th of August, 1616, and came to New England in 1629.   He was educated in the Colony, was chaplain at Saybrook from 1636 to 1640, and was located at Guilford and Hartford, Conn., at different periods.   He left Guilford with the intention of returning to England in 1659, but, being driven into Salem by stress of weather, he left his ship and accepted an invitation to settle over the church there.   He was ordained August 29, 1660, and continued in the ministry until his death, Dec. 9, 1708.   During his ministry (July 4, 1667), the brethren and sisters on the Bass River side applied for dismission to form a church by themselves. Sept, 20, 1667, the new organization was effected, and the Rev. Mr. Hale was ordained as their minister.   The church at Marblehead was formed Aug. 13, 1684, its members having formally withdrawn from the mother church the 6th of June previous.   Nov. 10, 1689, the members of the church from Salem Village presented their petition for dismission to form a new society.   On March 8, 1703, brother John Massey was presented with the old worn-out great Church Bible, he being considered as the first "town-born child."* It was given to him and delivered to him before the brethren. A new church edifice had also been built in the year 1670.

The Rev. Nicholas Noyes was born in Newbury, Dec. 22, 1647; took his degree at Harvard in 1667; was ordained teacher of the First Church, Nov. 14, 1683; and died Dec. 13, 1717.   He was a fine scholar and able preacher, but was swept away with others by the witchcraft delusion.   Mr. Noyes was the last ordained teacher under the old title.   The church at the middle precinct, now Peabody, withdrew and was dismissed June 25, 1713.

The Rev. George Curwin, son of Hon. Jonathan Curwin, was born in Salem, May 21, 1683; graduated at Harvard in 1701; was ordained pastor and colleague, May 19, 1714, and died Nov. 23, 1717.

The Rev. Samuel Fisk was the grandson of John Fisk, the assistant of Hugh Peters.   He was born in 1689; graduated from Harvard in 1708, and was ordained pastor over the First Church, Oct. 8, 1718. On this occasion the assembly met in a new house of worship on the same site as the others.   This latter house was commenced May 21,

---

* Massey was the first town-born child then living.

1718, and was opened for public worship July 13. The settlement of Mr. Fisk caused another division, and Nov. 14, 1718, the members living in the east part of the town applied for dismission, which was granted Dec. 25, and the company withdrew to form the present East Church.

Nov. 4, 1727, a public meeting was held to take proper observance of a terrible earthquake which visited the town on the "Lord's day night last, at half an hour after ten," — October 29, 1727. Both parishes met on this occasion, and there was a vast assembly.

Mr. Fisk introduced so many new practices in church management differing from those of his predecessors as to cause great disaffection and uneasiness in the parish. He refused to call regular church meetings and held them only when he stayed the church after the religious exercises. His course finally led to his expulsion from the church and pulpit in 1735. He and his followers claimed to constitute the First Church after their dismission. Mention is made by the pastor in his records of the house of Joseph Orne, as being "the dwelling house where the First Church met and worshipped God for several Lord's days after it was (with its Pastor) driven together from the public meeting house, on Lord's day, April 27, 1735." A fierce controversy continued for some time after this event in regard to the matter. The church thus formed at Joseph Orne's, subsequently became the Third Church. Mr. Fisk died in Salem, April 7, 1770.

After Mr. Fisk's expulsion the members remaining in the old church proceeded to reorganize. Aug. 5, 1736, the brethren adhering to the ancient principles of the church, met at the house of Benjamin Lynde and renewed the ancient covenant. Mr. John Sparhawk was chosen at this meeting to be the minister. He was born in September, 1713; graduated at Harvard in 1731; settled Dec. 8, 1736; died April 30, 1755.

The Rev. Thomas Barnard was born at Andover, Aug. 16, 1716; graduated at Harvard in 1732; installed pastor of the First Church Sept. 17, 1755; died Aug. 5, 1776. The North Church withdrew upon the settlement of Mr. Barnard's colleague, the Rev. Asa Dunbar, and organized July 19, 1772.

The Rev. Asa Dunbar was born in Bridgewater, May 26, 1745; graduated at Harvard in 1767; ordained as colleague with the Rev.

Thomas Barnard, July 22, 1772; resigned April 23, 1779. He died in Keene, N. H., June 22, 1787.

The Rev. John Prince, LL. D., was born in Boston, July 22, 1751; graduated from Harvard in 1776; ordained pastor of the First Church Nov. 10, 1779. In 1817 the church received a legacy of $3,000 from Charles Henry Orne, which when accumulated to $5,000 was to form a permanent fund for the support of the minister. The church was at the same time incorporated as the "First Congregational Society in Salem." In February, 1824, a meeting was called to settle a colleague. Mr. Henry Colman having preached as a candidate, a number were in favor of his settlement, but the majority were opposed, and his supporters withdrew and formed the Barton Square Church. Dr. Prince died June 7, 1836.

The Rev. Charles W. Upham was ordained as colleague Dec. 8, 1824. He continued in the pastorate until his resignation, Dec. 8, 1844.

The Rev. Thomas T. Stone was installed as pastor July 12, 1846, and his ministry terminated by vote of the church in February, 1852.

The Rev. George W. Briggs was installed as pastor Jan. 6, 1853, and continued in the ministry until March, 1867, when he resigned to accept a pastorate in Cambridge. He was the second minister who came to the church from the ancient church of Plymouth.*

* These sketches of pastors and teachers of the First Church are mainly from "New England Congregationalism," by Daniel Appleton White. Felt's "Annals of Salem" mentions George Burdet as a preacher, 1635–1637; John Whiting, 1657–1659. Dr. Bentley's "Description and History of Salem" says that, in 1672, Mr. Charles Nicholet, from Virginia, came to Salem and was invited to tarry for a year as an assistant minister. After two years he was chosen to continue for life, the vote being "taken in the congregation and not in the church." The church remonstrated, and in 1675, the General Court declared its disapprobation of a vote taken contrary to a law of the jurisdiction, and the established usages of the church. The pastor objected to Mr. Nicholet, stating that in his judgment the doctrine preached was "inconsistent in terms, the measures unfriendly to peace, and the duty without any mutual assistance." Mr. Nicholet explained, corrected his expressions, and promised caution, but the animosity could not be removed. A new meeting-house was built "on the northern part of the Common." [Although Dr. Bentley says "the northern part of the Common," it is definitely settled by the town records that the location of this meeting-house was not far from the present north-eastern gate of the Common. The building of this church seems to indicate a desire on the part of people living in the eastern portion of the town to form a new society, which they did later. See "East Church."] Mr. Nicholet saw no prospect of peace, and "after many farewell sermons," in 1676, departed from America forever.

The Rev. James T. Hewes succeeded Dr. Briggs in 1868, remaining with the society till 1875. The present pastor is the Rev. Fielder Israel, who was installed March 9, 1877.

The society will observe its two hundred and fiftieth anniversary in August, 1879.

The Friends Society. — There were Quaker services as early as 1657. They were first held in private houses. In 1688 Thomas Maule built the first Friends meeting-house, which stood on the south side of Essex Street, next east of the late Rev. Dr. Emerson's dwelling-house. This was sold to Maule for £25 in 1716, the Friends having built another meeting-house on Essex Street, on a part of the site of the Quaker burying-ground. The Quakers now worship in a brick church on Pine Street, built in 1832. This sect has no settled ministry, their ministers, like Paul in his day, working with their hands, or pursuing some lawful occupation, to provide for their own support and that of their families. Women, as well as men, are acknowledged as ministers. Among the ministers acknowledged and recorded as such, from time to time, by the Salem monthly meeting of Friends (comprising the meetings of Salem and Lynn), are the names of Micajah Collins, Mary Newhall, Moses H. Bedee, Avis Keene, Elizabeth Breed, Jane Mansfield, Benjamin H. Jones, William O. Newhall, Abigail Bedee, Sophronia Page, Henry Chase, Hannah Hozier, Lydia Dean, Mary Chase, Daniel Page, Ruth Page. Three of these, Micajah Collins, Moses H. Bedee, and Sophronia Page (all now deceased) travelled very extensively in the ministry, attending meetings of the society, and preaching publicly otherwise, through New England and at the South and West.

The East Church.—On Nov. 14, 1718, the brethren and sisters residing in the eastern part of the town applied to be released from their covenant obligations in the First Church, that they might organize a church of their own, and settle the Rev. Robert Stanton as their pastor. This is the first mention on the records of any desire on their part to leave the parent church, but prior to this time steps had been taken to establish a new church organization, and a new house had been built. This house was raised Aug. 27, 1717, and was opened for public worship in May, 1718. For a long period before this, efforts had been made for a separation, but the First Church opposed it. The old records tell us, that for a long time before the new church was built, those members of the old society residing in this eastern district had neglected to attend the meetings at the First Church on the Lord's Day, and some of them had pretended to be members of the Church of England in Marblehead, and had made a practice of going back and forth in boats "across our harbor, until it appeared more like a day of frolicking than the Lord's day." The new church stood on "Grafton's Lane," upon what is now the corner of Hardy and Essex streets. This house was used for public worship until the erection of the present edifice, which was dedicated Jan. 1, 1846. The Rev. Samuel Wigglesworth preached at the first opening of the church, in May, 1718. There continued to be trouble between the people and the First Church about a separation, and an appeal was made to the General Court. Dec. 25, 1718, the First Church finally voted the desired dismission, and on the 8th of April, 1719, the Rev. Robert Stanton was ordained as pastor of the new church, the third within the present limits of Salem, which from its location was known as the East Church. The Rev. Cotton Mather, of Boston, preached the ordination sermon on this occasion. The first pastor was ordained April 8, 1719, and died May 3, 1727, in his thirty-ninth year. William Jennison, his successor, graduated at Harvard in 1724; ordained over the East Church May 22, 1728; resigned in September, 1736; and died April 1, 1750. James Diman was born Nov. 29, 1707; ordained over the East Church May 11, 1737; and died the 8th of Oct., 1788. He was a native of Long Island, graduated at Harvard in 1730, and was librarian of the University from 1735 to 1737. William Bentley, the famous divine of 1812, was born June 22, 1759. He was ordained over the East Church, as colleague to the Rev. Mr. Diman, Sept. 24, 1783, and continued in the ministry until his death, in Salem, Dec. 29, 1819. He graduated at Harvard in 1777, and was tutor at the University for three years. He took an active part in the politics of the day, and was editor for several years of the "Essex Register." He was the author of an historical sketch of Salem. He took strong Arminian grounds, and under his lead the church became practically Unitarian in 1785, and was one of the first churches in America to adopt that faith. In the war of 1812, on one occasion, when the frigate "Constitution" was chased into Marblehead by British frigates, this patriotic pastor locked up his church, and at the head of his people, in full ministerial garb, hastened to

Marblehead to aid in the defence of the town and frigate. Dr. Bentley died in December, 1819, and Edward Everett preached his funeral discourse. James Flint was born in Reading, Dec. 10, 1779; graduated at Harvard in 1802; and was installed over the East Church Sept. 19, 1821. A colleague pastor, the Rev. Dexter Clapp, was settled in 1851. Dr. Flint continued as associate pastor till his death, March 4, 1855. During Mr. Flint's pastorate the old church was abandoned, and the present freestone edifice was erected on Brown Street, opposite Newbury. It was dedicated Jan. 1, 1846. Dexter Clapp was born July 15, 1816; installed Dec. 17, 1851, and resigned in February, 1864, on account of ill-health. Samuel C. Beane was born Dec. 19, 1835; installed, Jan. 1, 1865; resigned, Dec. 8, 1877. George H. Hosmer, of East Bridgewater, accepted the invitation to become the pastor of the East Church, Nov. 17, 1878, and was installed Jan. 2, 1879.

St. Peter's Church was erected on "Prison Lane" in 1733, on land given by Philip English and his connections, and was opened for worship June 25, 1734. It was the fourth church in Salem. The first Episcopal preacher was the Rev. John Lyford, who came with Conant in 1626. At the end of a year he accepted an invitation to preach in Virginia. There were Episcopal services, from time to time, after Lyford's departure, but no movement to form a church organization until 1733. The Rev. Charles Brockwell was the first rector of St. Peter's Church. He was a graduate at Cambridge, Eng., and entered on his duties Oct. 8, 1738. He resigned in 1746, and died April 20, 1755, aged fifty-nine. Mr. Brockwell was succeeded by the Rev. William McGilchrist. He was born 1703; was settled in 1747; and died April 19, 1780. He was obliged to suspend his ministerial functions in 1777, because the Legislature passed a law prohibiting the reading of the Episcopal service, under a penalty of £100 and one year's imprisonment. He resumed his duties as rector shortly before his death. The church was in a very dilapidated condition, from the depredations of its violent and angry opponents. The Rev. Robert B. Nichols was chosen an assistant to Mr. McGilchrist, and was paid by subscription. The Rev. Nathaniel Fisher followed, and next came the Rev. Thomas Carlile, a famous divine of his day. He was born at Providence, R. I., in 1792; was a graduate of Brown University in 1809; became rector of St. Peter's Church in 1817; resigned Oct.

6, 1822; and died March 28, 1824. The rectors succeeding Mr. Carlile, in the order of their ministry, have been the Revs. Henry W. Ducachet, Thomas W. Coit, Alexander V. Griswold, John A. Vaughan, Charles Mason, William R. Babcock, George Leeds, William Rawlins Pickman, James O. Scripture, E. M. Gushee, and Charles Arey. The present Gothic stone structure was erected in 1833. A willow-tree in the angle of the church, at the corner of St. Peter's and Brown streets, has grown from a slip from the tree over the grave of Napoleon at St. Helena.

The Tabernacle Church resulted from a division of sentiment among the members of the First Church. In 1735, the Rev. Samuel Fisk was pastor of the First Church. On the 27th of April of that year, according to a record kept by himself, he and his supporters, or, as he states it, "the First Church," were driven from the public meeting-house by their opponents, and were obliged to hold their services in the dwelling-house of Joseph Orne. Mr. Fisk claims that he carried the majority of the church with him, and that they were of right the First Church; and there followed a long and bitter controversy between the two parties. Mr. Fisk carried the church book, containing the records with him, and continued to use it in the new church, refusing to give it up to those who stayed behind. It was not until 1811 that the book was recovered from the heirs of Mr. Fisk. Dr. Bentley says, " Mr. Fisk was dismissed from the First Church in 1735, and accepted a new house provided by his friends in the same street, westward on the north side of the street." The late Samuel M. Worcester states, that " for twenty years, the present Tabernacle Church alone was called the First Church." The minority of the First Church, by the aid of a Council and the Legislature, dismissed Mr. Fisk, the pastor, on the 18th of April (O. S.), 1735. Having held together and hired preaching for about a year, they were duly organized as a church in 1736, under the style of " the Church and Parish of the Confederate Society in Salem." More briefly, they were called the " Confederate Church," while their brethren, who had been separated from them, were called by others "the First Church of Christ in Salem." The records of the First Church show that Mr. Fisk departed from the ancient usages and customs, and introduced many innovations which caused the separation. The present Tabernacle Church was the result of this separation, and in 1762 surrendered the title of First Church. The new society took the name of the "Third Church of Christ in Salem." The designation of Tabernacle formally appears in the church records of 1786. The new house was built in 1735, according to Bentley, on the same street, a little "farther to the westward, on the north side of the street." It stood for nearly forty years, until burned down on the night of the 6th of October, 1774. The ancient site of this meeting-house was probably that of the present "King" Building.

The Rev. Mr. Fisk became the pastor in 1735, and so continued until 1744. The Rev. Dudley Leavitt, his successor, was ordained Oct. 23, 1745, and died Feb. 7, 1762. The Rev. John Huntington was ordained Sept. 28, 1763, and died May 30, 1766. The Rev. Nathaniel Whitaker, D. D., the fourth pastor, was installed July 28, 1769. Previous to his installation, the church unanimously voted, to adopt "his plan of Church government," which was Presbyterian. The government of the church was by an eldership or session, of which the pastor was moderator, and member *ex officio*. April 27, 1772, some forty or fifty families, being offended, withdrew to form a new church.

On Nov. 27, 1773, a majority of the church requested the pastor to join with them in applying to the Boston Presbytery, "to take the Church under their watch and care." This action was taken in accordance with the conditions of Dr. Whitaker's settlement. The church was accordingly received in May, 1774. The church voted, Feb. 11, 1784, to reassume the congregational mode of church government. The relation with Dr. Whitaker was dissolved Feb. 26, 1784. Dr. Whitaker was endowed with great energy and determination. He was the first to introduce Presbyterian doctrines in Salem, and in so doing encountered great opposition. His ministry was not altogether harmonious. His congregation, although agreeing to become Presbyterian, in 1769, was not formally so until June, 1774. Upon the destruction of the first meeting-house, the doctor at once set about the construction of a tabernacle in the form of a tent, a rectangular parallelogram, and pyramidal in roof, — on the model of Whitefield's Church in London. The society was much crippled by the withdrawal in 1772. Of the £536 subscribed for the new house, £238 came from abroad. The house was raised in 1776, and opened for public worship in 1777. It was not finished at this time. The house

12

stood in a large field, in a somewhat unsettled neighborhood, on about the present site. From the time of the burning of the first house, Dr. Whitaker had no fixed salary. Collections were taken every Sunday for his support. He was an ardent patriot through the Revolution, but he became very unpopular with his congregation, and the feeling against him continued to grow stronger, until it culminated in his dismission in 1784. He died Jan. 21, 1795.

The Rev. Joshua Spaulding was ordained Oct 26, 1785, and was dismissed April 23, 1802. During his ministry, the church, built by Dr. Whitaker, was greatly improved. It was not until 1794, twenty years after it was undertaken, that this house was decently and tolerably finished. In 1804, the dome and belfry were carried away entire in a gale, and landed in an adjoining garden. A steeple was raised in 1805, at the front of the church, and in its improved form the church remained until demolished, March 9, 1854. Chief among the many associations hovering around this old tabernacle, is the fact that it was the cradle of the Massachusetts Missionary Society and of the American Board of Commissioners for Foreign Missions. It was in this church, Feb. 6, 1812, that the first foreign missionaries to India were ordained. The Rev. Samuel Worcester, D. D., was born in Hollis, N. H., Nov. 1, 1770, and died June 7, 1821. He graduated at Dartmouth, 1795, and was installed as pastor of the Tabernacle Church April 20, 1803, after a five years' ministry in Fitchburg. The Rev. Elias Cornelius was settled as his associate July 21, 1819. The Rev. Mr. Cornelius was dismissed Sept. 29, 1826. The Rev. John P. Cleaveland, D. D., was ordained Feb. 14, 1827; dismissed April 23, 1834. The Rev. Samuel M. Worcester, D. D., installed Dec. 3, 1834, was born at Fitchburg, Sept. 4, 1801; graduated at Harvard in 1822; studied at Andover Theological School, and was assistant teacher at Phillips Academy in Latin and Greek; professor of rhetoric and oratory at Amherst College from 1823 to 1834; pastor of the Tabernacle Church for a quarter of a century, until Dec. 3, 1859. He represented the town of Amherst in the General Court; was a member of the State Senate, and a representative from Salem in 1866. He died at Salem Aug. 16, 1866. Dr. Worcester was a man of remarkable talents, and an able preacher. The present church edifice was erected in 1854, during Dr. Worcester's pastorate. The corner-stone was laid April 26th, and the building was dedicated

December 3d of that year. The Rev. Charles Ray Palmer was ordained Aug. 29, 1860, and was dismissed June 13, 1872. The Rev. Hiram B. Putnam was installed Dec. 31, 1873, and was dismissed March 15, 1877. The Rev. DeWitt Scoville Clark is the present pastor. He accepted the call to the pastorate Nov. 17, 1878, and was installed Jan. 15, 1879.

The North Church is the sixth religious society in point of age in Salem. Its first proprietors, on account of a division among the members of the First Parish in regard to the settlement of a colleague pastor in 1770, separated from that parish, and on the 14th of February, 1772, purchased land for a church-site on the corner of North and Lynde streets. This estate is now occupied by the Hon. Otis P. Lord. This separation was harmonious, and the relations between the churches continued to be of the most friendly character. There were forty-two associates in the purchase, and John Nutting, who sold them the land, was the forty-third proprietor. March 3d, following, the proprietors of this land met at the town hall, and organized the society known as "The Proprietors of the North Meeting House," popularly called "the North Society." William Browne, Edward Augustus Holyoke, Joseph Blaney, Samuel Curwen, John Felt, Richard Ward, and Clark Gayton Pickman were chosen a committee to superintend the building of a church. The foundation of the house was laid May 11, 1772, and the building was opened for public worship, Aug. 23, 1772. The structure was of wood, with a tower and spire, on Lynde Street. In 1796, the spire, being deemed unsafe, was taken down, and replaced by a cupola. This house was known as "the large new meeting-house," and was frequently used for civic celebrations. It continued to be used as a house of worship for sixty-four years, until the erection of the present stone edifice on Essex Street. The building passed from the hands of the society in 1836, and remained standing for many years, being used for manufacturing purposes. It was last used as a manufactory of floor oilcloths.

On the 16th of May, 1772, fifty-two brethren and sisters were dismissed from the First Church, at their own request, to form the new society ; and July 19th, this company met at the Pickman house, opposite St. Peter's Street, still standing on Essex Street, in the rear of the stores numbered 167 to 171, and proceeded to effect a church organization.

The covenant of the First Church was adopted as that of the new church; and twenty to thirty more members were added, prior to the ordination of the minister. It was voted, Aug. 20th, that this should be called the North Church. On the same day, Thomas Barnard, Jr., was chosen pastor. Dr. Barnard was ordained Jan. 13, 1773. His ministry continued until Oct. 1, 1814, the date of his death, a period of nearly forty-two years. He was peculiarly fitted for his high calling. A little more than two years after his ordination, came that memorable Sabbath afternoon in February, 1775, when Col. Leslie, with a battalion of the British 64th, marched past his church, through Lynde and North streets, on the way to the North Bridge to seize cannon supposed to be concealed thereabouts. An account of the stirring scenes that took place there, and the part performed by Mr. Barnard, have been recounted in a preceding chapter. Dr. Barnard was born in Newbury, Feb. 5, 1748; graduated from Harvard in 1766; studied theology with Dr. Williams of Bradford, and received the degree of Doctor of Divinity from the Universities of Edinburgh and Providence, in 1794. His father, an uncle, a grandfather, and a great-grandfather were all ministers. He died suddenly, on the 1st of October, 1814. Dr. Barnard was a fine scholar. He delivered the Dudleian lecture at Cambridge, in 1795; and a discourse at Salem, upon the death of Washington, in 1799, which was printed "by desire of the town." John Emery Abbot, Dr. Barnard's successor, was born at Exeter, N. H., Aug. 6, 1793; graduated at Bowdoin in 1810; studied for the ministry at Cambridge University, and also with the Rev. W. E. Channing; was ordained pastor of the North Church, April 20, 1815; and died at Exeter, N. H., on the 7th of October, 1819. He was the son of Dr. Benjamin Abbot, for more than half a century the principal of Phillips Academy at Exeter. John Brazer, the third pastor, was born at Worcester, Mass., Sept. 21, 1789; graduated from Harvard in 1813; tutor of Greek at Harvard, 1815 to 1817; professor of Latin, 1817 to 1820; ordained pastor of the North Church, Nov. 14, 1820; delivered Dudleian lecture at Harvard in 1836, and received the degree of Doctor of Divinity in the same year; died, Feb. 26, 1846, at Huger plantation, Cooper River, near Charleston, S. C. During Dr. Brazer's ministry, the present stone church was erected. It was dedicated June 22, 1836. Octavius B. Frothingham succeeded Dr. Brazer, and was ordained March 10, 1847. He resigned April 9,

1855, to accept a pastorate in Jersey City, N. J. The Rev. Charles Lowe was installed pastor, Sept. 27, 1855, and resigned July 28, 1857. The Rev. Edmund B. Willson, the present pastor, was installed June 5, 1859.

South Church. — When the old "Third Church" meeting-house was burned, Oct. 6, 1774, the greater portion of the society, on account of dissatisfaction felt with the pastor, the Rev. Dr. Whitaker, purchased the old Assembly House, on Cambridge Street, as their place of worship. This society claimed to be the "Third Church," just as Dr. Whitaker's church had claimed to be the First Church when it left the parent society with the Rev. Samuel Fisk. On Dec. 19, 1774, it was voted that the new meeting-house should be called the "South Meeting House"; but the name Third Congregational Society was retained until the subscribers to the purchase of the Assembly House were incorporated as "The Proprietors of the New South Meeting House in Salem," March 15, 1805. The corporate name was changed to the South Church by an Act passed April 14, 1838. The present edifice was erected in 1804, on the present site, adjoining the old Assembly House, which stood where the vestry does now. Its dimensions were 66 by 80 feet, and it had a spire 166 feet high. Its architect was Samuel Mackintire. The first spire was blown over by the violent gale of September, 1804, but was replaced by the present symmetrical and beautiful piece of architecture. The church was dedicated Jan. 1, 1805, and was remodelled in 1860.

The Rev. Daniel Hopkins was the first settled pastor, and was ordained Nov. 18, 1778. He was born in Waterbury, Conn., Oct. 16, 1734; graduated from Yale College in 1758; he came to Salem in 1766, and preached in the Third Church for a time, after the death of Dr. Huntington. In 1775, he became a member of the Provincial Congress, which position he accepted at the urgent demands of his townsmen, and to the detriment of his private interests. He was chosen pastor of the South Church, March 15, 1776; but his duties as Congressman prevented his ordination until Nov. 18, 1778. He continued in the ministry until his death, Dec. 14, 1814. The Rev. Brown Emerson was ordained as Dr. Hopkins's colleague, April 24, 1805. He was born in Ashby, Mass., Jan. 8, 1778; he graduated at Dartmouth College in 1802; and was licensed to preach in February, 1804, by the Essex North Association. Dr. Emerson celebrated the fiftieth anniversary of his pastorate in 1855, and retained his connection with the church until his death, July 25, 1872. The Rev. Israel E. Dwinell was ordained as colleague pastor to Dr. Emerson, Nov. 22, 1849. He was born in East Calais, Vt., Oct. 24, 1820, and graduated at the University of Vermont, in 1843. He resigned his pastorate in 1863, and was succeeded by the Rev. E. S. Atwood, the present pastor, who was installed Oct. 13, 1864.

The First Baptist Society was organized in 1804, in a vestry erected near the site of the present meeting-house, on Federal Street. The church was regularly constituted, Dec. 24, 1804, with sixteen members. The society was incorporated in 1806. A new church was dedicated Jan. 1, 1806. It was remodelled in 1868; partially destroyed by fire, Oct. 31, 1877, and restored and repaired in 1878.

The Rev. Roger Williams, third pastor of the First Church, from 1633 to 1636, is claimed as the first Baptist preacher in New England. The first pastor of the First Baptist Church was the Rev. Lucius Bolles, D.D., who was born Sept. 25, 1779; graduated at Brown University in 1801; was settled over the First Baptist Church, Jan. 9, 1805; resigned, Aug. 6, 1834; died in Boston, Jan. 5, 1844. His succcessors, in the order of their pastorates, have been the Revs. Rufus Babcock, John Wayland, Thomas D. Anderson, Robert C. Mills, D.D., for twenty-five years; and George E. Merrill, the present pastor.

The Howard Street or " Branch Church," as it was originally called, was formed Dec. 29, 1803, its members being a number who left the Tabernacle Church on account of dissatisfaction felt at the dismissal of the pastor, the Rev. Joshua Spaulding. After uniting with the church at Rowley for a time, the disaffected members held services in Salem, in Jacob Lord's house, Carpenter Street; then in a vestry, built in 1802, on Baptist Hill, and, in 1804, a meeting-house was built on Howard Street, and Mr. Spaulding was installed April 17, 1805. On Aug. 23, 1813, the bodies of Capt. James Lawrence and Lieut. Augustus C. Ludlow, who had been killed on board the frigate "Chesapeake," in her engagement with the "Shannon," were buried from this church, Judge Story delivering a eulogy. Dr. Spaulding resigned May 4, 1814, left Salem, and moved to South-East, in New York. He died Sept. 26, 1825. The Rev. Henry Blatchford was the next regular pastor, and he was followed by the Rev. William

Williams, the Rev. John Todd, the Rev. George B. Cheever, the Rev. Charles T. Torrey, the Rev. Joel Mann, the Rev. M. H. Wilder, the Rev. E. W. Allen, and the Rev. C. C. Beaman. The church changed from Congregational to Presbyterian, March 25, 1815, and was restored to the original faith, June 4, 1828. The church several times suffered from depressions, and finally, Oct. 2, 1864, its pastor, Mr. Beaman, resigned, and the society quietly passed into history. The church was let for a time to the New Jerusalem Society, and by authority of the Legislature, granted by request of the proprietors, the church property was sold at auction, June 28, 1867. The proceeds of the sale of the communion plate were divided among those members of the church who remained in its fellowship at the time of sale.

The Freewill Baptists, sometimes called Christians, formed a society in Salem, in the year 1806, with the Rev. John Rand as its pastor. A meeting-house was erected for this society, on English Street, in 1807. In 1819, a second house was erected at the corner of Essex and Carlton streets. In 1828, the third house was built on Herbert Street. In 1840, the latter house passed into the hands of the Seaman's Society, and the Freewill Baptists became extinct as an organization. A portion of them continued with the Free Church or Campbell wing until 1850. Mr. Rand's successors in the ministry were, the Revs. Abner Jones, Samuel Rand, Moses How, Abner Jones, George W. Kelton, William Andrews, William Coe, and Christopher Martin.

The Universalist Church dates its organization from Feb. 5, 1810. Universalism was first preached in Salem, by the Rev. Samuel Smith, in 1804. From this time meetings were held in private houses by the leaders of the infant church: Ballou, Murray, Turner, Jones, and Barnes. The corner-stone of a church edifice was laid August, 1808, and the building was dedicated June 22, 1809, the Rev. George Richards being the preacher of the sermon. The succession of clergymen has been Edward Turner, June, 1809, to June, 1814; Hosea Ballou, Sept., 1815, to Oct., 1817; Joshua Flagg, Dec., 1817, to March, 1820; Barzillai Streeter, June, 1820, to Aug., 1824; Seth Stetson, June, 1825, to March, 1828; Lemuel Willis, Dec., 1828, to May, 1837; Matthew H. Smith, Nov., 1837, to April, 1840; Linus S. Everett, May, 1841, to April, 1846; Eben Fisher, May, 1847, to

Oct., 1853 ; Sumner Ellis, Jan., 1854, to Sept., 1858 ; Willard Spauld-ing, March, 1860, to Dec., 1869 ; Edwin C. Bolles (the present pastor), June, 1871.

The church edifice, of brick, is one of the oldest in the city, the South and the First Baptist only exceeding it in age. It has several times been remodelled,—in 1840, 1855, and 1878. At the last date, as well as in 1857, extensive changes were made in the outside of the building or its surroundings, as also in its interior arrangement and decoration. Its pews have sittings for one thousand people. Over three hundred families are connected with the parish ; and its Sun-day school, organized in 1829, numbers nearly six hundred mem-bers.

In this parish was formed, in 1832, the Female Samaritan Society, one of the most efficient charities of Salem. During the war, 1861-64, this society sent more than two hundred young men to the ranks of the United States Army. The church celebrated its fiftieth anniver-sary in 1859, and, with the published proceedings of that occasion, may be found much historical and biographical material relating to its early years.

A Roman Catholic Church was organized in Salem, in 1811. The first Roman Catholic services in Salem were held in 1806, by the Rt. Rev. John Cheverus, Bishop of Boston ; and were subsequently held in the intervening years, until 1811, by the bishop and Father Matig-non. In the latter year, a church was organized in a school-house on Hardy Street, by the Rev. Dr. O'Brien, who officiated as its priest for two years. From 1813 to 1819, services were held occasionally by Matignon and Cheverus. The meetings were of a missionary character. The Rev. Paul McQuade was the settled pastor from 1818 to 1822. During his pastorate, the St. Mary's Catholic Church, a wooden edifice, was erected in 1821, at the corner of Mall and Bridge streets, on land deeded for the purpose, in 1810, by Simon Forrester, an Irishman by birth, and a successful merchant. The land was to be used only for Catholic religious purposes forever. In 1826, the Rev. John Mahoney was settled as pastor, and from his time the succession has been unbroken. In 1842, the church was enlarged, and the first Catholic parochial school was taught in this city. In 1849, the congregation at St. Mary's having greatly increased, the St. James Church, on Federal Street, was built, and the "upper parish" organized. St. Mary's Church continued to be occupied until 1857, when the Church of the Immaculate Conception was erected on Walnut Street, and the old edifice abandoned. It remained standing, unused, for twenty years longer, when it was torn down, in 1877, as unsafe.

A Methodist Episcopal Church was first organized in Salem, in 1821. In 1823, the wooden church in Sewall Street (now Wesley Chapel) was built by the Rev. Jesse Fillmore, the first pastor. His ownership of the property caused dissension in the society, and its early history was stormy and troubled. The Rev. Mr. Fillmore was settled in 1822, and remained for a period of ten years, the church not then being a member of the General Conference. It did not unite with the latter until February, 1835. In March, 1841, a second Methodist Society was formed, by a withdrawal from the first; the Rev. N. S. Spaulding was its first pastor. A new house of worship was erected in Union Street. The second society continued to occupy this meeting-house, until 1851, the members of the first church gradually joining with it, until the two societies were merged, in 1844, and the house in Sewall Street passed into the hands of the Second Universalist Society.

In 1851, a new and larger house was deemed necessary, and the present house, at the corner of Lafayette and Harbor streets, was dedicated, Jan. 5, 1853. The pastors are changed every three years. The present pastor is the Rev. Daniel D. Steele, D. D.

In 1872, the meeting-house in Sewall Street was repurchased, and consecrated as "Wesley Chapel." It is occupied by a Methodist Society, formed by the withdrawal of members from the Lafayette Street Church. Its first pastor was the Rev. Joshua Gill. The present pastor is the Rev. W. H. Meredith.

The *Seaman's Society* was formed in August, 1823. Its first meetings were held under the auspices of the Moral Society. It was intended to furnish a place for religious worship for sailors in port, and sea-faring men generally. Eleazer Barnard, settled in 1824, was its first pastor; he was followed by Benjamin H. Pitman, and Michael Carlton. The society first worshipped on Derby or "Long Wharf." Subsequently the chapel in Herbert Street was purchased from the Freewill Baptists, and was occupied for many years, until, with the decline of Salem's commerce, the society gradually diminished, and

13

finally ceased to exist. The chapel is now owned and occupied by the St. Joseph's French Catholic Church.

The Independent Congregational Church in Barton Square, or, as it is more generally termed, the Barton Square Unitarian Church, was formed in 1824. On the 10th of May in that year, $13,000 was sub-scribed to build the house, and to pay the salary of the pastor, the Rev. Henry Colman. The corner-stone of the church edifice was laid July 4, and in December the dedication ceremonies took place. The society was incorporated Jan. 24, 1825, and the Rev. Mr. Colman was in-stalled Feb. 16. Mr. Colman's ministry lasted seven years, when he resigned and retired to private life, his health failing him. The Rev. J. W. Thompson was pastor of the church from March 7, 1832, to March 7, 1859; the Rev. A. M. Haskell from Jan. 1, 1862, to May 2, 1866; the present pastor is the Rev. George Batchelor. The society observed its semi-centennial in 1874. Its place of worship has been once remodelled; and refitted in 1877.

The Central Baptist Church, formerly called the Second Baptist, was organized in 1825. Its first pastor, the Rev. George Leonard, was settled August 23, 1826. The church was regularly constituted in January of the latter year, with "eleven brothers and twenty-one sisters," who were dismissed from the First Baptist Church for the purpose. In June, 1826, the present meeting-house was dedicated. It was remodelled in 1867, and again improved in 1877. Mr. Leon-ard's successors have been the Revs. Robert E. Pattison, Cyrus P. Grosvenor, Joseph Banvard, D. D., Benjamin B. Brierly, William H. Eaton, D. D., Daniel D. Winn, D.D., S. Hartwell Pratt, David Weston, D. D., and W. H. H. Marsh. The church is located at the foot of Federal Street, on St. Peter's Street.

A Mission Chapel, for the use of the colored people, was erected in 1828, on South Street, afterwards Mill Street, and now New Wash-ington Street. It stood on the hill between New Washington Street and Harbor Street. James P. Lewis was a missionary among the colored people in 1831. This church was originally known as the "Union Bethel Church." February 25, 1839, it was reorganized, under the title of the Wesleyan Methodist Church, with John N. Mars as its pastor. In 1842 it held the name of Zion's Methodist Church. Samuel Palmer was its minister in 1845, and it was known as the Wesleyan Methodist Connection. The society continued, with varying fortunes, till about 1861, when it ceased to exist.

The Crombie Street Church was founded in 1832, a church organization being effected on May 3d of that year. There were 139 members, who withdrew from the Howard Street Church in 1831, upon the resignation of the Rev. William Williams as pastor of that church, on account of a difference of views on the slavery question. His resignation was prompted by a desire to promote harmony. Those who withdrew worshipped under Mr. Williams, at first holding meetings in Lyceum Hall. In 1832, the old Salem Theatre building, on Crombie Street, was purchased, and the Rev. Mr. Williams was settled as pastor November 22d of that year. He was dismissed March 1, 1838, and the pastors since that time have been the Rev. Alexander J. Sessions, from June 6, 1838 to Aug. 22, 1849; the Rev. James M. Hoppin, March 27, 1850, to May, 1859; the Rev. J. H. Thayer, Dec. 29, 1859, to Feb. 19, 1864; the Rev. Clarendon Waite, April 10, 1866, to Nov. 26, 1866; and the present pastor, the Rev. Hugh Elder, ordained Jan. 29, 1868.

The Free Church was formed in 1839. In 1837, Campbellite opinions were embraced by a portion of the Freewill Baptists, which caused a division in the society of the latter, and two years later resulted in a separation. The new society rejected all creeds, and, according to its own phraseology, desired to be called an "assembly of Christians," and not "Christ-ians." A church was formed in 1840, with its place of meeting in Masonic Hall, No. 27 Washington Street. William W. Eaton was the first settled pastor, in 1843. He was succeeded by David O. Gaskill, in 1847. During the latter's pastorate the society ceased to exist, about 1850.

A Mormon Church was formed Jan. 1, 1842. Ten years previous, Joseph Smith, the famous Mormon prophet, came to Salem, with two elders, and preached the new dispensation. Erastus Snow and another made a second visit in September, 1841. Snow remained as a preacher, and organized a church, which, in 1843, had a membership of one hundred. During this year a number removed to Nauvoo, then the seat of the Mormon faith in Illinois, and the society was dissolved in 1844.

The Second Universalist Society was organized in 1844, and the first public meeting was held in Lyceum Hall, on May 12th of that year, the Rev. Thomas Whittemore supplying the desk. Subsequently, meetings were held for a time in Mechanic Hall; then in the

Sewall Street Church, and finally in Phœnix Hall, Lafayette Street. The Rev. Day K. Lee was the first settled pastor. He was succeeded by the Revs. Benjamin F. Bowles, S. C. Hewett, and E. W. Reynolds. On June 6, 1852, the society voted to discontinue its meetings.

A Second Advent Church was formed April 13, 1845. On Oct. 10, 1842, a camp-meeting had been held, by the disciples of Miller, in North Salem. Arrangements were subsequently made for holding public worship. The society now worships in Holyoke Hall, Essex Street.

Grace Church, Episcopal, was organized in 1858, by members who withdrew from St. Peter's Parish. The present Gothic meeting-house was erected in that year, on land adjoining the Brown Emerson estate, on Essex, between Monroe and Flint streets. Its rectors have been the Rev. George D. Wildes, the Rev. Joseph P. Kidder, and the Rev. James P. Franks.

New Jerusalem Church. — On July 7, 1794, William Hill, boarding in town, strongly maintained the doctrines of Emanuel Swedenborg. Maj. Joseph Hiller is mentioned as one of the first converts to the faith in Salem. The first meeting for worship was held in 1840, at the house of Mrs. Burleigh, on Lynde Street. But four persons were present. The Rev. O. P. Hiller, a grandson of the collector, preached the new faith at Lyceum Hall, to an audience of four hundred persons, on the evening of July 24, 1844. Eighteen years later, the Rev. T. B. Hayward was invited to come to Salem, by the people then interested in the "heavenly doctrines." From his efforts sprang "Salem Society of the New Jerusalem Church," consisting of thirteen members. The society was organized Jan. 25, 1863. The present meeting-house, on Essex Street above North, was erected in 1871, and dedicated April 18, 1872. The pastors have been the Revs. Abiel Silver, L. G. Jordan, and A. F. Frost.

The Calvary Baptist Church was formed in October, 1870, being the third Baptist society. It was constituted with about ninety members, who withdrew from the Central Baptist Church upon the settlement of the Rev. David Weston. It was designed as a free church, and was organized in Mechanic Hall, March 7, 1871. The church continued to worship there until February, 1873, when it removed to the Bethel in Herbert Street. The present meeting-house was erected in the last-named year on land presented by Mrs. John

Dwyer. It was dedicated Nov. 17, 1873. Its pastors have been the Revs. S. Hartwell Pratt, D. Henry Taylor, and William A. Keese. The church is located at the corner of Herbert and Essex streets. It was incorporated March 17, 1874.

French Church. — The St. Joseph's French Catholic Society worships in the Seamen's Bethel, on Herbert Street. It was formed in 1874. Services in French are also conducted at the rooms of the Young Men's Christian Association, these services being in the Protestant form.

Sunday Schools. — Nearly every church in the city has connected with it a Sunday school, for the religious training of the children and younger portion of the society. The Sunday-school libraries of Salem contain an aggregate of over 8,000 volumes, and some of the churches have libraries for the adult portions of the societies and for the pastors.

*

CHAPTER VI.

SKETCH OF THE ESTABLISHMENT OF THE PUBLIC SCHOOLS OF SALEM.

In New England the school-house and the church were considered inseparable, and we naturally turn from the history of the churches to an account of the establishment of the schools. The honor of leading in the establishment of a public school is claimed in behalf of both Salem and Boston. This claim cannot, with absolute confidence, be awarded to either city. The earliest recorded votes of the people (in Boston, 1635; in Salem, 1640) mention the employment of teacher in such terms as to indicate the prior existence of that office. Further, it is known that, in fact, the Rev. John Fisk did discharge the stated duties of teacher in Salem as early as 1637. Besides, the arrival of Endicott preceded by two years the settlement of Boston.

Latin and High School. — The records of the first school show at the earliest moment a tree of vigorous fibre and no uncertain hold. Mark the continuity of this school's existence! A complete pedagogical succession, with scarcely a missing link in the line of descent, and with none at all for more than one hundred years. Probably not a school in the world can bring such proof of continuous existence during two hundred and forty-one years. The identity is indisputable.

The masters of the Latin Grammar School have been: John Fisk, 1637–39; Edward Norris, 1640–70; Daniel Eppes, Jr., 1670–72; Edward Norris, 1672–76; Daniel Eppes, Jr., 1677–99; Samuel Whitman, 1699–99; John Emerson, 1699–1712; John Barnard, 1712–13; Obadiah Ayres, 1713–16; Samuel Andrews, 1716–18; John Nutting, 1718–47; Peter Frye, 1747–51; Jonathan Sewall, 1751–56; William Walter, 1756–58; Daniel Eppes, 1758–59; Nathan Goodale, 1759–70; James Diman, Jr., 1770–72; Antipas Steward, 1772–82; Belcher Noyes, 1782– ; Thomas Bancroft, –96; Nathaniel Rogers, 1796–97; David Kendall, 1797–98; Daniel

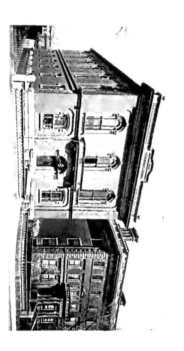

PLUMMER HALL.

HIGH SCHOOL.

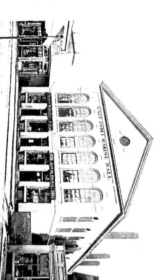

PEABODY ACADEMY OF SCIENCE.

STATE NORMAL SCHOOL.

Heliotype Printing Co., Boston.

Parker, 1798–1810 ; Moses Stevens, 1810–18 ; James Day, 1818–23 ; Theodore Eames, 1823–30 ; George Nichols, 1830–30 ; Amos D. Wheeler, 1830 33 ; and Oliver Carlton, 1833–56.

The masters of the English High School have been : Henry K. Oliver, 1827–30 ; Elisha Mack, 1830–30 ; William H. Brooks 1830–38 ; Rufus Putnam, 1838–52 ; Richard Edwards, 1852–53 ; and Albert G. Boyden, 1853–56.

The masters of the Girls' High School have been : Edwin Jocelyn, 1845–49 ; Charles N. Wheeler, 1849–54 ; and Moses P. Chase, 1854–56.

In 1856, the three schools were consolidated into the present High School, and the masters have been : Jacob Batchelder, 1856–61 ; William J. Rolfe, 1861–62 ; George H. Howison, 1862–64 ; Abner H. Davis, 1864–68 ; and John W. Perkins, 1868– .

The sites of the original school have been, as far as known, the following : On "Court" Street, upon the eastern half of the present Washington Street, over against Mr. Robert Brookhouse's residence ; in 1760, in the centre of Washington Street, over the northern end of the tunnel, occupying a new brick building ; in 1785, for awhile in hired quarters, awaiting the erection of a two-story wooden building, just north-east of the same end of the tunnel, the chamber of that house being its room ; in 1819, on Broad Street, in a new brick building, now (1878) occupied by a primary school. It was here that the Boys' English High School was established, afterwards to be united with the Latin School. In 1856, the consolidated school, the Girls' High School being combined with the foregoing schools, was located in a new edifice of brick, where it still remains.

The year 1845 was the first time that names of citizens were bestowed upon the public schools. The old Latin School was called the Fisk School ; the Boys' High, the Bowditch ; the Girls' High, the Saltonstall ; the English Grammar Schools, in the various parts of the city, the Phillips, Hacker, Pickering, Browne, Higginson, Bentley, and Epes. The Fisk and the Bowditch, in 1854, were united and received the title Bowditch ; in 1856, the Saltonstall was incorporated with them into the present High School, which bears no honorary name. The branches of instruction in the Latin School were, at first, English, Latin, Greek, good manners, and the "principles of Christian religion" (1677). Later (1699), writing, ciphering, and reading are mentioned. Then (in 1801), English grammar, composition, and geography are added to the list of studies, and writing and arithmetic are mentioned, as though for some reason — perhaps, as being taught in the English School — they had been temporarily discontinued. Term time, in the good old days, was "all the year round," or nearly so. The vacations prescribed in 1770 were as follows: General election, commencement day and the rest of that week, fasts, thanksgivings, trainings, Wednesday and Saturday afternoons. These were, properly, holidays, and not vacations as we now term them. The "glorious Fourth" was not yet ushered into being. The boys of 1700 were obliged to rise and breakfast early. From March to November, school opened at seven, A. M.; the rest of the year at eight, A. M. The school day ended at five and four, P. M., for the respective seasons.

Grammar Schools.—In 1712 the first grammar school, anciently called a writing school, was established, Nathaniel Higginson teacher. The site was the old watch-house "in the north end of the town"; *i. e.*, upon ground extending to Essex Street and into Washington Street, west of the location of the Stearns building. The successors of Higginson, till 1785, were Swinerton, Gerrish, Gale, Hart, Ford, Dawson, and Edward Norris. In 1785 the Centre School-house is erected; the upper story occupied by the Latin school and the lower part by this English school. At the same time the number of English schools increases: One is established in Dean Street, Isaac Hacker teacher; one on East (now Forrester) Street, John Watson teacher. In 1807 another is added, on School Street, taught by William B. Dodge. In 1819 South Salem is similarly favored: William Carnes is placed in charge of a school on South (now Washington) Street. In 1821 a like school was opened in Williams Street, with Samuel Burrill for teacher. These schools were the progenitors of our present grammar schools. They were originally organized for boys. In 1793 girls were admitted to the three schools then existing; namely, the Centre, Dean Street, and East Street schools, but not as associates and equals of the boys. To them an hour following the morning session and an hour after school at night was given. In 1827 they were granted two schools for themselves: on Beckford Street, Henry J. Hamilton, teacher; and on East Street, Rufus Putnam, Jr., teacher. In 1835 they are admitted to equal privileges with boys in the North Salem school ; and, in 1841, likewise to the South Salem school, in which year additional provision for both boys and girls is made by the establishment of a grammar school on Aborn Street, under Charles Northend. There are now (1841) four boys' grammar schools : two for girls, and three for both sexes. In the same year (1841) the Centre, Williams Street, and East Street schools (three of the boys' schools) are united and suitably called the Union School, located between Bath (now Forrester) and Essex streets. In 1845 this school is called by the honored name, Phillips ; the boys' school on Dean Street is called the Hacker ; the Beckford Street girls' school is yclept Higginson ; and that on East Street, Bentley ; the mixed school in North Salem receives the appellation, Pickering ; that in South Salem, Browne ; and that in Aborn Street, Epes. The consolidation of the Hacker, Higginson, and Epes, under the title Bowditch, in 1870, completed the present system of grammar schools : one for boys, one for girls, and three for both sexes. After some changes, the names and locations of these schools and the date of erection and material of their present edifices, are as follows : Phillips, Herbert Street, 1869, wood ; Bentley, Essex Street, 1861, brick ; Bowditch, Dean Street, 1870, brick ; Pickering, School Street, 1862, brick ; Browne (now called Holly Street School), Holly Street, 1874, wood. Though the first English (grammar) school was established in 1712, it was nearly one hundred years (1807) before the fourth school was opened. The population of Salem in 1712 is computed at 2,600 ; in 1800, it was 9,457 ; now (1878) it is set at 26,000. The number of pupils in 1718, at the first school above named, was 54. In 1803, the three English (grammar) schools and the Latin school contained 213 boys ; of whom perhaps 180 were in the former schools : now the number is above 1,200. In 1816 grammar and geography were added to the course, which had consisted of the "three R's." Up to that time private schools seemed to eclipse the public schools. Better management and an adjustment of the course of studies to the popular needs gave larger success to these schools. At the present day, in addition to studies named above, spelling, history, music, drawing, and some study of the Constitution of the United States, are embraced in the school-work. Female assistants in the boys' grammar schools, all under masters, began to be employed in 1839 ; for a year or two previously such teachers had

14

been serving in the East Female School. Now one of the five principals is a female, as are all of the assistant teachers in this class of schools : four male teachers, twenty-five female teachers.

Primary Schools. — The first record of a primary school is in 1729, when Samuel Browne donated to the town £240, the interest of half this sum to be devoted to the education of poor children in the grammar (Latin) school, one-quarter to be similarly applied for poor children in the English school, the remaining fourth part to be similarly invested " for the learning of six very poor children their letters and to spell and read " in " a woman's school." The same gentleman, in 1731, remembers the Latin, the English, and " the woman's school " by a donation of £50 each. We have also other incidental mention of the public care to bestow instruction upon the young and unlettered. In 1773 a class of boys not fitted to remain in masters' schools are put under female teachers. In 1801 three public schools are opened to children of both sexes of five years old and upwards. These, with their teachers, were as follows : Lynn Street, Mrs. Holman ; Church Street, Mrs. Lamperel ; East Street, Miss Carlton. This number increases to seven in 1820. There are now twelve primaries, employing forty-eight female teachers.

Colored School. — A school for colored children was organized in 1807, Chloe Minns being appointed teacher, and was supported till 1823 : the same teacher, apparently, having continued in charge all the time. In 1826 a school of the rank of writing school is kept by a colored man for colored children. An effort, in 1827, to re-open the primary is unsuccessful. In 1830 the right of a colored girl to enter the girls' high school was questioned, but affirmed. In 1834, in consequence of a remonstrance against permitting colored girls to attend that school, instruction for them is provided in the chamber of the Centre School-house, which the Latin school once occupied ; William B. Dodge is teacher till 1841, and Thomas B. Perkins then till 1843, when race distinction in public schools ceases.

Evening School. — An evening school of a private character was taught in 1770, and again, in 1772. Mr. Steward proposed to instruct twelve poor boys, from January to April, 1774, on Monday, Wednesday, and Friday evenings. His compensation came from the Brown fund, placed at the disposal of the committee. In 1823 an appropriation of seventy-five dollars is made for an evening school for young men over fifteen years of age, Mr. Hood, teacher. In 1847 the city missionary provides free evening instruction. The next year Mr. Ball, assisted by "many ladies and gentlemen," conducts schools two evenings a week for males and two evenings for females. This school is generously continued until, in 1850, the city authorities come to its support with an appropriation of three hundred dollars, the same gentleman remaining in charge. In 1854 a school was maintained one season at the charge of the city, under instructors already employed in the day schools. Finally, from 1869 to the present time, there have been public evening schools free to males and females who would be benefited by them. The one for males is now in charge of a female principal, with six young teachers as assistants ; that for females is conducted by a female principal, with three such assistants.

The Naumkeag School was opened in 1869, as a half-time and factory school. Such it continued until 1878, the present year, when it lost both these distinctive features. Miss Margaret A. Dunn was its teacher during that entire period. This school is now a miscellaneous one, supplementary to the graded system. In 1869 the school committee made the study of drawing a regular branch in all the day schools. In 1872 evening schools of drawing were inaugurated. There has been no discontinuance of either policy to the present time. From 1872 to 1877 a special instructor of the art was employed in the day schools.

Music. — In 1842, a teacher of vocal music in all the public schools, under masters, except the Latin, was employed ; compensation, $150. The next year, twice that amount was paid for such instruction, under three teachers. In 1848, the exercise seems to have been generally neglected, but the committee feel unable to put the study upon a permanent basis. In 1868, the branch receives due attention, and, from that time to 1877, a regular instructor is employed in all the day schools. By the dismissal of special instructors of these arts in the day schools, the committee did not intend to allow the neglect of the arts themselves ; but relied upon the educated skill of the teachers in the schools to continue and direct the practice.

School Committee. — Originally it was the custom for the voters to manage the schools at town-meetings. As schools grew more numerous, and more frequent attention to details was required, it was found impossible to exercise the proper control in this way. The selectmen were first intrusted with this responsibility; but, in 1712, an occasion calls for a board of committee,—the selection of a teacher for the Latin school. These men were Samuel Browne, Josiah Wolcott, Stephen Sewall, John Higginson, Jr., and Walter Price. Samuel Browne, in 1729, stipulated that the schools upon which his donations were bestowed should be committed to men chosen for that special duty. The people elected the committee till 1836, when, at the incorporation of the city, this power was delegated to its council; but it was restored to the people in 1859, where it still resides. From 1836 to 1847, the number of members was twenty-five; since then it has been a board of eighteen elected, and the mayor and president of the common council, *ex officio.* The committee have made annual reports in print, regularly, since 1848. For some time previously, statements concerning the schools were included as part of the city government's report. The executive office of superintendent was established in 1865. Jonathan Kimball was the first superintendent, and held the office until 1872, when it was discontinued for a year. Augustus D. Small has filled the office from 1873 to the present time.

The Salem State Normal School was founded in 1854; the Resolve of the Legislature for its establishment having been approved April 16, 1853. The State board of education decided June 2, 1853, to locate the school at Salem, and the city furnished the site and erected the building, receiving from the State $6,000, the amount appropriated by the Legislature. The site was formerly occupied by the registry of deeds, and the buildings of that department were removed for the school building. The cost to the city, over and above the $6,000 appropriation by the State, and $2,000 contributed by the Eastern Railroad, was about $5,200. The building was dedicated Sept. 14, 1854, Gov. Emory Washburn presiding. An address was delivered by the Hon. George S. Boutwell. The school was opened Sept. 13, 1854, Richard Edwards being the first principal. He is now principal of the Bloomington (Ill.) State Normal School. His successor was the late Alpheus Crosby. He was a celebrated Greek scholar, and was a man of note among literary people. He resigned in July, 1865, and devoted the remainder of his life to literary pursuits. He died April 17, 1874, aged sixty-three. Prof. Daniel B. Hagar succeeded Prof.

Crosby, and the school to-day is under his supervision. The school has always been a prosperous institution of learning, and the attendance of pupils never was so large as within the last three years. The expenses of pupils at this school are very moderate. Tuition is free to those who comply with the condition of teaching in the public schools of Massachusetts. For the assistance of those who find even the moderate expenses burdensome, the State makes an annual appropriation, one-half of which is distributed, at the close of each term, among pupils from within the Commonwealth who merit and need aid. The institution has a valuable library, containing, in works of general reference and reading, and in text-books, about nine thousand volumes. It has, also, a fair supply of philosophical apparatus, and a museum containing a large collection of specimens illustrating various departments of science.

Originally the school building was sixty-seven feet square; but an addition has been built, and a French roof added, making it now one of the finest public buildings in the city.

CHAPTER VII.

THE LITERARY, BENEVOLENT, AND OTHER SOCIETIES OF SALEM.

Sketches of institutions that have an educating or refining influence on the people appropriately follow an account of the churches and schools ; next come benevolent institutions and societies, and those akin to them ; and, lastly, miscellaneous societies.

The Salem Athenæum was incorporated in 1810, being formed by a union of the Social and Philosophical Libraries.   The first of these dates its origin to a time when Salem was a small provincial town, 1760.   In that year, a library was formed, and called the Social Library.   It was the outgrowth of a social evening club, composed of gentlemen of extended literary attainments : among them, Benjamin Lynde and Nathaniel Ropes, judges of the superior court; Andrew Oliver, judge of the court of common pleas ; William Pynchon, a lawyer; the Rev. William McGilchrist; the Rev. Thomas Barnard ; Stephen Higginson, a merchant ; William Browne, judge of the superior court; Col. Benjamin Pickman, and Dr. E. A. Holyoke.   In 1797, this library received an Act of incorporation.   The Philosophical Library was founded in 1781.   An American privateer had captured the vessel on which a part of the library of the celebrated Dr. Richard Kirwan had been shipped across the Irish Channel, and the books were brought to Beverly and sold.   These were purchased by a company of Salem gentlemen, and the library was thus started.   It was the combination of these two libraries that formed that of the Salem Athenæum, which institution was incorporated in March, 1810. The call for the first meeting was signed by E. A. Holyoke, William Orne, Nathaniel Silsbee, and Samuel Putnam.   Rooms in the Central Building, Central Street (then Market Street), were opened July 11, 1810.   In 1815, the library was removed to rooms in Essex Place ; in 1825, to rooms over the Salem Bank ; in 1841, to Lawrence Place ;

and in 1857, to the present rooms in Plummer Hall. This building was erected from a fund of $30,000 bequeathed to the Athenæum for the purpose in 1854 by Miss Caroline Plummer. The building was completed in 1857. It is occupied jointly by the Athenæum and Essex Institute. The present number of volumes in the Athenæum library is about sixteen thousand. They have been principally obtained by money arising from the annual assessments and from the sale of shares, though the library has received valuable donations and several legacies.

The Essex Institute was formed in February, 1848, by the union of the Essex Historical Society and the Essex County Natural History Society, the Act of incorporation receiving the approval of the governor Feb. 11, 1848. As a preface to a sketch of the Institute it will be appropriate to allude briefly to the two societies by the union of which it was formed.

The Essex Historical Society was formed April 21, 1821, mainly through the efforts of the late Mr. George A. Ward. It had for its objects "the collection and preservation of authentic memorials relating to the civil history of the county of Essex, and the eminent men who had resided within its limits ; also all facts relating to its natural history and topography." In response to a petition to the General Court signed by Dr. Edward A. Holyoke and twenty-five others, an Act of incorporation was granted and approved June 21, 1821. Dr. Holyoke was the first president of the society. It had been expected that a valuable collection of material for a library, chiefly manuscripts, belonging to the Rev. Dr. William Bentley, who had died several months previously, would be placed in the possession of the society, by the executors of his will, but in this its founders were disappointed. However, the institution flourished, and a good collection of portraits and curiosities was soon gathered ; and besides, the nucleus of a library. These collections were first deposited in Essex Place ; then in a room over the Salem Bank, and afterwards in Lawrence Place, till the formation of the Institute.

The Essex County Natural History Society was formed Dec. 14, 1833, with Dr. Andrew Nichols, of Danvers, as president, and Mr. John M. Ives, of Salem, as secretary. An Act of incorporation was not petitioned for until 1836, and bears date February 12th of that year. A meeting to complete the organization was held in Topsfield April 16, 1834, and the society immediately commenced the collection of a library of standard works and a cabinet of specimens in natural history. The cabinet and library were first deposited in Essex Place; subsequently in the Franklin Building; in Masonic Hall, Washington Street; and in Pickman Place, Essex Street — this being the last place of deposit before the union with the Essex Historical Society.

Soon after the organization of the Natural History Society, attention was directed to horticulture, and the first public exhibition was held July 11, 1834. The series of exhibitions that followed were very instrumental in diffusing throughout the community a general and extensive taste for horticultural pursuits. The society issued one volume — three numbers, dating in 1836, 1838, and 1851 — of the "Journal of the Essex County Natural History Society," and during the winter of 1837-8, a course of six lectures was delivered under its auspices.

During the autumn of 1847, several meetings of the two above-described societies were held to effect a union, and a plan drafted by a committee chosen for the purpose, was adopted Jan. 14, 1848. An Act of incorporation was obtained on the 11th of the following month, and on the 1st of March, by its acceptance, the Essex Institute was formed. The Hon. Daniel A. White was the first president. The Institute at first consisted of three departments — the historical, the natural history, and the horticultural. A department of fine arts has since been added. The president of the Institute is chief officer of each department, but a special vice-president is assigned to each, with as many curators as are required for the successful advancement of the work. The means of carrying out the plans of the institution are secured by a library, embracing not only books, but documents, newspapers, and manuscripts; by a museum comprising all collections of history and science; by meetings at the rooms, or in various parts of the county, in the summer season, for the discussion of historical or scientific subjects; by courses of lectures or musical entertainments; by exhibitions under the charge of the horticultural or fine arts departments; by publications.

The library now contains about 30,000 volumes and 100,000 pamphlets, embracing valuable works on history, art, science, religion, and the classics; besides files of newspapers, public documents, pro-

LIBRARY ROOM, PLUMMER HALL.

HISTORICAL ROOM, ESSEX INSTITUTE.

Heliotype Printing Co., Boston.

ceedings of historical, scientific, educational, agricultural, and other societies. This large and extremely valuable library has been obtained principally by donations or exchanges. Among the largest donors of valuable books have been the Hon. Daniel A. White, who at various times gave large numbers of books, in all about 8,000; Mrs. Eliza L. Rogers, Ichabod Tucker, Thomas Cole, Nathaniel Silsbee, Jr., W. D. Pickman, and Mrs. J. S. Cabot. Any person residing in the county of Essex may be chosen a resident member, and any person without the county, a corresponding member. The annual fee is three dollars, and this entitles to the taking from the library of any circulating books, and the privilege of reading at the rooms any book belonging to the Salem Athenæum Library.

The natural history collection is now in charge of the Peabody Academy of Science, having been so disposed in 1867, together with the museum of the East India Marine Society. At the time of this arrangement, the Institute collection numbered over 125,000 specimens, and in a number of classes of the animal kingdom was inferior to only one or two in the country. The historical collections are still preserved separately, and are extremely valuable also. They include valuable portraits of people of local and general prominence.

The regular, special, and field meetings are free to the public, and all are cordially invited to attend them. They attract large numbers of people inclined to historical and scientific matters. The "field meetings," as those held in the summer season about the county are styled, are an Essex Institute feature, and are a very successful means of reaching the general public, and securing a vastly more extended interest in scientific branches, and a more liberal support for the work of the institution.

The lectures and concerts given under the auspices of the Institute are of the very highest order, and exert a powerful influence in elevating the public taste for history, science, and music. Some of the leading men of this and other countries have been introduced to Salem audiences, and even to the American people, by the Essex Institute; and some of the finest music performed in the city has been at the concerts at the Institute rooms.

The exhibitions have uniformly been successful, whether of agricultural and horticultural products, or of works of art or antiquities. The former are held annually, with an occasional special exhibit, and

15

the contributions are not confined to Salem, but frequently towns in remote parts of the county send valued acquisitions to the collections. The art exhibitions bring before the public eye many beautiful and valuable paintings and other works of art, that would not be allowed to be taken from their places in libraries and parlors under any other auspices. Only one collection of antique relics has been exhibited. This was in 1875, and was the wonder and admiration of all who attended. There were displayed for the first time in public the very choicest and most highly treasured antiquities, that are preserved in the old Salem families, and carefully guarded by successive generations. Such relics as were displayed at this exhibition are never allowed to become parts of any museum or public collection.

The publications have always been valuable. From 1848 to 1868, inclusive, six volumes of the "Proceedings of the Essex County Institute" were published. In April, 1859, the publication of "The Historical Collections" was commenced. This is still continued. It contains abstracts from old town and church records, old journals and diaries, and papers of an historical character read before the meetings. One volume of the "American Naturalist," commenced in 1867, was published under the auspices of the Institute, and its publication was then transferred to the Peabody Academy of Science. "The Bulletin" was started in January, 1869, and its publication is still continued, one volume per year being issued. It contains a record of the meetings of the society, short papers of an historical character read before the Institute, scientific communications, and a general report of its proceedings. Other publications have occasionally been issued.

The rooms of the Institute are in Plummer Hall, which is shared with the Salem Athenæum, by a vote of that society, the objects of the Institute being in accordance with those which Miss Plummer mentioned in her will as those to which the building was to be devoted. The library and other collections of the Essex Institute have grown from modest beginnings to magnificent and unusually valuable collections. The institution is thoroughly appreciated, and its name and fame have reached all quarters of the country and world. Under the direction and personal supervision of Dr. Henry Wheatland, its president, the work of the Institute is successfully carried forward by a devoted corps of workers, and its usefulness increases yearly.

At the rooms in Plummer Hall are also deposited the libraries of the Essex Agricultural Society, and the Essex South District Medical Society.

Peabody Academy of Science. — In this institution Salem has a substantial remembrance of the wise liberality of the late George Peabody, the famed London banker and philanthropist. Under date of Feb. 26, 1867, Mr. Peabody addressed to Francis Peabody, Esq., of Salem, Prof. Asa Gray, of Cambridge, the Hon. William C. Endicott and George Peabody Russell, Esq., of Salem, Prof. Othniel C. Marsh, of New Haven, Conn., Dr. Henry Wheatland and Abner C. Goodell, Jr., Esq., of Salem, Dr. James R. Nichols, of Haverhill, and Dr. Henry C. Perkins, of Newburyport, a letter, enclosing an instrument of trust, naming them as trustees of a fund of $140,000, "for the promotion of science and useful knowledge in the county of Essex."

After naming the trustees and the amount given, the letter read as follows : " Of this, my native county, I have always been justly proud, in common with all her sons, remembering her ancient reputation, her many illustrious statesmen, jurists, and men of science, her distinguished record from the earliest days of our country's history, and the distinction so long retained by her as eminent in the education and morality of her citizens. I am desirous of assisting to perpetuate her good name through future generations, and of aiding, through her means, in the diffusion of science and knowledge ; and after consultation with some of her most eminent and worthy citizens, and encouraged by the success which has already attended the efforts and researches of the distinguished scientific association of which your chairman is president, and with which most of you are connected, I am led to hope that this gift may be instrumental in attaining the desired end. I therefore transmit to you the enclosed instrument, and a check for the amount therein named, one hundred and forty thousand dollars, with the hope that this trust, as administered by you and your successors, may tend to advancement in intelligence and virtue, not only in our good old county of Essex, but in our Commonwealth and in our common country."

According to the terms of the instrument of trust, $40,000 was applied to the purchase of the East India Marine Hall, containing the extensive and valuable museum of that society, and of land under and adjoining that building. The $100,000 forms a permanent fund. Arrangements were soon made for the transfer of the collections of the East India Marine Society, and the natural history collection of the Essex Institute, to the charge of the trustees of the Peabody Academy; and these two valuable museums were combined in one, and re-arranged in the hall of the East India Marine Society, which had been refitted for the purpose. An Act of incorporation was granted to the Peabody Academy by the State Legislature, April 13, 1868. Prof. F. W. Putnam was elected director of the museum; and associated with him in the great work of re-arranging and properly classifying the collections, Dr. A. S. Packard, Jr., Prof. Alpheus Hyatt, Prof. Edward S. Morse, and Mr. Caleb Cooke, all curators in the natural history department of the Essex Institute.

From the organization of the academy, its work has been steadily progressive. From 1868 to 1876, the "American Naturalist," a monthly magazine, devoted to science and natural history, was published under its auspices. It has since been transferred to a Philadelphia publishing house. The museum has been open free to the public six days in each week, thousands visiting it each year. No better general collection exists in the country; and in some departments, it is unrivalled. A "Summer School of Biology" was organized in 1877, and was continued the following season. It was under the direction of Dr. A. S. Packard, Jr., who was assisted by a corps of scientific gentlemen, including Mr. James H. Emerton, Mr. John Robinson, the Rev. E. C. Bolles, and Mr. Caleb Cooke. This school furnished to students in natural history valuable facilities for the conduct of their studies.

The Salem Lyceum dates back to Jan. 18, 1830, when the organization was started. The earlier lectures were given in various churches; but the present Lyceum Hall was built in 1831, and the success of the institution increased from that time. Judge Daniel A. White, the president of the Lyceum, delivered the first lecture, Feb. 24, 1830, and an effort was made to have home talent largely represented in the list of lecturers. Among the Salem lecturers who appeared in Lyceum courses in the earlier days of the institution, were Francis Peabody, Jonathan Webb, Henry K. Oliver, Dr. Abel L. Pierson, Charles W. Upham, and Rufus Choate. Some of the most noted men of the time have, year after year, lent their talents to the success of the Salem

INTERIOR—PEABODY ACADEMY OF SCIENCE.

INTERIOR—PEABODY ACADEMY OF SCIENCE.

Heliotype Printing Co., Boston.

Lyceum : among them, Daniel Webster, Edward Everett, Ralph Waldo Emerson, Oliver Wendell Holmes, Charles Francis Adams, A. P. Peabody, Horace Mann, Robert C. Winthrop, Jared Sparks, George Bancroft, and Caleb Cushing. The Lyceum has always maintained a high standard in the selection of its lecturers, and few similar organizations can show such a fine record. The fiftieth annual course of entertainments was opened Nov. 13, 1878, with a lecture by the Hon. Henry K. Oliver, mayor of Salem; his lecture being an historical sketch of the society.

The Young Men's Union was organized in 1855. It maintains a reading-room in Peck's Block, Washington Street; and each season presents a fine course of lectures, concerts, and other entertainments. As a rule these have been largely patronized. They have always been of a high order.

Musical Societies. — Salem has always been noted for its musical talent, and its devotion to musical study and practice. Early in this present century, an attempt succeeded in the publishing, by Mr. John Appleton, of a work intended to supplant the imperfect and unique church music then in general vogue, by a more sober, solemn, and devotional style, and, at the same time, pleasing in melody, accurate and rich in harmony. No organized music society, however, appears till 1818, when the Handel Society was formed, continuing about three years, and studying the highest order of music. In 1821, but existing a very short time, the Haydn Society started.

The first more permanent association was the Mozart Association, organized by the efforts of Gen. Henry K. Oliver, in May, 1825. It had a very successful career of about ten years, giving concerts, with music from the classic authors, and exerting a marked influence upon the taste and skill of the several church choirs in the city, the leading members of which were enrolled among its numbers. Hon. John Pickering was its president, Henry K. Oliver vice-president, conductor, and organist, and the Hon. Leverett Saltonstall first director. The first organ ever built by the celebrated brothers Hook, of Boston, was used by this society. Their concerts were always well patronized, and the prospect of a permanent existence was so very favorable that an application was made in 1834 to the Legislature for an Act of incorporation to enable the society to purchase and hold real estate whereon to erect a music hall. The Act passed both branches, but was vetoed by Gov. Lincoln, on the ground that he considered it " inexpedient to encourage the incorporating of institutions of so limited a public benefit ! " This discouragement seems to have operated unfavorably on the continuance of the society.

The next association for musical purposes was the Salem Glee Club, organized in 1832, of which the leading spirits were Gen. Henry K. Oliver, John Chadwick, Warwick Palfray, William Kimball, Charles Lawrence, Charles G. Putnam, William Brown, Leverett Saltonstall, and W. H. Prince. The club was under the presidency and instruction of Gen. Oliver, who selected its library, comprising all the best works of Horsley, Callcott, Spofforth, Lord Mornington (father of the Duke of Wellington), Danby, Bishop, and others. The club continued about twenty-two years. On its breaking up, its library was presented to the Harvard Musical Association, of Boston.

The Salem Academy of Music was organized Aug. 31, 1846, with W. H. Prince as president. It existed for several years.

The Salem Choral Society was organized Feb. 5, 1855, and gave its first concert Dec. 25, 1855. It rendered sacred music. J. F. Tuckerman was its first president, and a council of advice consisted of Asahel Huntington, Leverett Saltonstall, James M. Hoppin, Alfred A. Abbott, W. H. Prince, O. B. Frothingham, Otis P. Lord, and Joseph Andrews.

Among organizations of less note may be mentioned the Salem Philharmonic Society, organized Sept. 25, 1849; the Union Singing School, 1847; and the Salem Musical Education Society, of later date.

The Salem Oratorio Society was organized Nov. 17, 1868, with a membership of about three hundred persons. It was gathered mainly by the personal efforts of Mr. Francis H. Lee, an amateur. Its success has been very great; mastering, under the instruction and lead of Mr. Carl Zerrahn, the principal works of Handel, Haydn, Mendelssohn, and rendering them to the public in a manner to excite the praise of the severest musical critics,—one of whom, in a leading musical journal, declared that there never had been heard in this country such marvellous chorus singing. The fame of the society spread far and wide, and it was selected, at the Peace of the World Jubilee at Boston, in 1872, as one of the societies to sing the double choruses of Handel's "Israel in Egypt," over against the Handel and Haydn Society of Boston.

The Salem Schubert Club was formed in May, 1878, for practice and performance of English glees and madrigals. Its membership is about sixty mixed voices. The society is under the direction of Mr. William J. Winch, of Boston. The first public performance was given at Plummer Hall, Jan. 14, 1879.

The Salem Marine Society, the most ancient organization in the city, originated in March, 1766, when eighteen shipmasters constituted the society. The Act of incorporation was received in 1772. The early meetings were held at the houses of members, and later at the public houses. The society now has rooms in Franklin Building, corner of Essex and Newbury streets, which it owns. The late Thomas Perkins bequeathed to the society his buildings known as Franklin Place, and the first meeting was held there Nov. 28, 1833. The building was badly damaged by fire Jan. 29, 1845, again Jan. 4, 1859, and totally destroyed Oct. 21, 1860. The last time the insurance had expired a few hours before the fire ; but the generosity of the insurance company, and liberal contributions of citizens, aided substantially in erecting the present fine structure. The subscriptions amounted to over $14,000. The objects of the institution, from its formation, have been charity, and progress in navigation. These principles have been closely adhered to.

The East India Marine Society is one of the oldest associations in the country, having been organized Oct. 14, 1799. Capt. Benjamin Hodges was the first president ; Jacob Crowninshield, treasurer ; and Capt. Jonathan Hodges, secretary. Its chief objects were "to assist the widows and children of deceased members, who may need it, out of the funds of the society"; "to collect such facts and observations as tend to the improvement and security of navigation"; "to form a museum of natural and artificial curiosities, particularly such as are to be found beyond the Cape of Good Hope, or Cape Horn." The by-laws provided that "any person shall be eligible as a member of this society, who shall actually have navigated the seas near the Cape of Good Hope or Cape Horn, either as master or commander, or as factor or supercargo of any vessel belonging to Salem, or, if resident in Salem, of any vessel belonging to any port in the United States." These conditions were always observed, and under them 348 joined the society up to the time that its museum was, with that of the Essex Institute, placed in charge of the Peabody Academy of

Science (1867). Of these, 278 had died, leaving seventy surviving members. The charity bestowed was frequently outside of the channels prescribed in the by-laws. Much attention was paid to improvement in navigation. The earliest journal written in the records of the society was by Nathaniel Bowditch, who was for some years master or supercargo on voyages from Salem to the East Indies. The museum of curiosities collected was a very remarkable and extremely valuable one, and makes a prominent part of the collections now displayed by the Peabody Academy. The society first occupied a room in a building on the corner of Essex and Washington streets; next a building in the rear of the present Downing Block, and in 1825 moved. into the East India Marine Hall, on Essex, nearly opposite St. Peter's Street. The opening of this new hall was celebrated by a procession and dinner, at which President Adams, Mayor Quincy, of Boston, Judge Story, of the United States Supreme Court, and President Kirkland, of Harvard College, were present. The organization of the society is still maintained, and its charity fund is continued.

The Salem Fraternity is an exceedingly worthy institution. It was organized in April, 1869, and maintains, free to all, a reading-room, amusement room, and library, in the Downing Block, Essex Street. The library contains upwards of 2,000 volumes, and free instruction is given in various branches by competent teachers. Its labors are mainly among such young people of both sexes as are employed in the city, but who have no home associations. Its objects are appreciated by the charitably disposed, and its influence is considerable.

The Young Men's Christian Association was organized in 1858. It has rooms at No. 194 Essex Street, which are open to all, day and evening, and where religious services are frequently conducted on week days and on each Sunday.

Temperance Societies. — Salem has had, first and last, a host of temperance organizations. Washington Total Abstinence Union, from 1841 to 1847; the Martha Washington Society, in connection with the first named; Young Men's Temperance Society, 1843; Henfield Division, Sons of Temperance, 1844, and still in existence; Salem Division, 1846; Young Men's Division, 1859 to 1865; Phillips Division, 1859, and Abraham Lincoln Division, 1866, both still maintained; Independent Division, Daughters of Temperance, and Zephyr Union

Daughters; Social Council, 1859; Essex Temple of Honor, 1856; Meteoric Temple of Honor, 1866, and still existing; Cadets of Temperance, 1848; Naumkeag Tent, Independent Order of Rechabites, 1844; Ocean Tent of Rechabites; Daughters of Rechab; Father Mathew Temperance Society, 1848, and still maintained; Temperance Watchmen, 1851; Young Men's Catholic Temperance Society, 1857, and still existing; Bands of Hope; Minnehaha Lodge, Order of Good Templars (1862), and Siloam Lodge, 1866, both in existence now; Young Men's Temperance Volunteers, 1867; the present Reform Clubs; Ladies' Christian Temperance Union, and others. Each one has done what was within its power to check the evil of intemperance, and with greater or less degree of success.

The Plummer Farm School is a reformatory institution for boys, founded by bequests of Miss Caroline Plummer,—one of $10,000; one of $8,000; and, besides, the residue of her property after paying other legacies. The legacies were accepted, according to the terms of Miss Plummer's will, by the city council, and the mayor and aldermen chose ten trustees to have charge of the institution. An Act of incorporation was granted by the Legislature, May 21, 1855. The amount of the fund July 1, 1856, was $25,462.23. To this the city added $8,000, and interest on the whole was allowed to accumulate till 1870, when the school building was erected on Winter Island, on lands owned by the national government, which granted their use for the school. The building is a handsome French-roof structure. Mr. C. A. Johnson is principal of the school. The school fund now amounts to $50,000.

The City Relief Committee is composed of the pastors and one delegate from each church, and delegates from charitable societies, who act with the assistance of an agent in dispensing charity among the worthy poor of the city. Funds are furnished by the churches and by general contribution.

The Salem Hospital was organized April 7, 1873, a fund having been contributed for its formation by Capt. John Bertram and other citizens. The hospital building is located on Charter Street. This institution supplies a want long felt in the community.

The Salem Dispensary, organized in February, 1820, and incorporated in 1831, had for its object the relief of poor people, by afford-

16

ing medicine and medical advice gratuitously. Its labors ended on the formation of the Salem Hospital, which assumed its mission.

Old Ladies' and Old Men's Homes. — About 1860, the late Robert Brookhouse tendered a large brick house on Derby Street, corner of Orange, to be converted into a "home" for old ladies. A fund was raised, mainly by subscription, the Rev. Michael Carlton, who had been the agent of the Moral Society, collecting a large part of the money, and "The Association for the Relief of Aged and Destitute Women" was incorporated April 4, 1860. The home was opened the following year, the building having been refitted for the purpose. This house was built in the early part of the present century, by B. W. Crowninshield.

The Old Men's Home, corner of Derby and Turner streets, was opened in 1877, and is maintained by its founder, Capt. John Bertram.

The Masons. — There are in Salem six branches of the Masonic fraternity. Essex Lodge, F. A. M., was erected March 9, 1779, under authority from the Massachusetts Grand Lodge, descending from the Grand Master of Scotland. This charter was returned to the Grand Lodge, March 6, 1789, it being found impossible to continue the lodge, as so many of its members were mariners and absent at sea. Another charter was granted, and the lodge formally constituted June 8, 1792. The lodge was suspended on account of the anti-Masonic excitement from 1833 to 1845. Starr King Lodge was chartered March 9, 1865, twenty-two members having demitted from Essex Lodge for the purpose of forming it. Washington Royal Arch Chapter was constituted in September, 1811; suspended from March 17, 1835, to September, 1852; since which time companions have demitted to constitute Sutton Chapter, Lynn; William Ferson Chapter, Gloucester; Amity Chapter, Beverly; Holton Chapter, Danvers. Salem Council of R. S. M. was constituted June 3, 1818. Winslow Lewis Commandery of Knights Templars, under the jurisdiction of the Grand Commandery of Massachusetts and Rhode Island, was instituted June 27, 1865. Sutton Grand Lodge of Perfection, under the authority of the Supreme Council of Inspectors-General of the thirty-third degree of the Ancient Accepted Scottish Rite of Freemasonry, for the Northern jurisdiction of the United States of America, was constituted and established April 8, 1864.

The Odd Fellows. — During the latter part of the summer of 1843, Adrian Low and Thomas Harvey, both residents of Salem, and members of the order of Odd Fellows, the former of Siloam Lodge, and the latter of Oriental Lodge, conceived the idea of organizing a lodge iu their own city, and the necessary steps were at once taken. A special meeting of the Grand Lodge of Massachusetts was held at Salem, Nov. 6, 1843, and Essex Lodge was formed, fifteen members being admitted. In January succeeding, this lodge had a membership of thirty, and in June, 1876, its members numbered 335. A charter for a new lodge in Salem was granted in 1846, and on the 18th of November, Fraternity Lodge was organized, with twenty-nine members, that number withdrawing by card from Essex Lodge. Its membership iu June, 1876, was 205. Both of these lodges have excellent records of work done within the order, and of charity bestowed on sick members. Both are in flourishing condition to-day, and have the promise of brilliant futures. Naumkeag Encampment was instituted June 26, 1845. Union Degree Daughters of Rebecca is the title of the female branch of Odd Fellowship in Salem.

Religious Associations. — Three religious associations, that are strictly county organizations, are so intimately connected with Salem that they properly find a place in this sketch.

The Essex Congregational Club, embracing in its membership prominent ministers and laymen, in the Trinitarian Congregational churches of Essex County, had its origin in the meeting of the "American Board of Commissioners for Foreign Missions," which was held in Salem in 1871. The arrangements for that meeting were in the hands of a committee from various towns and cities in the county. After the session of the "Board," the committee assembled for a social evening; and at that meeting a committee was chosen to take measures for the formation of an Essex County Congregational Club, in order, in the words of the resolution, "to perpetuate the pleasant intimacies formed, and to promote better acquaintance among the churches of the vicinity." For various reasons no further steps were taken until Nov. 12, 1872, when a meeting of representative Congregationalists was held in the South Chapel, all preliminaries arranged, and a constitution drafted. The first regular meeting was held in Central Hall, Central Street, Jan. 6, 1873. The constitution adopted, was, with two or three slight alterations, the same as that of the "Boston

Congregational Club," which was organized in 1869, and was the pioneer association of the kind in the United States.

The exercises of the club are a supper, a brief social meeting, and a formal session, at which carefully prepared essays on practical topics are read, and the reading is followed by a general discussion. Although the club is organized on a denominational basis, it is widely catholic in its spirit, and from time to time the presence and utterances of men of all varieties of religious faith have been welcomed. The representatives of the local and metropolitan journals are uniformly present; and the public press has given wide currency to papers that were considered of special importance. Its growth in strength and usefulness, and its extended reputation, entitle it to be ranked as one of the institutions of Essex County, and an institution that exerts no small influence for good over the religious communions that are represented in it. It holds six meetings a year, usually on the second Monday of alternate months.

The Salem Baptist Association was formed in 1826, and was then composed of nineteen churches, made up of 2,178 members. Its first session was held at Lynn in 1828. It now includes twenty-four churches, composed of about 4,500 members. The Salem Pastoral Union is an organization of thirty-five years' standing, and is connected with the Salem Baptist Association, its members consisting of pastors of the churches composing that association.

The Salem Charitable Mechanic Association was organized Oct. 1, 1817, and the Mechanic Hall Corporation in 1839. The former has a library and reading-room in the Mechanic Hall Building. For many years, commencing in 1828, this society maintained lecture courses under the name of the Mechanic Lyceum.

The Salem Mutual Benefit Association is a mutual life-insurance company, as is also a lodge of the Royal Arcanum recently organized in the city. The headquarters of the Essex County Odd Fellows' Mutual Benefit Association are also in Salem.

The Harmony Grove Cemetery Corporation was organized in 1839, and incorporated in 1840; cemetery consecrated June 14, 1840. The cemetery contains about sixty-five acres, and is beautifully laid out, and finely kept. The remains of George Peabody, the philanthropist, are here interred.

Miscellaneous Societies. — The American Association for the Advancement of Science has its headquarters in Salem, occupying a room on the second floor of the Bank building, on Central Street. Prof. F. W. Putnam is the permanent secretary. The library of this association is a very large and valuable one, and its volumes are sent all through the country among the leading scientists. The business of the association is done almost wholly by mail and express, and few people comprehend its wide scope. The Salem Female Charitable Society was organized in 1801, and incorporated in 1804; the Samaritan Society was organized Dec. 10, 1832; the Salem Female Employment Society was incorporated May 1, 1867; the Seamen's Widow and Orphan Association was formed in 1833, and incorporated in 1844; the Seamen's Orphan and Children's Friend Society organized Feb. 25, 1839, and received an Act of incorporation in 1841. A new "home" has just been completed and opened on Carpenter Street. The City Orphan Asylum of Salem Sisters of Charity is the successor of the Looby Asylum, founded by the late Thomas Looby in 1866. It is situated on Lafayette Street, the building being a new one of brick, and perfectly adapted for the uses to which it is put. St. Peter's Guild, organized in 1872, is devoted to charitable work, under direction of the rector of St. Peter's Church. There are also in the city at the present time lodges of the United Order of American Mechanics, Knights of Pythias, Knights of Honor, American Protestant Association, United Order of Red Men, and others of lesser note.

CHAPTER VIII.

SKETCH OF THE COMMERCIAL HISTORY OF SALEM, WITH BIOGRAPHICAL
NOTICES OF PROMINENT MERCHANTS.

The commercial record of Salem, the most brilliant chapter in her history, is yet to be written. The old shipmasters, whose record is a part of that history, are many of them still living among us ; but their numbers are gradually diminishing, and before many years nothing will be left for the historian to glean from but the written and printed page. This history is so full of important events, and so crowded with interesting details, that it is not possible in the limits of a single chapter to do more than touch, in the briefest manner possible, upon some of the salient points. Perhaps the facts here stated may show what a wealth of material lies ready to be moulded into shape, and induce some chronicler worthy of the theme to undertake the interesting task of gathering it together for preservation. So, ere it be too late, the record may be preserved and handed down as a precious legacy from Salem of the past to Salem of the future.

Salem was undoubtedly chosen as a good place for settlement by Roger Conant, who describes it as " a fruitful necke of land," because of its harbors and rivers. Situated on a peninsula, with North River on one side, and South River on the other, all parts of the town were readily accessible by water. Salem was from the first, and of necessity, a maritime place. The Massachusetts Company that sent John Endicott to Salem was a trading company, and the Home governor, Matthew Cradock, writes to Endicott, in 1629, to send as return cargoes " staves, sarsaparilla, sumach, two or three hundred firkins of sturgeon, and other fish and beaver."

The early, long-continued, and staple trade of Salem was in the product of the fisheries. The harbor and rivers swarmed with fish, and so plenty were they that they were used for manure. From 1629 to 1740, Winter Island seems to have been the headquarters of the Salem fishing trade, and that trade was the staple business of Salem down to a much later period. In 1643, the merchants of Salem were trading with the West Indies, with Barbadoes and the Leeward Islands.

Between 1640 and 1650, the commercial career of Salem received an impetus, and her vessels made voyages not only to the mother country, but to the West Indies, Bermudas, Virginia, and Antigua. Her wealth was great in proportion to her population, and Josselyn, writing in 1664, says, " In this town are some very rich merchants." In 1663, William Hollingworth, a Salem merchant, agrees to send one hundred hogsheads of tobacco from the River Potomac by ship from Boston to Plymouth in England, the Island of Jersey, or any port in Holland, and thence to said island, for £7 sterling per ton.

From 1670 to 1740, the trade was to the West Indies and most parts of Europe, including Spain, France, and Holland. From 1686 to 1689, inclusive, Salem is trading to Barbadoes, London, Fayal, Pennsylvania, Virginia, and Antigua. The great majority of her vessels are ketches from twenty to forty tons, and carrying from four to six men. Only one ship appears among them, and her tonnage is but one hundred and thirty tons. In 1698–99, registers are taken out for two ships of eighty and two hundred tons, a barque, three sloops, and twenty ketches. John Johnson, of Salem, in 1693, "having for nigh three years followed the trade of boating goods," to and from Boston, " sometimes twice a weeke," complains to Gov. William Phipps, of the cost of entering and clearing.

In 1700, the foreign trade of Salem is thus described by Higginson : " Dry Merchantable Codfish for the markets of Spain, Portugal and the Straits. Refuse fish, lumber, horses and provisions for the West Indies. Returns made directly to England are sugar, molasses, cotton-wool, logwood and Brasiletto wood, for which we depend on the West Indies. Our own produce a considerable quantity of whale and fish oil, whalebone, furs, deer, elk and bear skins are annually sent to England. We have much shipping here and freights are low."

Philip English. — A good type of the Salem merchant of this period may be found in Philip English. He came to Salem before 1670, and in 1675 married the daughter of another Salem merchant, Mr. William Hollingworth. In 1676, he is at the Isle of Jersey, commanding the ketch " Speedwell." He had so flourished in 1683 that he put up a stylish mansion on the eastern corner of Essex and English streets. It was one of those ancient mansion-houses for which Salem was once noted — a venerable, many-gabled, solid structure, with projecting stories and porches. Down to 1753 it was known as English's great house. It stood until 1833, long tenantless and deserted, and when torn down a secret room was found in the garret, supposed to have been built after the witchcraft furor as a place/ of temporary security in case of a second outcry.

In 1692, Philip English was at the height of his prosperity. He was trading with Bilboa, Barbadoes, St. Christopher's, and Jersey, as well as with several French ports. He owned twenty-one vessels, besides a wharf and warehouse on the neck, and fourteen buildings in the town. It is probable that his wife was over-elated by their prosperity, and forgot her humble friends of former days; for she is now called "aristocratic," and the prejudice thus engendered against her doubtless led to her being "cried out" against for witchcraft. Both Mr. English and his wife were so accused. From 1694 to 1720, Mr. English sends ketches to Newfoundland, Cape Sable or Acadia, to catch fish, and sends these fish to Barbadoes or other English West Indies, Surinam, and Spain. He also had a number of vessels running between Salem and Virginia and Maryland. The ketch of those days was two-masted, with square sails on the foremast, and a fore and aft sail on the mainmast, which was shorter than the foremast. The schooner, which gradually supplanted the ketch, first appears in our Salem marine about 1720.

Mr. English was put into Salem jail, so says Felt, in 1725, for refusing, as an Episcopalian, to pay taxes for the support of the East Church. About 1734 he retired from trade, and in 1735, he was put under guardianship as being clouded in mind. He died in 1736, aged about eighty-six years, and was buried in the Episcopal church-yard.

Richard Derby. — About the time that Philip English retired from trade we find Richard Derby the master of the sloop "Ranger," about to sail from Salem for Cadiz and Malaga. Salem, at this time, has about thirty fishing vessels, much less than formerly, and the same number which go on foreign voyages to Barbadoes, Jamaica, and other West India Islands; some to the Wine Islands; others carry fish to Spain and Portugal. In 1739, Mr. Derby sails in the "Ranger" to St. Martin's, and in 1742 he is master and part owner of the "Volant," bound for Barbadoes and the French Islands. In 1757, he retired from the sea and became a merchant of Salem, relinquishing his vessels to his sons, John and Richard.

The commerce in which Mr. Derby was engaged was pursued in vessels ranging from fifty to one hundred tons. His vessels, laden with fish, lumber, and provisions, cleared for Dominica, or some Windward Isle in the British West Indies, and then ran through the islands for a market. The returns were made in sugar, molasses, cotton, rum, and claret, or in rice and naval stores, from Carolina. With the returns from these voyages, assorted cargoes were made of oil, naval stores, and the produce of the islands, for Spain and Madeira; and the proceeds remitted partly in bills on London, and partly in wine, salt, fruit, oil, iron, lead, and handkerchiefs, to America. The commerce of these days was bold and adventurous. Few vessels exceeded sixty tons burden, and they were exposed not only to the dangers of the seas, but also to the buccaneers and French and English cruisers. During the French War, from 1756 to 1763, Mr. Derby owned several ships, as well as brigantines, carrying each eight or ten cannon. He was owner of part of the cannon which Col. Leslie was sent down from Boston by Gen. Gage to capture in 1775. He was born in Salem, Sept. 16, 1712, and died there Nov. 9, 1783.

Dr. Edward A. Holyoke, writing of the commerce of Salem in 1749, says : — "The commerce of this town was chiefly with Spain and Portugal, and the West Indies, especially with St. Eustatia. The cod fishery was carried on with success and advantage. The schooners were employed on the fishing-banks in the summer, and in the autumn were laden with fish, rum, molasses, and the produce of the country, and sent to Virginia and Maryland, and there spent the winter retailing their cargoes, and in return brought corn and wheat and tobacco. This Virginian voyage was seldom very profitable, but as it served to keep the crews together, it was continued till more advantageous employment offered."

The commerce of Salem did not receive any decided impetus till the close of the Revolutionary War. From that period until the embargo preceding the War of 1812, the commercial prosperity of Salem was at the zenith. The three most prominent merchants of that period were Elias Hasket Derby, William Gray, and Joseph Peabody. They owned a large proportion of the shipping of Salem, and their vessels penetrated every port and brought home the offerings of every clime. They made the name of Salem familiar wherever trade penetrated or civilization ventured, and the name of the Salem merchant a synonym for honor, intelligence, and vigor the world over.

Elias Hasket Derby. — The second son of Richard Derby, Elias Hasket, was born in Salem, Aug. 16, 1739. At an early age, he entered the counting-room of his father, and from 1760 to 1775 he took charge of his father's books and engaged extensively in trade with the English and French islands. At the commencement of the Revolutionary War, he had seven sail of vessels in the trade of the West Indies. Many of the rich men clung to the mother country, but Mr. Derby espoused the cause of the colonists. His trade and that of Salem was ruined by the war. Indignant at the oppressive course of Great Britain, Mr. Derby united with his townsmen, and Salem fitted out at least 158 armed vessels during the Revolution.

From 1771 to 1785 the tonnage of Salem declined, and did not revive till the opening of the India trade, when it increased with astonishing rapidity, as appears by the following table : —

Tonnage of Salem. — In 1768, 7,913 tons ; 1771, 9,223 tons ; 1781, 8,652 tons ; 1791, 9,031, tons ; * 1800, 24,862 tons ; 1807 (252 vessels), 43,570 tons.

On the 15th of June, 1784, the barque "Light Horse" was sent by Mr. Derby to St. Petersburg, with a cargo of sugar, and opened the American trade with that place. For a short time Mr. Derby sent ships to Spain and the West Indies. But his daring and venturesome spirit was not content to follow only in the footsteps of his predecessors, and he turned his eyes to the Cape of Good Hope and the far-distant Indies, and determined to measure his strength with the incorporated companies of England and France and Holland, which then entirely monopolized the commerce of the East.

In November, 1784, he despatched the ship "Grand Turk," of 300 tons, Capt. Jonathan Ingersoll, on the first voyage from Salem to the Cape of Good Hope. Although this voyage was not very successful, it gave Mr. Derby an insight into the wants and prices of the Indian market, and Nov. 28, 1785, he cleared the same vessel under command of Ebenezer West, for the Isle of France, with the purpose to visit Canton ; went to the Isle of France, Batavia, and China, and

---

* This table is from a list of Salem property, valued and returned to the General Court. A return from the custom-house puts the tonnage in 1791 at 14,570 tons, and in 1794 at 16,788 tons.

returned to Salem in June, 1787, with a cargo of teas, silks, and nankeens, making the first voyage from New England to the Isle of France, India, and China.

In December, 1787, Mr. Derby again despatched his ship "Grand Turk" on a voyage to the Isle of France, under the charge of his son, Elias Hasket Derby, Jr. The "Grand Turk" was sold at a great profit, and the son remained at the Isle of France until the arrival, about a year afterwards, of the ship "Atlantic," when he proceeded to Surat, Bombay, and Calcutta, and first displayed our ensign at those ports. He bought at the Isle of France the ship "Peggy," sent her to Bombay for cotton, and then back to Salem, where she arrived June 21, 1789, with the first cargo of Bombay cotton. One of his vessels was the first to display the American flag at Siam, and another made the first voyage from America to Mocha.

In February, 1789, Mr. Derby sent, for the first time, the ship "Astrea" on a direct voyage to Canton. American ships were now following the lead of the "Grand Turk," and we find fifteen there in 1789, five of them belonging to Salem and four to Mr. Derby. In 1790 he imported into Salem 728,871 pounds of tea. In May, 1790, the brig "William and Henry," Capt. Benjamin Hodges, owned by Gray & Orne, entered this port with a cargo of tea, which was among the first of such cargoes imported in an American bottom. When Mr. Derby first engaged in the India trade there were no banks, and he rarely purchased or sold on credit. While his large ships were on their voyages to the East, he employed his brigs and schooners in making up the assortment for cargoes by sending them to Gottenburg and St. Petersburg for iron, duck, and hemp; to France, Spain, and Madeira for wine and lead; to the West Indies for spirits; and to New York, Philadelphia, and Richmond, for flour, provisions, iron, and tobacco. In the brief space of fourteen years, from 1785 to 1799, he made 125 voyages, by at least thirty-seven different vessels; of which voyages, forty-five were to the East Indies or China. Among the officers of his ships who were afterwards distinguished, were the Hon. Nathaniel Silsbee, late United States senator from Massachusetts, and Dr. Nathaniel Bowditch.

In 1798, the nation appeared to be on the eve of a war with France, and was without a navy. John Adams was president, and the administration, in June, 1798, passed an Act authorizing the president to accept such vessels as the citizens might build for the national service, and pay for them in a six per cent. stock. Subscriptions were opened in Salem, and Mr. Derby and Mr. William Gray each subscribed $10,-000, and William Orne and John Norris, each $5,000, and in a brief period some $74,700 was subscribed. Mr. Enos Briggs, who had built many of Mr. Derby's fastest ships, was instructed to build a frigate, to be called the "Essex." The keel was laid April 13, 1799, and September 30th following she was successfully launched. She proved the fastest ship in the navy, and captured property to the amount of two million dollars. Admiral Farragut served on the "Essex" as a midshipman.

Mr. Derby erected a costly edifice on the site now occupied by Derby Square, and laid out walks and gardens from Essex Street to a terrace which overhung the South River. This mansion he occupied but a few months before his death. Mr. Derby made one more brilliant voyage before he closed his career, although he did not live to ascertain its results. Hostilities between France and the United States had commenced when Mr. Derby sent a ship of 400 tons, called the "Mount Vernon," equipped with twenty guns, manned by fifty men, and loaded with sugar, to the Mediterranean. The cost of the cargo was $43,275. The vessel was attacked by the enemy, but escaped, and arrived safely in America with a cargo of silks and wines, and realized a net profit of $100,000. Before her arrival, Mr. Derby died, Sept. 8, 1799, and left an estate which exceeded a million dollars, and was supposed to be the largest fortune left in this country during the last century.

Among the many eminent merchants of Salem, Mr. Derby should be named first. He led the way to India and China, and opened for Salem that extensive foreign commerce which will always hold a prominent place in her history.

William Gray. — During Mr. Derby's later years William Gray was a prominent merchant of Salem. He was born in Lynn, June 27, 1760, moved to Salem at an early age, and entered the counting-room of Richard Derby. He became one of the largest ship-owners in Salem, and followed the lead of Mr. E. H. Derby in sending ships to Canton and ports in the East Indies. In 1805, Salem had fifty-four ships, eighteen barques, seventy-two brigs, and eighty-six schooners, five ships building, and forty-eight vessels round the Cape. In 1807, sixty ships, seven barques, forty-two brigs, forty schooners, and three sloops in the merchant service, and 100 fishermen and schooners ; and of these William Gray owned fifteen ships, seven barques, thirteen brigs, and one schooner, or one-fourth of the tonnage of the place.

From 1801 to 1810 inclusive, the duties collected at Salem amounted to $7,272,633.31, and these were the years of Mr Gray's greatest activity. His former mansion is now the Essex House. About 1808, he left the Federal party and joined the Democrats, upholding Jefferson in the Embargo Act of that year. Party feeling ran high, and Mr. Gray, finding a growing coolness towards him among many of his former associates, left Salem in 1809 and moved to Boston, where in 1810 and 1811 he was chosen lieutenant-governor, and where he died, Nov. 3, 1825. During his life he accumulated a great property. As a merchant he was industrious, far-seeing, and energetic ; as a citizen, patriotic and public-spirited, and he may well be classed among Salem's "princely merchants."

Joseph Peabody. — Contemporary with Mr. Gray was another eminently successful merchant, Joseph Peabody, who lived to see the decline of that commercial prosperity to which he had contributed so largely. He was born in Middleton, Dec. 9, 1757, and during the Revolutionary War he enlisted on a privateer, and made his first cruise in E. H. Derby's "Bunker Hill," and his second in the "Ranger." In 1782, he made a trip to Alexandria in the "Ranger," as second officer ; and on his return the vessel was attacked by the enemy and Mr. Peabody was wounded. After peace was restored he was promoted to a command in the employ of the Messrs. Gardner, of Salem, and soon realized a sufficient sum to purchase the vessel known as the "Three Friends." He retired from the sea in 1791, and engaged actively in commerce. The brig "Three Friends," Joseph Peabody, master, entered from Martinico in June, 1791, with a cargo of molasses and sugar consigned to Mr. J. Gardner, and this was probably his last voyage. During the early years of the present century he built and owned eighty-three ships, which in every instance he freighted himself. His vessels made thirty-eight voyages to Calcutta, seventeen to Canton, thirty-two to Sumatra, forty-seven to St. Petersburg, and thirty to other ports of Europe. He shipped at different times 7,000 seamen, and advanced thirty-five to the rank of master, who entered his employ as boys.

The disastrous effects of the embargo and war were shown in the diminution of vessels in the foreign trade of Salem, from 152 in 1807 to fifty-seven in 1815. In 1816, forty-two Indiamen had sailed and sixteen returned since the war. In 1817, Salem had thirty-two ships, two barques, and eighteen brigs in the India trade, and from 1808 to 1817 the arrivals from foreign ports were 936; which yielded an annual average of duties of $378,590. In 1821, 126 vessels were employed in foreign commerce, fifty-eight of them in the India trade, the largest being the ship "China," H. Putnam, master, 370 tons.

A few facts relating to the connection of Mr. Peabody about this time with the China trade are interesting. In 1825 and 1826, the "Leander," a little brig of 223 tons, brought into Salem cargoes from Canton, which paid duties amounting, respectively, one to $86,847.47, and the other to $92,392.94. In 1829, 1830, and 1831, the "Sumatra," a ship of only 287 tons, brought cargoes from the same port, paying duties of $128,363.13, in the first case; $138,480.34, in the second; and $140,761.96, in the third,—the five voyages paying duties to an aggregate of nearly $587,000. No other vessel has entered Salem paying $90,000 in duties. Both brig and ship were owned by Mr. Peabody, and were commanded on each voyage by the same gentleman, Capt. Charles Roundy, who still lives in Salem, a good type of that class of master mariners whose energy and fearlessness carried the name of Salem to the remotest ports, and whose uprightness and business integrity made that name an honored and respected one in those far-off countries. Among the commanders of Mr. Peabody's vessels still living in Salem, are Charles Roundy, Oliver Thayer, Joseph Winn, Peter Silver, and Thomas M. Saunders. Mr. Peabody died at Salem, Jan. 5, 1844.

John Bertram. — These brief notices of a few of the prominent merchants of Salem, should not be closed without some reference to the last of their number, whose vessels arrived in her harbor from ports beyond the Cape of Good Hope. It is a curious coincidence, that our first merchant, Philip English, is supposed to have been born on the Isle of Jersey, and that our last merchant, John Bertram, first saw the light on that same island, Feb. 11, 1796. Mr. Bertram came to Salem at an early age; and in December, 1813, we find him sailing from Boston in the schooner "Monkey" as cabin-boy. He arrived in Charleston, S. C., early in 1814, and left there in an American privateer in March. The privateer was captured, and he was taken to Bermuda and confined in the Bermuda and Barbadoes prison-ships. Having been born on the Isle of Jersey, and being familiar with the French language, he was released, as a Frenchman, after which he shipped on an American schooner and started for home, but was again taken prisoner, and carried to England, where he arrived in April, 1815, after peace had been declared.

In 1824, with P. I. Farnham and others, Mr. Bertram chartered the schooner "General Brewer," and, in company with Capt. W. B. Smith, sailed for St. Helena. When a few days out, he met the brig "Elizabeth," of Salem, Story, master, bound also for St. Helena. Capt. Story came on board the "General Brewer," and took tea with Capt. Bertram; and each was desirous that the other should not know his destination. They each announced themselves as bound for Pernambuco. Capt. Bertram suspected, however, that the "Elizabeth" was bound to St. Helena, and he was extremely anxious to arrive there first, and dispose of his cargo. As night came on, in order to lighten his vessel, he had his entire deck-load of lumber passed aft and thrown overboard, and by crowding on all sail, day and night, he arrived at St. Helena, disposed of his cargo, and was coming out of the harbor just as the "Elizabeth" arrived. From St. Helena, Capt. Bertram went to Pernambuco, on his way to Salem. After his return home, he purchased the "Velocity," of 119 tons burden, and, with Capt. W. B. Smith, again set sail for St. Helena. He went from there to the Cape of Good Hope, and thence to the Rio Grande and the coast of Patagonia, at which latter place he remained, engaged in trading for hides, while Capt. Smith made trips up and down the coast in the "Velocity." After being at Patagonia for some time, Capt. Bertram and Capt. Smith both sailed for Pernambuco in the "Velocity," and there found Capt. Thomas Downing, of Salem, in the brig "Combine," of 133 tons burden. They purchased the "Combine" of Capt. Downing, and Capt. Bertram returned in her to Patagonia. Capt. Smith came back to Salem in the "Velocity," and arrived there in August, 1826, with a cargo of 208,291 pounds of beef, consigned to Peter E. Webster. After trading for awhile on the coast, Capt. Bertram returned to Salem in the "Combine," arriving Dec. 14, 1826. He afterwards made another trip to Patagonia in the "Combine," returning to Salem in July, 1827, with 135,122 pounds of beef. He was on the coast of Patagonia for about three years.

On his final return to Salem, the firm of Nathaniel L. Rogers & Bros. offered him an interest in the ship "Black Warrior," of 231 tons burden, and he sailed in command of her from Salem in December, 1830, for Madagascar, Zanzibar, and Mocha. Capt. Henry F. King, of Salem, was with him on this voyage, serving as his clerk. He loaded with a large quantity of gum-copal in bulk, and established a trade there which he has continued to the present time. He returned from this voyage March 31, 1832. Mr. Bertram was connected in this business in the early years with Michael Shepard, Nathaniel Weston, and Andrew Ward.

From 1845 to 1857 he was trading with Para. He sent, in December, 1848, one of the first vessels from Massachusetts to California after the gold discovery, and the favorable accounts he received from her induced him to send three vessels from Salem the next spring with full cargoes, and two others shortly after. He also engaged in the California trade with Messrs. Glidden & Williams, of Boston. While Capt. Bertram was engaged in the California trade he built, with others, the ship "John Bertram," 1,100 tons, at East Boston, and she was launched in sixty days from the time of laying her keel, and in ninety days was on her way down Boston harbor with a full cargo on board, bound for San Francisco. Although many predicted that a vessel built so hastily would not last long, their predictions have not been verified, and the ship is still afloat sailing under a foreign flag. She sailed for San Francisco on her first voyage Jan. 10, 1851. Capt. Bertram has been connected with the building and management of several railroads in the West. He founded, and has maintained at his own expense, the "Old Men's Home," and he was largely instrumental in establishing the Salem Hospital. As a merchant, he was enterprising and energetic; as a citizen, public-spirited and charitable. His name worthily closes the long list of eminent merchants who have given Salem a history unparalleled in the annals of commerce.

Salem Merchants. — Among other prominent Salem merchants, were John Turner, who died in 1742; Edward Kitchen; and Thomas Lee, who died July 14, 1747. These men followed Philip English. The name of Pickman has been intimately connected with the commerce of Salem. Benjamin Pickman,. who was born in 1706, and died in 1773, was very successful as a merchant. His trade was largely with the West Indies. Timothy Orne, who died July 14, 1767; Joseph Cabot, who died Nov., 1781; William Orne, who was born Feb. 4, 1751, and died Oct. 14, 1815; George Crowninshield, who was born Aug. 6, 1734, and died June 17, 1815, and who lived in a house on the site of the present custom-house; George Crowninshield, Jr., who was born May 28, 1766, and died Nov. 26, 1817; Thomas Perkins, who was born Apr. 2, 1758, and died Nov. 24, 1830; Nathaniel West, who was born Jan. 31, 1756, and died Dec. 19, 1851; Joseph Lee, born May, 1744, and died in 1831; Pickering Dodge, Gideon Tucker, Robert Stone, Dudley L. Pickman, Jerathmael Peirce, Aaron Wait, Nathaniel Silsbee, John W. Rogers, Nathaniel L. Rogers, Robert Brookhouse, Robert Upton, David Pingree, Tucker Daland, Michael Shepard, Stephen C. Phillips, Edward D. Kimball, and Charles Hoffman — were all prominently connected with the commerce of Salem, and their individual careers would well repay the labors of the biographer.

The enterprise and vigor displayed by Salem merchants, in seeking new ports for trade, is something almost unparalleled. Reynolds, who made a tour round the world in the U. S. vessel "Potomac," writing of Salem, in 1835, says: "When peace arrived, and our independence was acknowledged, the merchants of Salem were among the first to explore new channels of trade, disdaining to confine themselves to the narrow track of a Colonial commerce. With a few erroneous maps and charts, a sextant, and ' Guthrie's Grammar,' they swept round the Cape of Good Hope, exhausted the markets of the Isles of France and Bourbon, and pushing onward entered the Straits of Babelmandel and secured the trade of the Red Sea. They brought from Madras, Calcutta and Bombay the best of their staples, and had their choice of the products of Ceylon and Sumatra."

Canton Trade.—The close of the War of the Revolution, found the merchants of Salem in possession of many large and fast-sailing vessels, which had been built for use as privateers. Being too large to be profitably engaged in the coasting-trade, or on the short voyages to the ports heretofore visited by Salem ships, their owners determined to open to distant countries new avenues of trade, and bring to Salem the products of lands lying in the remotest quarters of the globe.

They boldly entered into competition with that great and powerful monopoly, the East India Company, which Queen Elizabeth incorporated on the last day of the sixteenth century; a company whose

18

governor, Josiah Child, formerly an apprentice, sweeping one of the counting-rooms of London, became the possessor of boundless wealth, the companion of nobles, and one from whom King Charles II. graciously accepted a gift of ten thousand guineas; a monopoly which held in its powerful grasp the whole trade of England with the distant East, issuing its edicts from the India House on Leadenhall Street, to its subjects in India, commanding them to disregard the votes of the House of Commons; and which, as late as the year 1800, when the ship "Active," of Salem, George Nichols, master, arrived at Liverpool from Salem, with a cargo of Surat cotton, compelled her to carry it to London and dispose of it from the warehouses of the company in that city.

Elias Hasket Derby opened the trade with China, and on the 28th of November, 1785, cleared the ship "Grand Turk," Ebenezer West, master, for the Isle of France, with the purpose to visit Canton. This vessel went to the Isle of France and China, and returned to Salem in June, 1787, with a cargo of teas, silks and nankeens, making the first voyage from New England to the Isle of France, India and China.

In the year 1790 there were three arrivals from Canton. The brig "William and Henry," Benjamin Hodges, master, 150 tons, in May, to Gray & Orne; the ship "Astrea," James Magee, master, and Thomas Handasyd Perkins, supercargo, of 330 tons, in June, to Elias H. Derby, with a cargo of tea paying $27,109.18 as duties; and the ship "Light Horse," Ichabod Nichols, master, 266 tons, in June, to Elias H. Derby, with a cargo of tea, paying $16,312.98 as duties. There is no year when the direct arrivals from Canton numbered more than three. The trade at this time must have been unprofitable, for Mr. Derby seems to have abandoned it, and we find no further arrival from Canton till 1798, when the ship "Perseverance," Richard Wheatland, master, enters in April, with a cargo of tea and sugar, to Simon Forrester, paying in duties $24,562.10. The ship "Elizabeth," Daniel Sage, master, arrived in June, 1799, to William Gray, and the ship "Pallas," William Ward, master, to Samuel Gray, William Gray, and Joseph Peabody, with a cargo of tea and sugar, paying a duty of $66,927.65, arrived in July, 1800.

In May, 1802, the ship "Minerva," M. Folger, master, belonging to Clifford Crowninshield and Nathaniel West, entered from Canton, and was the first Salem vessel which circumnavigated the globe. She sailed round Cape Horn, stopped one degree south of Chiloe, went to the Island of Mas-a-Fuera, where she took seals, wintered south of Lima, and proceeded to China. She came home round the Cape of Good Hope.

The ship "Concord," Obed Wyer, master, entered from Canton in July, 1802, with a cargo of tea, to Gideon Tucker and Pickering Dodge, paying a duty of $20,477.53; and in April, 1803, the ship "Union," George Hodges, master, to Ichabod Nichols and thirty-nine others, entered with a cargo of tea, paying a duty of $43,190.79. The ship "Friendship," William Story, master, arrived from Canton, Sumatra, and the Isle of France, in August, 1804, to Jerathmael Peirce, with tea, coffee and pepper, paying a duty of $31,514.19. The ship "Eliza," William Richardson, master, arrived in May, 1807, to Peirce & Wait, and the ship "Hercules," James M. Fairfield, master, with a cargo of tea and cassia, paying a duty of $45,575.98, in March, 1808, to Nathaniel West. In April, 1810, the brig "Pilgrim," Charles Pearson, master, arrived to Richard Gardner, and the ship "Hunter," Philip P. Pinal, master, with a cargo of tea, sugar-candy, and cassia, to Jerathmael Peirce, in May, 1810.

The brig "Active," William P. Richardson, master, arrived with a cargo of tea and cassia, consigned to James Cook, and paying duties to the amount of about $32,000. The "Active" left Salem June 1, 1810, and went to the Feejee Islands, where she remained till July 26, 1811. She arrived in Salem March 27th, 1812, 118 days from Canton.

The brig "Canton," Daniel Bray, Jr., master, arrived in May, 1817, from Canton and Marseilles, to Joseph Peabody and Gideon Tucker, having performed the voyage to Canton and Europe in eleven months and twenty-five days. The ship "China," Benjamin Shreve, master, cleared for Canton May 24, 1817, and arrived in Salem March 30, 1818, with a cargo of tea, nankeens and silks, to Joseph Peabody and others, and paying a duty of $15,348.56. In January, 1819, the ship "Hercules," James King, Jr., master, arrived with a cargo of tea and sugar, paying a duty of $51,765.49, and consigned to Nathaniel West, Jr., and others. The ship "Osprey," Stephen Brown, master, arrived from Canton, via Boston, in July, 1819, 117 days from Canton, to William P. Richardson, and the ship "Midas," Timothy Endicott, master, entered from Canton via Boston, to Pickering Dodge, with a cargo of tea, cloves and sugar, in September, 1819, 143 days from Canton. In February, 1820, the ship "Friendship," Thomas Meek, master, entered from Canton to Pickering Dodge and others, with a cargo paying a duty of $21,677.44.

The brig "Leander," owned by Joseph Peabody, made three voyages direct from Canton, entering in March, 1825, in April, 1826, and in July, 1829. Charles Roundy was master on the first two voyages, and N. Smith on the last; the cargoes paying duties of $86,847.47, $92,392.94 and $84,043.82 respectively. The ship "China," H. Putnam, master, entered from Canton in April, 1825, to Joseph Peabody and others, paying a duty of $22,987.32.

The ship "Sumatra," owned by Joseph Peabody, made six voyages direct from Canton, entering in April, 1829, in April, 1830, in October, 1831, in June, 1834, in December, 1836, and in October, 1841. Charles Roundy was master on the first four voyages, and Peter Silver on the last two. When returning on the last voyage, Capt. Silver speaks the ship "Echo," dismasted, with 140 passengers, bound for New York. He could not board the distressed vessel at once, because of the storm then prevailing, but lay by until he was able to send his boat and supply her with sails and provisions. He took on board his own vessel 24 of the passengers, including several sick ladies, and landed them at Holmes' Hole. For the kind and timely assistance rendered, Capt. Silver was presented by the passengers with a silver pitcher, and each of his mates with a silver cup.

The ship "Eclipse," William Johnson, master, entered from Canton in August, 1832, consigned to Joseph Peabody.

The above-named comprise all the vessels that entered at the Salem custom-house direct from Canton, bringing a full cargo of Canton goods. There were many other Salem vessels that went there in the course of their voyages, or that cleared from Salem for Canton and returned to other ports. The ship "St. Paul," Charles H. Allen, master, and owned by Stephen C. Phillips, went to China from Manila, and on her return to Salem in March, 1845, brought part of a cargo of tea and other merchandise from China. All the direct trade from Canton to Salem after 1825, was carried on by Joseph Peabody.

Among the vessels that cleared for Canton was the ship "Brutus," Richard Crowninshield, master, March 7, 1798. The ship "Gov. Endicott," Benjamin Shreve, master, cleared for Canton, May 5,

1819, and experienced a tremendous gale on July 31st, during which the whole watch, consisting of the second mate and seven men were washed overboard and lost, and her mizzen-mast and rudder were carried away. She arrived at St. Salvador in a crippled condition on the 26th of September.

India Trade.—India was visited soon after the close of the Revolutionary War by Salem vessels. The trade was opened by Elias Hasket Derby, and the ship "Atlantic," commanded by his son, was the first vessel to display the American ensign at Surat, Bombay and Calcutta. This was in the year 1788. The ship "Peggy" arrived in Salem June 21, 1789, with the first cargo of Bombay cotton brought to this country, consigned to E. H. Derby. The brigantine "Henry," Benjamin Crowninshield, master, of 125 tons burden, and manned by eight men, arrived at Salem from Madras, Bengal and the Isle of France, consigned to E. H. Derby and John Derby, Jr., January 10, 1791, and on May 13, 1793, the ship "Grand Turk," Benjamin Hodges, master, of 564 tons burden, and owned by E. H. Derby, arrived from Madras with 1,031,484 pounds of sugar, 500 bags of saltpetre, 464 pieces of redwood, 3,900 hides, 709 bags of ginger, 830 bags of pepper, and 22 chests of tea, the cargo paying a duty of $24,229.65. The schooner "Polly and Sally," George Crowninshield, master, and consigned to Richard Crowninshield, with sugar, pepper and coffee, arrived from Bengal in May, 1794. The brig "Enterprise," William Ward, master, entered in August, 1794, from India, consigned to William Gray. The ship "Henry," Jacob Crowninshield, master, entered from India and Cowes, in November, 1794, to E. H. Derby. The ship "Washington," Benjamin Webb, Jr., master, entered July 11, 1795, from Calcutta via Boston, with a cargo of sugar to John Fisk. The ketch "Eliza," Stephen Phillips, master, appears to be the first vessel to arrive at Salem direct from Calcutta. She entered October 8, 1795, with a cargo of sugar to E. H. Derby. The "Eliza" cleared from Salem for the East Indies, December 22, 1794, with an outward cargo of 48 casks of brandy, 22 barrels of naval stores, and 106 pairs of silk stockings.

There were five arrivals from India in 1796. February 23d, the brig "Friendship," George Hodges, master, to Joseph Osgood, Jr., from Calcutta; April 18th, the snow "Peggy," Joseph Ropes, master, to E. H. Derby, from India; April 18th, the ship "John," Jona.

Moulton, master, to William Gray, from Calcutta; August 16th, the brig "Hind," Jona. Hodges, master, from Calcutta, and September 20th, the ketch "Eliza," Stephen Phillips, master, to E. H. Derby, from Calcutta. There were four entries from India in 1797. In May, the bark "Essex," John Ropes, master, to William Orne, from Calcutta; in May, the ship "William and Henry," John Beckford, master, to William Gray, from Bengal; in May, the ship "Benjamin," Richard Gardner, master, to E. H. Derby, from Calcutta and the Cape of Good Hope; and in July, the ship "Betsey," Nathaniel Silsbee, master, from Calcutta and Madras, consigned to Daniel Peirce and Nathaniel Silsbee, with sugar, coffee and pepper, paying a duty of $10,753.20.

During the year 1798 there were nine entries from Calcutta; the largest number of entries in any single year. The years 1803 and 1818 show the same number. The entries, all from Calcutta, were, in January, the ship "Recovery," Joseph Ropes, master, to E. H. Derby; in January, the ship "Lucia," Thomas Meek, master, to William Gray; in March, the bark "Sally," Benjamin Webb, master, to Thomas Saunders & Co.; in March, the brig "Good Hope," Edward West, master, to Nathaniel West; in March, the brig "Adventure," James Barr, Jr., master, to John Norris; in March, the ship "Betsey," Josiah Orne, master, to Samuel Gray & Co.; in March, the ship "Mary," Nicholas Thorndike, master; in May, the ship "Sally," Josiah Obear, master; and in July, the ship "Belisarius," John Crowninshield master, to George Crowninshield & Sons, with a cargo of sugar, 10,767 pounds of sugar-candy, and 118,215 pounds of coffee, from Calcutta and the Isle of France.

There were but two entries in 1799. The ship "Recovery," Joseph Ropes, master, entered May 7th to E. H. Derby. This vessel had touched at Mocha on her outward passage, and displayed the American flag for the first time at that port. The ship "Ulysses," Josiah Orne, master, entered July 10th, to William Gray. Both entries were from Calcutta. The above-named vessels comprise all that arrived from India prior to the year 1800.

The limits of this chapter will not permit a full list of the subsequent entries, but the names of a few are given as showing the Salem merchants and shipmasters engaged in this trade. The ship "Active," Timothy Bryant, master, with a cargo of 180,000 pounds of cotton to Bryant & Nichols, entered from Bombay in August, 1800. The ship "Vigilant," James Clemmons, master, entered from Bombay in February, 1801, with a cargo of cotton to Simon Forrester. The bark "Eliza," Benjamin Lander, master, entered from Calcutta in July, 1801, with a cargo of sugar and other merchandise to Joseph White. The ship "Hazard," Henry Tibbetts, master, entered from Calcutta in May, 1802, with sugar, cigars, and cordage to John and Richard Gardner, paying a duty of $16,298.

The brig "Sally," William Ashton, master, entered from Calcutta in February, 1803, to Jacob Ashton & Co., with a cargo of sugar paying a duty of $10,631.54. The ship "Lucia," Solomon Towne, master, entered from Calcutta in August, 1804, with a cargo of sugar, indigo, and cheroots, to William Gray and others, and paying a duty of $24,001.08.

The ship "Argo," Stephen Field, master, entered from Calcutta in March, 1805, with a cargo of sugar to Philip Chase and others, and paying a duty of $32,799.47. The ship "Mary Ann," Edward Norris, master, entered from Calcutta in April, 1806, with a cargo consigned to John Norris, and paying a duty of $14,797.68. The ship "Franklin," Timothy Wellman, 3d, master, entered from Calcutta in October, 1806, with a cargo of sugar to Joseph Peabody, and paying a duty of $19,734.60. The ship "Friendship," Israel Williams, master, entered from Madras in November, 1806, with a cargo of pepper, coffee, and indigo to Peirce & Wait, paying a duty of $21,093.21. The ship "Exeter," Thomas B. Osgood, master, entered from Bengal in October, 1807, with 356,043 pounds of cotton, 11,141 of indigo, and 80,731 of sugar, paying a duty of $16,331.21, and consigned to Benjamin Pickman, Jr.

The ship "Union," William Osgood, master, entered from Calcutta in September, 1811, with a cargo to Stephen Phillips, and paying a duty of $26,408.23. The ship "Restitution," David D. Pulsifer, master, entered from Calcutta in October, 1812, with a cargo to Simon Forrester, and paying a duty of $51,526.33. The brig "Caravan," Augustine Heard, master, entered from Calcutta in March, 1813, with a cargo to Pickering Dodge, paying a duty of $26,975. The bark "Patriot," Nathan Frye, master, entered from Calcutta in March, 1816, to John H. Andrews.

In October, 1816, forty-two vessels had cleared for India since the close of the war of 1812, and sixteen of them carried out three million hard dollars. The ship "Malabar," Josiah Orne, master, entered from Bombay in June, 1817, with a cargo of cotton and pepper to John W. Rogers, paying a duty of $18,769.40. The ship "Endeavour," Timothy Bryant, Jr., master, entered in September, 1817, to Dudley L. Pickman. The brig "Alexander," David A. Neal, master, entered from Bombay in September, 1817, with cotton to Jonathan Neal.

The ship "Gentoo," Nathaniel Osgood, master, entered from Calcutta in June, 1818. The cargo of this vessel, as was often the case with large vessels sent on distant voyages, was the property of a large number of persons. It consisted principally of sugar and cotton, and the consignees were Pickering Dodge, Nathaniel Silsbee, Francis and George Lee, John Belknap, Francis Quarles, Samuel P. Gardner, Baker & Hodges, Henry Pickering, John Derby, Philip & A. Chase, Samuel G. Derby, John W. Rogers, John Stone, Humphrey Devereux, Nathaniel Osgood, and Samuel G. Perkins. The whole duty paid was $29,270.55. The brig "Lawry," John Holman, master, entered from Calcutta in May, 1820, to John Derby, and paying a duty of $20,693.99.

The brig "Naiad," Nathaniel Osgood, master, arrived from Calcutta in January, 1821, with a cargo to Pickering Dodge, paying a duty of about $24,000. The ship "Aurora," Robert W. Gould, master, arrived from Siam in January, 1823, with a cargo of pepper and coffee to Willard Peele. The brig "Ann," Charles Millett, master, arrived from Bombay, in November, 1825, to Henry Prince. The brig "Reaper," J. F. Brookhouse, master, entered from Bombay in February, 1830, consigned to Robert Brookhouse. The brig "Nereus," Thomas Farley, master, entered from Bombay in April, 1830, consigned to John W. Rogers. The ship "Catherine," Joseph Winn, Jr., entered from Calcutta in October, 1831, consigned to Joseph Peabody. The brig "Quill," S. I. Shillaber, master, entered from Bombay in October, 1832, consigned to N. L. Rogers & Brothers. The brig "Cherokee," W. B. Smith, master, entered from Bombay in February, 1837, consigned to Michael Shepard. The ship "William and Henry," Charles H. Fabens, master, entered from Bombay in September, 1839, consigned to David Pingree.

In 1842, there were three entries from Calcutta. The ship

"Gen. Harrison," W. Lecraw, master, in February; the ship "Isaac Hicks," Newell, master, in September; and the ship "New Jersey," Barry, master, in December; all with cargoes consigned to Francis Peabody. The last entry at Salem from ports in India was that of the bark "Brenda," H. Bridges, master, in August, 1845, with a cargo of pepper and cordage to Michael Shepard, paying a duty of $31,793.65.

A detailed history of these India voyages could not fail to be interesting, and would contain many thrilling accounts of the perils of the sea. In January, 1788, the ship "Juno," Henry Elkins, master, and owned by E. H. Derby, cleared for the East Indies, and when forty hours out was found to be sinking. Every effort was made to free her, but without success, and in twenty minutes she went down. The crew escaped in one of the ship's boats, and were picked up and taken to Demerara. In 1793, the ship "Astrea," on a trading voyage from Madras to Pegu, was seized by the king of the latter place as a transport for stores to his army in Siam, who had gone thither to attack its forces. Capt. Gibant and his second mate were detained as hostages for the performance of the voyage. In March, 1802, the ship "Howard," Benjamin Bray, master, from Calcutta, was lost at Grapevine Cove, Gloucester. The captain, second mate, and two seamen were drowned. On Thursday, Oct. 28, 1819, the brig "Naiad," Nathaniel Osgood, master, arrived at Salem from Calcutta, with a cargo consigned to Pickering Dodge. On the Monday night previous the "Naiad" was struck by lightning, and the second mate, Mr. William Griffen, of Salem, was instantly killed. He was on the maintopsail yard at the time, and on being struck fell into the water with his clothes on fire. The first mate was knocked down, and one of the men severely injured. The vessel received but trifling damage.

From the year 1800 to 1842, inclusive, only the years 1809, '14, '15, '38, '39, and '41 passed without an entry at Salem from some of the ports of India. The whole number of entries during that period from Calcutta were 115, the years 1805, '6 and '7 showing 17, and the years 1816, '17 and '18 showing 21. There were twenty entries from Bombay during the same time; six from Bengal; six from Madras; three from Siam; and two from Ceylon. During the periods from 1802 to 1807, and from 1816 to 1822, there was the greatest activity in the Calcutta trade.

19

From 1816 to 1840 the Salem trade with Calcutta was mainly carried on by Joseph Peabody. He was the owner of the famous ship "George," which made voyages between Salem and Calcutta with the regularity of a steamer. The "George" was built in 1814, for a privateer, by an association of ship-carpenters, who were thrown out of employment by the war of 1812. Peace came on before she was sold, and Capt. Peabody bought her for $16 per ton. She measured 328 tons, and was a full-rigged ship. The "George" made twenty voyages to Calcutta between 1815 and 1837. She sailed from Salem May 23, 1815, on her first voyage, and arrived home June 13, 1816, 109 days from Calcutta. The length of her voyages was surprisingly regular, varying but a few days in all her passages between Calcutta and Salem. She sailed from Salem Aug. 5, 1836, on her last voyage, reaching Salem on her return May 17, 1837, 111 days from Calcutta. Her commanders were William Haskell, Thomas West, Samuel Endicott, Thomas M. Saunders, Jonathan H. Lovett, Jr., and Benjamin Balch, Jr. Her supercargoes were Daniel H. Mansfield, Ephraim Emmerton, Jr., George W. Endicott, Samuel Endicott, Samuel Barton, and James B. Briggs. Her cargoes paid in duties $651,743.32. After her last voyage to Calcutta she was sold to Jefferson Adams and Caleb Smith, and went to Rio Janeiro, where she was condemned, about Jan. 12, 1838. Mr. Peabody imported from Calcutta, between 1807 and 1840, about 1,050,000 pounds of indigo, of which the ship "George" brought, in seventeen voyages, 755,000 pounds.

Batavia Trade. — In the Indian Ocean, near the island of Sumatra, lies the island of Java, and here again Salem vessels were the first to display the American ensign. There was quite an extensive trade with this island in the early days of Salem's commerce. Of the seventy-two arrivals from Batavia, between the years 1796 and 1855, thirty-five were previous to the year 1807, and seventeen during the years 1817, '18, '19, and '20. From 1806 to 1816 there was no arrival.

The brig "Sally," Benjamin Webb, master, cleared for Batavia, Sept. 30, 1795, and entered from the same place Sept. 6, 1796, with a cargo of pepper and sugar to Thomas Saunders & Co. The schooner "Patty," Edward West, master, cleared for Batavia Sept. 26, 1795, with wine, brandy, gin, tobacco, lead, and iron, and entered from

Heliotype Printing Co.

Ship "George," 1820.

Boston.

that place, on her return, Oct. 3, 1796, with pepper and sugar, consigned to Nathaniel West. The bark "Vigilant," John Murphy, master, entered in February, 1797, with 238,746 pounds of coffee, and 168,604 pounds of sugar, consigned to Simon Forrester. The brig "Eunice," Enoch Sweet, master, entered in July, 1797, with coffee, sugar, and pepper, to George Dodge and others. The brig "Star," John Burchmore, master, entered in November, 1797, to John Norris & Co. The bark "Eliza," Gamaliel Hodges, master, entered in February, 1798, and again in December, 1799, to Joseph White. The brig "Olive Branch," Jonathan Lambert, Jr., master, entered in 1798, consigned to Ashton & Lambert. The ship "Friendship," Israel Williams, master, entered July 4, 1798, with 301,687 pounds of coffee, and 111,087 pounds of sugar, to Peirce & Wait, and paying a duty of $18,376.13. The brig "Exchange," William Richardson, master, entered in August, 1798, to Ezekiel H. Derby. The ship "Hazen," Jonathan Hodges, master, entered in August, 1798, consigned to William Orne. The ship "Franklin," James Devereux, master, entered in October, 1801, with 315,742 pounds of coffee, 164,699 of pepper, and 155,797 of sugar, consigned to Joseph Peabody, and paying a duty of $29,709.40. The same vessel, with the same master and consignee, entered in March, 1804, and May, 1805.

The ship "Margaret," Samuel Derby, master, entered in June, 1802, with coffee and other merchandise, consigned to John Derby and Benjamin Pickman. The "Margaret" cleared for Sumatra Nov. 19, 1800, with $50,000 in specie, twelve casks of Malaga wine, and two hogsheads of bacon. She left Salem Harbor on the 25th of November, and anchored in Table Bay, Cape of Good Hope, Feb. 4, 1801. Leaving Table Bay February 10, she reached Bencoolen Roads, Sumatra, on the 10th of April, 136 days from Salem. Without stopping to trade at Sumatra, the vessel proceeded to Batavia, arriving there on the 25th of April. While at Batavia, Capt. Derby made a bargain with the Dutch East India Company to take the annual freights to and from Japan; and left for that place with his cargo June 20, 1801.

The "Margaret" arrived at the port of Nagasaki July 19, being obliged to fire salutes, and dress the vessel with flags, before entering port. Mr. George Cleveland, who was clerk for Capt. Derby, gives an interesting description of his visit to the city of Nagasaki.

" In the first place," he says, " we went to Facquia's, an eminent stuff merchant. Here we were entertained in such manner as we little expected. We had set before us, for a repast, pork, fowls, meso, eggs, boiled fish, sweetmeats, cake, various kinds of fruit, and sacky, and tea. The lady of the house was introduced, who drank tea with each of us, as is the custom of Japan. She appeared to be a modest woman. The place we next visited was a temple, to which we ascended from the street, by at least two hundred stone steps. Adjoining this was the burying-ground. We went next to the glasshouse, which was on a small scale; thence to a lac-ware merchant's, where we were entertained with great hospitality. Thence we went to a tea-house, or hotel, where we dined. After dinner, we were entertained with various feats of dancing and tumbling. Towards dark, we returned to the island, and so great was the crowd in the streets to see us pass, that it was with difficulty that we could get along. The number of children we saw was truly astonishing. The streets are narrow, and at the end of every street is a gate, which is locked at night. The houses are of two stories, built of wood.

" The Japanese observed one fast when we were there. It was in remembrance of the dead. The ceremonies were principally in the night. The first was devoted to feasting, at which they fancy their friends to be present; the second and third nights, the graves are lighted with paper lamps, and, situated as they are on the side of a hill, make a most brilliant appearance. On the fourth night, at three o'clock, the lamps are all brought down to the water, and put into small straw barques, with paper sails made for the occasion, and, after putting in rice, fruit, &c., they are set afloat. This exhibition was very fine.

" As the time was approaching for our departure, we began to receive our returns from the interior, brought many hundred miles. These consisted of the most beautiful lacquered ware, such as waiters, writing-desks, tea-caddies, knife-boxes, and tables. We also received a great variety of silks, fans in large quantities, and a great variety of porcelain. The East India Company's cargo had already been put on board. The principal article was copper in small bars. The company's ships have been obliged to take their departure from the anchorage opposite Nagasaki on a certain day to the lower roads, no matter whether it blew high or low, fair or foul, even if a thousand boats should be required to tow them down. We, of course, had to do as our predecessors had done. Early in November, we went to this anchorage, and remained a few days, when we sailed for Batavia, where we arrived safely after a passage of a month."

This account is interesting, because the "Margaret" was the first Salem vessel, and the second American vessel, to visit Japan. The ship "Franklin," of Boston, commanded by Capt. James Devereux, of Salem, was the first American vessel which traded with Japan, having been employed to make the same voyage as the "Margaret," two years previously. Commercial intercourse was not opened with Japan till half a century later; the American treaty, the result of the expedition, under Commodore Perry, which opened her ports to the world, being dated March 31, 1854. Previous to this time, all the trade with Japan was in the hands of the Dutch, who were obliged to submit to the grossest indignities.

The ship "Henry," John Barton, master, entered from Batavia in July, 1802, to John Derby and Benjamin Pickman. The ship "Herald," Zachariah F. Silsbee, master, entered in May, 1804, to Nathaniel Silsbee. The brig "William," arrived Aug. 31, 1802, consigned to Jonathan Mason. She lost her captain, John Felt, and her mate, by sickness, during the voyage. The ship "Mary and Eliza," Nathaniel Hathorne, master, arrived in October, 1804, with coffee, nutmegs, sugar, and mace, to Joseph White. The bark "Georgetown," George Ropes, master, arrived in April, 1806, to Stephen Phillips. The ship "Henry," Benjamin Russell, master, arrived in May, 1806, to Edward Russell and others. The ship "Hercules" made two voyages, entering in March, 1816, and March, 1817, to Nathaniel West, commanded on the first voyage by Edward West, and on the second by James King, Jr. The ship "Erin," Nathan Cook, master, entered in November, 1819, to Henry Pickering. The brig "Franklin," John White, master, entered in September, 1820, to Stephen White. The brig "Roscoe," J. M. Ropes, master, entered in August, 1827, to Charles Saunders. The bark "Henry," R. Wheatland, master, entered in December, 1835, consigned to Samuel Cook and others.

The ship "Union," William Osgood, master, from Pulo Penang, with a cargo of pepper and tin, consigned to Stephen Phillips, was cast away on the north-west point of Baker's Island Feb. 24, 1810, during a snowstorm, and lost, with most of her cargo.

The brig "Java," Nathaniel Osgood, master, from Batavia, went ashore on the bar off Nauset, Cape Cod, on the night of February 9, 1832, in a snowstorm. The crew narrowly escaped, in the boats. The cargo, consisting of 585,000 pounds of coffee, 13,500 pounds of nutmegs, and 94,000 pounds of block-tin, was owned by Jonathan Neal. The vessel was a total wreck.

The ship "Sumatra," Peter Silver, master, made two voyages from Batavia, arriving at Salem in September, 1842, and August, 1843, consigned to Joseph Peabody. Capt. Silver had a strange experience on one of these voyages. He sees a vessel in distress, and, bearing down, finds her to be the bark "Kilmars," of Glasgow, with no person on deck except a female, who seems almost frantic. He sends a boat and brings her on board. She was about eighteen years old, and wife of the commander of the bark. Two months before, the vessel had sailed from Batavia, with a cargo of sugar for Europe. The crew, shipped at Batavia, were many of them discharged convicts. The captain received an intimation that the crew contemplated obtaining possession of the vessel, and, when it became certain that such was their intention, he charged the ringleader with the design, and, in the altercation that followed, shot and wounded him. He then succeeded in confining the crew in different parts of the vessel, and endeavored, with the help of two boys, to navigate his vessel back to Batavia. In the early morning, before the vessel was discovered by Capt. Silver, the captain with the two boys had started in a boat for the shore to procure help. The captain's wife, finding her husband missing, was fearful that he had been killed by the mutineers, but she found that they were still confined. Dreading lest they would soon break out, she took her stand on the rail, determined to throw herself overboard if they regained the deck. Only twenty minutes after she was taken from the "Kilmars," the crew broke out, took charge of the vessel, and made sail. In order to avoid a collision, Capt. Silver steered away from the vessel, and arrived at Batavia, where he placed the lady under the charge of the Dutch Government. The "Kilmars" subsequently reached Angier, where the authorities took possession of her, and adopted measures for the trial of her crew. The captain and the boys were picked up in the Straits of Sunda. Anxiety and overwork had made him partially insane. When he left his vessel he had expected to be able to return at once with help.

The ship "Rome," Nathaniel Brown, master, arrived from Batavia in December, 1842, consigned to B. W. Stone. The last arrivals in our harbor from Batavia, were the bark "Buckeye," in August, 1853, and the bark "Witch," in November, 1855, both consigned to Edward D. Kimball.

Sumatra Trade.—Salem sent the first vessel that ever sailed direct from this country to Sumatra, and a Salem captain commanded the last American vessel that brought a cargo of pepper from that island. In the year 1793, Capt. Jonathan Carnes, of Salem, being at the port of Bencoolen, learned that pepper grew wild on the north-western coast of Sumatra. On his return to Salem he made known his discovery to Mr. Jonathan Peele, who immediately built a schooner, and gave Carnes the command. The vessel was called the "Rajah," and was of 130 tons burden, carrying four guns and ten men. In 1795 he set sail for Sumatra, the destination of the vessel and the object of the voyage being kept a profound secret. The "Rajah" cleared at Salem, Nov. 3, 1795, for India, having on board 2 pipes of brandy, 58 cases of gin, 12 tons of iron, 2 hhds. of tobacco, and 2 boxes of salmon. The vessel was absent eighteen months, during which time her owner, Mr. Peele, had no tidings from her. At last she enters Salem harbor, with a cargo of pepper in bulk, the first to be so imported into this country. This cargo was sold at a profit of seven hundred per cent. Such an extraordinary voyage created great excitement among the merchants of Salem, and they were all anxious to discover in what part of the Eastern world the cargo had been procured. But the matter still remained a secret. Capt. Carnes was preparing for another voyage ; and the Salem merchants, determined if possible to penetrate the mystery, despatched several vessels to the port of Bencoolen, where it was known Carnes got his first knowledge of the trade. They were not successful, however, and had to make up their voyages in some of the ports of India. But the secret voyages to Sumatra did not long continue. By the first of the present century the mystery was penetrated, and the whole ground open to competition.

The brig "Rajah" made several voyages to Sumatra under command of Capt. Carnes, entering at Salem in October, 1799, with 158,544 pounds of pepper, and in July, 1801, with 147,776 pounds, the last time consigned to Jonathan & Willard Peele.

The firm of George Crowninshield & Sons were largely engaged in the early Sumatra trade. The ship "Belisarius," Samuel Skerry, Jr., master, made several voyages for this firm, entering at Salem in July, 1801, with 320,000 pounds of pepper, in July, 1802, with 306,542 pounds, and in September, 1803, with 276,459 pounds. The ship "America" made two voyages, commanded by John Crowninshield on the first, and Jeremiah Briggs on the second, and entering in November, 1801, with 815,792 pounds of pepper, paying a duty of $53,-842.27, and clearing January 2, 1802, on the second voyage, returning in October, 1802, with 760,000 pounds, paying $50,031.76. The ship "Concord," Jonathan Carnes, master, made two voyages, entering in November, 1803, and in August, 1805. The ship "John," John Dodge, master, entered in October, 1807, and the ship "Fame," Holten J. Breed, master, in April, 1812, with 623,277 pounds of pepper, paying a duty of $37,396.62, consigned to this firm.

Joseph Peabody entered upon this trade early. Among his vessels were the ship "Cincinnatus," John Endicott, master, which entered in September, 1803, with 307,824 pounds of pepper; and in November, 1807, commanded by William Haskell, with 347,000 pounds. The ship "Franklin," Samuel Tucker, master, which entered in September, 1810, with 539,585 pounds. The ship "Janus," John Endicott, master, which entered in December, 1809, with 537,989 pounds, and in December, 1810, with 547,795 pounds. The "Janus" sailed from Salem April 1, 1810, and arrived at the Vineyard on her return, November 26, 1810, making one of the shortest voyages ever made from Salem to Sumatra and back. These were among Mr. Peabody's early voyages. He continued the trade until about the time of death, in 1844. The ship "Sumatra," Peter Silver, master, which entered in July, 1838, and the ship "Eclipse," George Whitmarsh, master, which entered in February, 1840, in February, 1841, and in December, 1842, and the ship "Lotos," Benjamin Balch, Jr., master, which entered in November, 1841, were among the later voyages.

Abel Lawrence & Co. were the consignees of the brig "George Washington," Timothy Bryant, master, which entered in November, 1803, and of the ship "Putnam," Nathaniel Bowditch, master, which entered in December, 1803, with 425,000 pounds of pepper, and 42,-000 pounds of coffee, from Sumatra and the Isle of France, and paying a duty of $27,634.67. Capt. Bowditch afterwards became distinguished for his mathematical works, and achieved a world-wide reputation by his treatises on navigation.

The ship "Good Hope," George Cleveland, master, entered in January, 1805, consigned to Nathaniel West. The ship "Freedom," John Reith, master, in January, 1805, consigned to Jonathan & Willard Peele. The bark "Eliza," Joseph Beadle, master, entered in August, 1806, consigned to Joseph White & Co. The ship "Union," George Peirce, master, entered in October, 1806, consigned to Stephen Phillips, with 465,271 pounds of pepper, paying a duty of $28,-506.26. The ship "Eliza," James Cook, master, entered in October, 1807, with 1,012,148 pounds of pepper, consigned to James Cook, and paying a duty of $66,903.90. The ship "Herald," Z. F. Silsbee, master, entered in December, 1809, consigned to James Devereux. The bark "Active," William P. Richardson, master, entered in December, 1809, consigned to John Dodge, Jr. The bark "Camel," Holten J. Breed, master, entered in July, 1816, consigned to William Silsbee. The bark "Eliza and Mary," Nathaniel Griffen, master, consigned to William Fettyplace, entered in April, 1823. The brig "Jane," Thomas Saul, master, entered in November, 1823, consigned to Willard Peele. The brig "Persia," Moses Endicott, master, in July, 1824, with 160,000 pounds of pepper to Dudley L. Pickman. The ship "Friendship," Charles M. Endicott, master, entered in July, 1831, consigned to William Silsbee, and the ship "Delphos," James D. Gillis, master, entered in October, 1831, consigned to Z. F. Silsbee and others. The bark "Malay," J. B. Silsbee, master, entered in November, 1836. The bark "Borneo," C. S. Huntington, master, in April, 1842, consigned to Z. F. Silsbee.

David Pingree was the consignee of the ship "Caroline Augusta," which entered in August, 1842, and in November, 1845. She was commanded on the first voyage by E. D. Winn. Tucker Daland was the consignee of the brig "Lucilla," which entered in June, 1842, and in November, 1846. H. W. Perkins was master on the first voyage, and D. Marshall on the second. This was the last vessel to arrive at Salem from the coast of Sumatra.

The trade with Sumatra was, at one time, mainly carried on by Salem merchants, and a large proportion of the pepper consumed, was distributed to all countries from the port of Salem. From the year 1799 to 1846 inclusive, but five years (1813, '14, '15, '22 and

'37) passed without an entry at Salem from the Island of Sumatra. During that period there were 179 arrivals, the years 1809, '10 and '23 showing ten each, the largest number in any single year.

Although the direct trade between Salem and Sumatra ceased in 1846, Salem vessels and Salem shipmasters were engaged in it until a much later date. The last Salem vessel on the coast was the ship "Australia," J. Dudley, master, owned by Stone, Silsbee & Pickman. She was there in 1860. There is no direct trade to-day between the United States and Sumatra. Capt. Jonathan Carnes, of Salem, commanded the first American vessel that ever procured pepper from the Island of Sumatra, and a Salem captain was master of the last American vessel that visited that coast. The bark "Tarquin," Thomas Kimball, master, and William F. Jelly, mate, both of Salem, arrived at New York in 1867, and this arrival closed the American trade with the Island of Sumatra. The "Tarquin" was owned by John L. Gardner, of Boston.

The energy and fearlessness of our early navigators was something almost marvellous. In vessels of but one hundred and fifty tons they boldly set sail for ports never before visited by Americans, and without chart or guide of any kind, made their way amid coral reefs and along foreign shores. Even as late as 1831, when a United States vessel was despatched to the island, no chart of the coast could be found in the possession of the government. The U. S. frigate "Potomac" sailed for the East Indies in 1831, and in the journal of her voyage it is stated that it was the original intention of the commander to prepare charts and sailing directions for the guidance of other mariners, but that "this duty has been much more ably performed than it could have been with our limited materials. For this important service our country is indebted to Capt. Charles M. Endicott and James D. Gillis, of Salem, Massachusetts. The former, who was master of the 'Friendship,' when she was seized by the Malays at Quallah-Battoo, has been trading on this coast for more than fifteen years, during which period he has, profitably for his country, filled up the delays incidental to a pepper voyage, by a careful and reliable survey of the coast, of which no chart was previously extant which could be relied on. Capt. Endicott has since published the result of his labors in a well executed chart, which comprises all that portion of the coast which is included between Sinkel, in 2° 18′ and 4° 15′ north. Actuated by a like commendable zeal for the commercial interests of his native country, Capt. Gillis has extended the surveys to latitude 5° north, and published an excellent chart, accompanied also with sailing directions. These are important acquisitions to our knowledge of this coast, and will increase the security of our merchants and mariners. We gladly embrace this opportunity to acknowledge our obligations to both these gentlemen for much valuable information and many interesting facts."

Salem, therefore, was not only the first at Sumatra, but the first to make it safe for others to follow her lead, and as long as American vessels visited the coast their commanders were provided with copies of the charts prepared by these Salem shipmasters.

The dangers of the coral reefs were not the only ones our mariners had to contend with. The natives of the island were cruel and treacherous, and ready to commit any atrocity for the sake of plunder. While the ship "Friendship," Charles M. Endicott, master, lay at Quallah-Battoo, she was attacked by the native Malays. The first mate, Charles Knight, was killed, and several of the seamen wounded. Capt. Endicott was ashore at the time, receiving the pepper to be sent on board. Observing something unusual in the conduct of those aboard the ship, Capt. Endicott determined to return to her at once, but hardly had he started with his men when crowds of Malays began to assemble on the banks of the river, brandishing their weapons and otherwise menacing him. At the same time three Malay boats, with forty or fifty men each, came out of the river and pulled toward the ship. Convinced that the only way to recover the ship was by obtaining assistance from some other vessel, Capt. Endicott directed his boat's course to Muckie, a port about twenty-five miles distant, where he knew two or three American vessels were lying. Arriving there he found three vessels, among them the brig "Gov. Endicott" of Salem, H. H. Jenks, master, and the ship "James Monroe," J. Porter, master, of New York. These vessels proceeded at once to Quallah-Battoo. The "Friendship" was meanwhile in the possession of the Malays, who plundered her of the specie and every other movable article. Four of her crew jumped overboard at the time of the attack, and swam a distance of two miles before they could find a safe place to land. After wandering about in the bushes, almost without food, for three days, they found a canoe and made their way to the residence of a friendly native named Po Adam, who furnished them with clothing and carried them aboard one of the American vessels. Upon the arrival at Quallah-Battoo of the three vessels, before mentioned, an attack was made upon the town, and the "Friendship" was boarded and recaptured. Her voyage having been broken up, the "Friendship" returned to Salem, where she arrived July 16, 1831. About a year thereafter the U. S. frigate "Potomac," before referred to, bombarded Quallah-Battoo as a punishment for the conduct of the natives towards an American vessel.

Another Salem vessel, the "Eclipse," had a somewhat similar experience on the coast of Sumatra, in 1838. While the mate and four hands were ashore, a party of Malays boarded the vessel and killed the captain, Charles P. Wilkins. The crew, finding themselves over-powered, escaped, some by ascending the shrouds, and some by jumping overboard and swimming ashore. The Malays then plundered the ship of specie, opium, and everything else of value, and departed with their ill-gotten gains. The men aloft descended, lowered their boat, and rowed to a French bark lying at an adjoining port. The next morning the crew returned to the vessel, and during the night they set sail and left the island. The "Eclipse" had a sad ending. She sailed from Sumatra July 10, 1849, under command of Capt. Daniel Cross, and was never after heard from. She had on board a cargo of pepper, consigned to Tucker Daland and Henry L. Williams.

Manila Trade. — In the early days of Salem commerce, when her enterprising and energetic merchants were seeking to establish trade with hitherto unknown countries, and her ships were ploughing the waters of seas which had never before floated an American vessel, the ship "Astrea," commanded by Henry Prince, and owned by that king among merchants, Elias Hasket Derby, entered the harbor of Manila, the capital city of the Philippine Islands, situated on the island of Luzon. Obtaining there a cargo of 750,000 pounds of sugar, 63,695 pounds of pepper, and 29,767 pounds of indigo, she entered at Salem in May, 1797, and paid a duty on her cargo of $24,020. A journal of this voyage, kept by Nathaniel Bowditch, afterwards so famous as a mathematician, is on the files of the East India Marine Society. The "Astrea" left Salem March 27, 1796, and went to Lisbon, Madeira and Manila, arriving at the latter place Oct. 3, 1796. On the passage home, Feb. 18, 1797, the ship sprung aleak, and two men were obliged to be kept at the pumps constantly from that time till the 22d day of May, 1797, when the vessel arrived at Salem.

From 1797 to 1858, the date of the last arrival from this port, there were eighty-two entries at Salem from Manila. The period from 1829 to 1839 shows the largest number of arrivals, thirty of the eighty-two entries being made during that time.

The ship "Folansbe," Jonathan Mason, Jr., master, entered in May, 1799, with sugar and indigo, consigned to John Collins & Co. The ship "Laurel," Daniel Sage, master, entered in July, 1801, with 115,-133 pounds of indigo and 124,683 of sugar, consigned to William Gray, and paying a duty of $32,382.26. The ship "Fame," Jeremiah Briggs, master, entered in March, 1804, consigned to Jacob Crowninshield. The ship "Essex," Joseph Orne, master, entered in May, 1805, with sugar and indigo, consigned to William Orne, and paying a duty of $18,443.70. The ship "Horace," John Parker, master, entered in May, 1806, consigned to William Gray. The ship "Exeter," Thomas B. Osgood, master, entered in June, 1806, with 14,589 pounds of indigo and 702,064 of sugar, consigned to Benjamin Pickman, Jr., and paying a duty of $23,526.33.

From 1806 to 1816, there seems to have been no entry from Manila at the port of Salem. The ship "Endeavour," Timothy Bryant, master, entered in May, 1816, consigned to Nathan Robinson. The ship "Perseverance," Samuel Hodgdon, master, in May, 1820, consigned to Willard Peele. The brig "Ann," Charles Millett, master, in July, 1824, consigned to Henry Prince. The brig "Peru," William Johnson, Jr., master, in April, 1825, consigned to Stephen C. Phillips. The ship "Endeavour," James D. Gillis, master, in September, 1826, consigned to Nathaniel Silsbee. The bark "Derby," Allen Putnam, master, entered in March, 1827; in April, 1829, J. H. Eagleston, master; and again in July, 1832, J. W. Chever, master, consigned to Stephen C. Phillips. The ship "Mandarin," William Osgood, master, entered in March, 1830, consigned to Pickering Dodge. The ship "Sumatra," Charles Roundy, master, entered in November, 1832, consigned to Joseph Peabody. The brig "Charles Doggett," William Driver, master, entered in November, 1832, consigned to Richard S. Rogers. The ship "Lotos," George W. Jenks, master, entered in June, 1832, consigned to Pickering Dodge. The ship "Brookline," Charles H. Allen, master, entered in April, 1837, consigned to Stephen C. Phillips. The ship "Caroline," Charles H. Fabens, master, entered in April, 1842, consigned to David Pingree.

The ship "St. Paul," belonging to Stephen C. Phillips, was almost as famous in connection with Salem's trade with Manila, as was the ship "George" in the Calcutta trade. The "St. Paul" made twelve voyages between Salem and Manila. She sailed on her first voyage from Salem June 3, 1838, and arrived at Manila in 100 days, which was the shortest passage made by the ship from Salem to Manila. She reached Salem on her return in April, 1839, 148 days from Manila. Joseph Winn, Jr., commanded the ship on this voyage, having also been master on her previous voyage from New York to Manila, and back to Salem, where she arrived for the first time April 29, 1838. On her second and third voyages she was commanded by George Peirce, and entered at Salem April 4, 1840, and July 7, 1841. Joseph Warren Osborn was master on the fourth and fifth voyages, and she arrived at Salem Aug. 8, 1842, and Jan. 8, 1844, making on the last voyage the long passage of 188 days. On her sixth, seventh, eighth and ninth voyages, she was commanded by Charles H. Allen, entering at Salem Mar. 17, 1845, Mar. 12, 1846, Mar. 19, 1847, and April 6, 1848. William B. Davis was master on her tenth voyage, sailing from Salem May 18, 1848, and returning Mar. 26, 1849. On her eleventh and twelfth voyages she was commanded by Charles H. Allen, returning to Salem on her eleventh voyage Jan. 7, 1851, and sailing from Salem on her twelfth voyage July 5, 1851. On the 9th of December, 1851, she went ashore on Masbata Island, in the Straits of San Bernardino. She was subsequently raised and sold to Spanish parties, but never returned to Salem.

The last arrival at Salem from Manila was the bark "Dragon," Thomas C. Dunn, master, which entered in July, 1858, with a cargo of hemp, consigned to Benjamin A. West. Salem merchants continued the trade with Manila for some time thereafter, but their vessels entered and cleared at other ports. Tucker Daland and Henry L. Williams, Henry Gardner, B. W. Stone & Brothers, and Silsbee & Pickman were extensively engaged in this trade. The two last named firms still continue the trade with Manila.

Isle of France Trade. — In the Indian Ocean, not far from the eastern coast of Madagascar, lies a small island, called the Isle of France, or Mauritius. The climate of this island is remarkably fine.

Throughout the year the thermometer ranges from 76° to 90° in the shade. The Dutch formed a settlement there in 1644, but subsequently abandoned it. A more successful attempt to form a permanent establishment was made by the French in 1721. It remained in French hands until the year 1810, when it was taken by the British in an expedition under Gen. Abercromby, and has since remained a British possession.

When the merchants of Salem, after the close of the Revolutionary War, sought to establish commercial intercourse with foreign ports never before visited by American vessels, the Isle of France was among the first places to which they sent their ships to bring home cargoes of sugar, which was the staple article of export. Elias Hasket Derby despatched the "Grand Turk," Ebenezer West, master, there in November, 1785, and she returned to Salem in June, 1787, making the first voyage from New England to the Isle of France. In December, 1787, the "Grand Turk" made another voyage to the Isle of France, under the charge of Elias Hasket Derby, Jr. He sold the vessel, and remained on the island about a year, when he went to India and thence back to Salem.

Of the arrivals at the Isle of France in 1789, ten were from Salem, five from Boston, two from Philadelphia, one from Virginia, three from Baltimore, one from Beverly, and one from Providence.

The schooner "Richard and Edward," George Crowninshield, master, entered Jan. 4, 1790, consigned to George Crowninshield. The brig "William," Thomas West, master, entered in December, 1791, consigned to William Gray. The ship "Henry," Jacob Crowninshield, master, cleared for the Isle of France June 25, 1791. She was of 190 tons burden, and carried ten men. Her outward cargo consisted of 60 boxes of wax and 50 boxes of sperm candles, 18 barrels hams, 3 M feet of oars, 14 tons iron, 13 hhds. tobacco, 17 casks oil, 102 bbls. beef and pork, 27 casks ale, 6 kegs flints, 287 bbls. flour, 424 cases and 190 jugs of Geneva, 25 boxes soap, 6 boxes chocolate, 43 kegs lard, 62 quintals fish, 6 hhds. W. I. rum, 12 bags pimento, 16 cannon, 88 cwt. shot, 1 hhd. 4 crates ware, 40 bbls. tar, 4 bbls. pitch, 30 M lumber, 175 casks powder, 7 saddles and bridles, 12 tables, and 5 desks. She entered on her return in November, 1792, with 172,749 pounds of sugar consigned to Elias Hasket Derby. The brig "Hind," John Beckford, master, entered in January, 1793, consigned to William

Gray. The brig "Peggy," Amos Hilton, master, entered in August, 1793, consigned to John Fisk. The ship "Aurora," Thomas Meek, master, entered in March, 1794, with 424,034 pounds of sugar consigned to William Gray.

The ship "Benjamin," 161 tons, Nathaniel Silsbee, master, cleared for India Dec. 10, 1792, and entered in July, 1794, from the Isle of France with cotton, indigo, sugar, and pepper consigned to Elias H. Derby. Her outward cargo consisted of tobacco, cordage, shooks, iron, lead, salt provisions, earthen ware, &c. Capt. Silsbee was but twenty years old when he assumed command of the "Benjamin." The brig "Peggy," John Edwards, Jr., master, entered in May, 1795, consigned to John Fisk. The brig "Rose," John Felt, master, entered in July, 1795, consigned to Elias H. Derby. The ship "Belisarius," George Crowninshield, Jr., master, entered in July, 1795, with tea, coffee and indigo consigned to George Crowninshield & Co., and again in October, 1796, with the same description of cargo. The brig "Hope," Samuel Lambert, master, entered in June, 1796, consigned to Ashton & Lambert. The ship "Martha," George Ropes, master, entered from the Isles of France and Bourbon in May, 1797, with 416,993 pounds of coffee, 136,617 of sugar, and 13,262 of cotton, consigned to Elias H. Derby, and paying a duty of $23,317.88. The ketch "Eliza," Stephen Phillips, master, entered in July, 1797, consigned to Elias H. Derby. The brig "Katy," Job Trask, master, entered in July, 1797, consigned to Benjamin Pickman, Jr.

There were nine entries at Salem from the Isle of France in 1798; the largest number in any single year. Among the entries were the ketch "Brothers," John Felt, master, in April, consigned to Ezekiel H. Derby; the ship "Martha," John Prince, Jr., master, in June, consigned to Elias H. Derby, with 260,000 pounds of coffee, 336,603 of sugar, and 17,803 of cotton, paying a duty of $24,943.47; and the bark "Vigilant," Daniel Hathorne, master, in October, consigned to Simon Forrester.

The trade with the Isle of France was largely carried on by Elias Hasket Derby, and after his death, in 1799, the Salem trade with this island decreased. The years 1797 and 1798 show seventeen arrivals and were the years when the most trade was carried on between Salem and this island. There were a few direct arrivals after 1798. The bark "Two Brothers," Samuel Rea, master, entered in April, 1806,

Nath'l Tilsbll   Dudley A Parkman.

Rob't Upton   N L Rogers

consigned to Thorndike Deland. The brig "Sukey," Henry Prince, Jr., master, entered in August, 1808, consigned to Stephen Phillips. There were a few arrivals in later years, and some vessels bound to or from other ports touched at this island; but the largest direct trade was prior to the year 1800.

Mocha Trade. — On the 26th of April, 1798, Capt. Joseph Ropes, in the ship "Recovery," left Salem, bound direct for Mocha, Arabia Felix, with $50,000 in specie, and arrived at that port on the 9th of September. This was the first American vessel that ever displayed the stars and stripes in that part of the world. The captain says that the arrival of the strange ship was viewed with great interest by the authorities, who could not divine from whence she came, and made frequent inquiries to know how many moons she had been coming. Capt. Ropes went from Mocha to Calcutta, and thence to Salem. The first vessel to arrive at Salem from Mocha with a full cargo of coffee was the ship "Recovery," Luther Dana, master, which arrived in October, 1801, with 216,286 pounds of coffee consigned to Elias H. Derby, 7,485 pounds to Henry Prince, 11,825 pounds to Nathaniel Bowditch, 34,917 pounds to Clifford Crowninshield, and 33,181 pounds to Nathan Robinson, and paying a duty of $16,844.39. The ship "Ulysses," Henry Elkins, master, entered from Mocha and Muscat in January, 1802, consigned to George Crowninshield & Sons. The brig "Edwin," Joseph J. Knapp, master, entered in November, 1803, consigned to Charles Cleveland & Co. The ship "Bonetta," Benjamin Russell, master, entered from Mocha in February, 1804, with 268,851 pounds of coffee consigned to Benjamin Pickman, Jr.

In 1805, there were eight arrivals from Mocha, the largest number in any single year; and during that year there was landed at Salem over two million pounds of Mocha coffee. The entries were: the ship "Margaret," Henry Elkins, master; the ship "Two Sons," Thomas Rall, master; and the ship "America," Benjamin Crowninshield, master, — all consigned to George Crowninshield & Sons; the brig "Suwarrow," William Leach, Jr., master, consigned to William Leach and others; the bark "Eliza," Joseph Beadle, master, consigned to Joseph White; the ship "Mary," Samuel King, master, from Aden, consigned to John Norris; the ship "Commerce," Thomas Bancroft, master, consigned to Nathaniel West; and the bark "Mary," Daniel Bray, Jr., master, consigned to Benjamin Pickman and John Derby.

21

George Crowninshield & Sons had three vessels which entered from Mocha in 1806 : the ship "Margaret," Henry Elkins, master; the ship "John," William Fairfield, master; and the brig "Telemachus," Benjamin Frye, master. The ship "Franklin," Timothy Wellman, 3d, from Mocha and Aden, entered in December, 1808, with 532,365 pounds of coffee consigned to Joseph Peabody, and paying a duty of $26,618.25. The brig "Coromandel," William Messervy, master, entered in October, 1813, with a cargo of coffee consigned to John Derby, and paying a duty of $28,587.60. The brig "Beulah," Charles Forbes, master, entered from Mocha in April, 1820, consigned to John W. Rogers. The brig "Ann," Charles Millett, master, entered in May, 1827, consigned to Michael Shepard. After the opening of the Zanzibar trade the vessels engaged in that trade visited Mocha and obtained a part of their cargo there, and to the account of that trade reference may be had for later dates.

Madagascar Trade.— The American trade with the Island of Madagascar was opened by Nathaniel L. Rogers & Brothers, eminent and enterprising merchants of Salem. Robert Brookhouse was also among the pioneers in this trade. The brig "Thetis," Charles Forbes, master, appears to be the first vessel to enter, with a full cargo, from that island. She arrived in November, 1821, with 216,-519 pounds of tallow consigned to J. W. & R. S. Rogers. The brig "Beulah," Charles Forbes, master, which entered from Mocha in April, 1820, consigned to John W. Rogers, touched at Madagascar on her passage, and brought from there a small quantity of tallow. This appears to be the first American vessel to trade at Madagascar. The brig "Climax," G. W. Grafton, master, entered in March, 1822, consigned to Robert Brookhouse. The brig "Thetis," William Bates, master, made three voyages, entering in January, 1823, in February, 1824, and in January, 1825, consigned to Richard S. Rogers. The brig "Reaper," Robert Brookhouse, Jr., master, entered in December, 1824, consigned to Robert Brookhouse. The brig "Nereus," B. W. Brookhouse, master, entered in December, 1825, consigned to Nathaniel L. Rogers. The brig "Susan," Stephen Burchmore, master, entered in August, 1826, consigned to Robert Brookhouse.

At the time of the opening of trade with Madagascar, Zanzibar was a small settlement, and no trade was carried on there,— gum-copal, the principal staple, being carried to India by the Sultan's vessels, to be cleaned. The trade with Zanzibar was an extension of the Madagascar trade. The vessels subsequently engaged in that trade usually touched at Madagascar and Mocha, and made up their cargoes in part in each place. In the account of the Zanzibar trade will be found the later arrivals.

Zanzibar Trade.— As Salem had been first at Sumatra and Madagascar, so she was first at Zanzibar. But little of the uncleaned gum-copal, which was the staple article of export, was brought to this country until after the "Black Warrior," belonging largely to N. L. Rogers, and commanded by John Bertram, was there in 1831. Capt. Bertram arrived in Zanzibar while the Sultan's frigate was lying in the harbor ready to carry the gum-copal to India, and made a bargain for what was on hand and for future cargoes. The "Black Warrior" arrived in Salem in March, 1832, with the first large quantity of uncleaned gum-copal that had been imported into this country. For some time thereafter, the gum-copal trade was monopolized by Salem merchants, and all the gum-copal used was distributed from the port of Salem.

But the "Black Warrior," although taking the first large cargo from Zanzibar, was not the first vessel to open trade with that port. The brig "Ann," Charles Millett, master, and owned by Henry Prince & Son, left Salem March 12, 1826, for Mocha. When she arrived there, in June, Capt. Millett found a great scarcity of breadstuffs, and, leaving a clerk in charge of the business, he left Mocha for Zanzibar and Lamo, where he obtained a cargo of small grain, and purchased ivory and other articles for the homeward cargo. The "Ann" went from Zanzibar to Mocha, and from thence to Salem, arriving May 9, 1827. This was the opening of American trade with Zanzibar. The same vessel made a second voyage to Zanzibar, leaving Salem August 9, 1827, and arriving home April 10, 1829, having visited many new ports on the east coast of Africa. On the passage home, February 20, the "Ann" lost her masts and was otherwise badly wrecked. She also lost her mate and two men. For their skill and success in navigating the vessel into port, the insurance companies presented the commander with a service of plate, his clerk, John Webster, with a silver pitcher, and the rest of his men with $330.

The three-masted schooner "Spy," Andrew Ward, master, appears to be the first vessel to enter at the Salem custom-house from Zanzibar. She arrived at Salem August 11, 1827, 110 days from Zanzibar, with a cargo consigned to Nathaniel L. Rogers & Brothers. Capt. Ward reported that the "Susan," Burchard, master, touched at Zanzibar about the 1st of March, and that the "Fawn" of Salem had also been there. The "Spy" was the first three-masted schooner seen hereabouts, such a rig at that time being very uncommon.

On the 12th of January, 1825, the brig "Laurel," Lovett, master, owned by Robert Brookhouse, left Salem for South America. Finding markets dull, the captain sailed for ports east of the Cape of Good Hope; and about the 10th of July left Port Louis, Mauritius, for Zanzibar, stopping at the Island of Johanna on the way. This was the first time the American flag was displayed at that island, and the king gave a reception in honor of the event. The vessel arrived at Zanzibar the 20th of July, 1825, and, although not the first to open trade, seems to be the first to have displayed the American flag at that port. From Zanzibar the "Laurel" proceeded to Mombas, and from there to Patta, Lamo, and other small places, in all of which she appears to have displayed the American flag for the first time. The "Laurel" arrived in Salem, on her return passage, June 3, 1826.

From the year 1827, when the "Spy" entered from Zanzibar, to the year 1870, when the last entry from that port was made at Salem, there were 189 arrivals from Zanzibar. The period from 1840 to 1860 was the time of the greatest activity in this trade, 145 of the 189 entries being made between those years. Nathaniel L. Rogers & Brothers, John Bertram, Michael Shepard, David Pingree, Joseph Peabody, Andrew Ward, Nathaniel Weston, James B. Curwen, Ephraim Emmerton, Tucker Daland, Michael W. Shepard, George West, and Benjamin A. West were among those engaged in this trade.

Among the earlier arrivals were the brig "Cipher," S. Smith, master, in March, 1834; the brig "Tigris," John G. Waters, master, in July, 1834, consigned to David Pingree; the brig "Thomas Perkins," J. P. Page, master, in November, 1834, consigned to Putnam I. Farnham; the brig "Leander," J. S. Kimball, master, in April, 1836, and again in August, 1837, consigned to Joseph Peabody; the brig "Palm," N. W. Andrews, master, in November, 1836, consigned to John Bertram; the brig "Cherokee," W. B. Smith, master, in April, 1837, consigned to Michael Shepard; the bark "Star," E. Brown, master, in November, 1839, again in 1842, W. B. Smith, master, and again in September, 1846, in October, 1847, and in January, 1849, William McFarland, master, consigned to Michael Shepard; the brig "Richmond," William B. Bates, master, in October, 1840, to Ephraim Emmerton; the brig "Rolla," A. S. Perkins, master, in January, 1841, and again in January, 1843, consigned to David Pingree; the brig "Rattler," F. Brown, master, in May, 1841, and again in 1843, J. Lambert, master, consigned to Michael Shepard; the bark "Brenda," Andrew Ward, master, in March, 1844, with 142,124 pounds of dates and other merchandise, consigned to Michael Shepard and John Bertram; the brig "Richmond," William B. Bates, master, entered in December, 1845, consigned to Ephraim Emmerton; the bark "Eliza," A. S. Perkins, master, entered in May, 1846, consigned to George West and David Pingree; the bark "Orb," W. Cross, master, entered in November, 1846, and again in March, 1848, C. F. Rhoades, master, consigned to Tucker Daland; the bark "Sophronia," B. R. Peabody, master, entered in January, 1849, and again, E. A. Emmerton, master, in October 1850, consigned to Ephraim Emmerton; the bark "Iosco," Groves, master, entered in January, 1852, consigned to Michael W. Shepard, and again in December, 1852, consigned to John Bertram.

Space will not permit the enumeration of any large proportion of the arrivals from this port, but enough have been given to indicate the merchants who were engaged in the Zanzibar trade. Many of the vessels touched at Madagascar and Mocha, and obtained a part of their cargoes at those places. For years this trade was largely in the hands of Salem merchants, and Salem was the principal point of distribution for ivory, gum-copal, and Mocha coffee.

Among the vessels lost while engaged in this trade, was the bark "Peacock," Joseph Moseley, master, and owned by John Bertram, which was wrecked on a reef near Majunga, Madagascar, August 6, 1855, and with the cargo was a total loss. The bark "Arabia," John Wallis, master, and owned by Benjamin A. West, sailed from Salem on her first voyage, July 4, 1857. On the passage home, on May 9, 1858, while off the Cape of Good Hope, she fell in with the "Ariadne," bound from Bombay to Boston. This vessel being in a crippled and sinking condition, her crew, twenty-three in number, were taken on board the "Arabia." The supply of water was inadequate for so large an addition to their number, and Capt. Wallis thought it prudent to enter Table Bay and procure an additional supply. At the entrance to the bay, the " Arabia" was becalmed. The night was dark, and about 2, A. M., the vessel struck on a reef and became a total loss. The cargo was saved and sold. The bark "Iosco," Claussen, master, and owned by John Bertram, was wrecked on a reef, off Zanzibar, July 7, 1858. Both vessel and cargo were lost. The bark "Guide," McMullan, master, and owned by John Bertram, was wrecked on the Ras Hoforn, east coast of Africa, on the night of September 4, 1860, and with her cargo was a total loss. The bark "Jersey," James S. Williams, master, and owned by John Bertram, was built at Salem in 1869, and was wrecked at Madagascar on her first voyage.

The large importation of uncleaned gum-copal, which prior to 1832 had been sent to India to be cleaned, led to the establishment, in Salem, of a factory, at the foot of Turner Street, by Jonathan Whipple, to clean and prepare the gum for the market. Prior to the establishment of Mr. Whipple's factory, Daniel Hammond had been engaged in cleaning the gum, but Mr. Whipple was the first to establish the business on an extensive scale. At first the gum was cleaned by being scraped with a knife. Mr. Whipple soon introduced the process of washing it with an alkali. The uncleaned gum was deposited in tubs of alkali liquor and allowed to stand over night. It was then taken and placed upon large platforms in the open air, and carefully dried and brushed. The gum was then sorted as to size and color.

This business was established about 1835, and increased very rapidly. Mr. Whipple commenced by employing four or five men, but at the time of his death, in 1850, the number of men employed averaged thirty-five or forty, and the amount of gum cleaned each year was about 1,500,000 pounds, the gum losing in weight about one-quarter part during the process of cleaning. Mr. Whipple was succeeded by his sons, who continued the business under the name of Stephen Whipple & Brothers. The business was prosperous until the year 1861, when an import duty of ten cents a pound was imposed on the uncleaned gum. The gum was thereafter cleaned on the coast of Africa before shipment, and the business diminished until it was finally abandoned altogether.

The trade with Zanzibar, Madagascar, Arabia, and the east coast of Africa has been continued by Salem merchants from the summer of 1826, when the "Ann" was there, to the present day. In 1846, Salem had nine vessels there. The firm of John Bertram still continue the trade, but their vessels no longer enter the port of Salem. The last arrival at Salem from Zanzibar was the bark "Glide," May 1, 1870, and this was also the last arrival at Salem of any vessel from beyond the Cape of Good Hope.

Cape of Good Hope Trade.—When the merchants of Salem, at the close of the Revolutionary War, sent their vessels on long voyages, the Cape of Good Hope was among the first places visited. In this, as in most other trades established with distant countries, Elias Hasket Derby was the first to lead the way. In 1781, he built at the South Shore a fast sailing ship of 300 tons, called the "Grand Turk," for use as a privateer. She carried twenty-two guns, and was remarkably successful in capturing prizes. In November, 1784, Mr. Derby despatched this vessel, under command of Jonathan Ingersoll, on the first voyage from Salem to the Cape of Good Hope. The cargo of the "Grand Turk" consisted in part of rum, which was sold to an English East Indiaman and delivered at the Island of St. Helena. From there she returned to Salem, via the West Indies, arriving in 1785. A striking incident is connected with this voyage of Captain Ingersoll. He bought in the West Indies Grenada rum enough to load two vessels, sent home the "Grand Turk," and returned himself in the "Atlantic." On his passage to Salem he rescued the master and mate of the English schooner "Amity," whose crew had mutinied and set their officers adrift in a boat. After their arrival at Salem, Capt. Duncanson of the "Amity" was sitting one day with Mr. Derby in his counting-room, and while using his spy-glass he saw his own vessel in the offing. Mr. Derby promptly manned one of his own brigs, put two pieces of ordnance on board of her, and, taking with him the English captain, boarded and recaptured the "Amity."

Mr. Derby purchased a vessel which had been captured from the British during the Revolutionary War. He named her the "Light Horse." This bark he sent, in January, 1787, to the Cape of Good Hope, under command of John Tucker, The captain wrote his first letter from Table Bay, dated May 15, 1787, giving an account of a sale of part of the cargo. From the Cape he went to the Isle of France, sold the remainder of his cargo, loaded with coffee, and some India goods, and returned to Salem, arriving in January, 1788.

The brig "Hope," of one hundred and sixty tons burden, carrying eight men, made an annual voyage between Salem and the Cape of Good Hope for six consecutive years, entering at Salem in February, 1790, in August, 1791, in July, 1792, in June, 1793, in May, 1794, and in July, 1795. She was commanded on the first three voyages by Jonathan Lambert, and on the last three by Samuel Lambert, and her cargo was consigned, on each voyage, to Jacob Ashton and others. The schooner "Ruth," Jonathan Lambert, Jr., master, entered in July, 1796, consigned to Jacob Ashton and others. The ship "Betsey," Jeremiah L. Page, master, entered in May, 1804, consigned to Abel Lawrence & Co.

Coffee, wine, pepper, sugar, ivory and aloes were among the articles imported. Most of the direct trade with the Cape of Good Hope, was carried on before the commencement of the present century, and Jacob Ashton and Jonathan Lambert appear to have been largely engaged in it.

Australian Trade. — Wherever a new channel of trade was opened for Americans, Salem was either the first to open it, or her vessels followed closely after the pioneers. She was found asking for admission to the port of Sydney, in 1832, and by a special order of the council, passed that year, the ship "Tybee," Charles Millett, master, was allowed to enter that port. This vessel was owned by Nathaniel L. Rogers, and others, and was the first American vessel to enter the ports of Australia. The "Tybee" entered at Salem from Sydney Jan. 20, 1835, again in March, 1836, and again in June, 1837. Joseph Rogers commanded her on these voyages, and her cargo consisted mainly of wool. The ship "Black Warrior," William Driver, master, entered from Sydney in September, 1835, and the ship "Shepherdess," J. Kinsman, master, in May, 1836, both bringing cargoes of wool. All the above-mentioned cargoes were consigned to Nathaniel L. Rogers & Brothers. This trade did not prove profitable, and it was not long continued, the direct entries at Salem, from Sydney, being confined to the years 1835, '36, and '37.

Feejee Islands Trade. — The enterprise of Salem merchants seems not to have been confined by the limits of the civilized world, but to have extended to all habitable countries, however remote and however peopled. Salem was as familiar a name to the cannibals of the Feejee Islands, during the first half of the present century, as it was to the savages of Africa and Madagascar. In many of those wild countries, the untutored inhabitants thought Salem comprised all the remainder of the outer world about which they knew so little. Capt. William P. Richardson, of Salem, was at the Feejee Islands, in the bark "Active," in 1811. He sailed from Salem June 1, 1810, and left the Feejee Islands, July 26, 1811, for Canton. He arrived at Salem March 27, 1812, 118 days from Canton. This was the first trading voyage from Salem to the Feejee Islands. Commercial intercourse with these islands began about 1806, probably by vessels of the East India Company.

When Commodore Wilkes went on his famous exploring expedition, he took with him, as pilot and interpreter, Capt. Benjamin Vanderford, a Salem shipmaster who, having made many voyages to these islands, was familiar with the customs and language of the natives. Capt. Vanderford died March 23, 1842, on the passage home ; and the commodore, writing of him, says : "During the cruise I had often experienced his usefulness. He had formerly been in command of various vessels sailing from Salem, and had made many voyages to the Feejee Islands. During our stay there, he was particularly useful in superintending all trade carried on to supply the ship." Commodore Wilkes was indebted to another Salem captain for bringing one of the vessels of his squadron, — the "Peacock," — safely into port, on the 12th of July, 1840. Capt. J. H. Eagleston, of Salem, who was trading there at the time, rendered him this important service. The commodore, iu his report to the government, says : "The squadron is much indebted to Capt. Eagleston for his attention and assistance. I am also indebted to him for observations relating to gales."

Capt. Eagleston made voyages to these islands between 1830 and 1840, in the bark "Peru," the ship "Emerald." the brig "Mermaid," and the ship "Leonidas." On one of his passages in the "Leonidas" he caught several albatrosses, and tied to the neck of each a quill containing a slip of paper, on which was written "Ship Leonidas, of Salem, bound to New Zealand." One of these birds was caught by a French vessel off the Cape of Good Hope, several hundred miles away from the spot where it was first caught by Capt. Eagleston. The news reached Salem March 21, 1840, and was the first news of this vessel since she sailed, on the 9th of August. Capt. Eagleston sailed for Stephen C. Phillips, who was a prominent merchant of

22

Salem, from about 1828 to the time of his death in 1857. Mr. Phillips was largely engaged in trade with the Feejee Islands, with Manila and other Eastern ports. In 1846, Salem had six vessels engaged in trade with the Feejee Islands. The usual voyage was from Salem to the Feejee Islands, where the vessel would remain collecting the beche-de-mer, a sort of sea-slug found on reefs and in shallow water, and after drying and preparing them for the market, carry them either to Manila to exchange for sugar and hemp, or to China to exchange for tea; the voyage usually consuming about two years. Salem almost monopolized this trade, and, in a work, written in London, in 1858, by Thomas Williams and James Calvert, missionaries at these islands, it is stated that the traffic in sandal-wood, tortoise-shell, and beche-de-mer, "has been, and still is chiefly in the hands of Americans from the port of Salem." There are many curious articles at the Peabody Academy of Science at Salem, which were brought from the Feejee Islands during the early voyages.

Among the Salem merchants engaged in this trade, were Nathaniel L. Rogers & Brothers, Stephen C. Phillips, Samuel Chamberlain & Co., and Benjamin A. West. The bark "Zotoff," Benjamin Wallis, master, made several voyages to the Feejee Islands. Capt. Wallis, on two of these voyages, covering a period from 1844 to 1850, was accompanied by his wife, who, upon her final return, wrote an account of her travels, in a book entitled "Life in Feejee." She mentions seeing the brig "Elizabeth," the bark "Samos," Capt. H. J. Archer, the bark "Pilot," Capt. Hartwell, and the brig "Tim Pickering," all of Salem, during the first voyage. The "Samos" was afterwards condemned at Manila. The "Tim Pickering," Walden, master, while lying at Ovalou, in the Feejee Islands, was driven ashore in a severe gale, April 5, 1848, and became a total loss. Capt. Benjamin Vanderford was at the Feejee Islands about 1819, in the ship "Indus," and about 1822, in the "Roscoe." The bark "Dragon," Thomas C. Dunn, master, sailed from Salem Feb. 22, 1854, and arrived at the Feejee Islands, a distance of 16,770 miles in eighty-five days, making the shortest passage ever made from the United States. She crossed the equator in twenty days, and passed Port Philip, New Holland, seventy-three days out. She reached Salem from Manila Sept. 4, 1856, with 1,170 bales of hemp, consigned to Benjamin A. West.

The seamen of Salem, visiting these islands, were exposed to peril of their lives from the ignorant and deceitful inhabitants, and to disaster to their ships from hidden reefs, of the existence of which they were unaware. In August, 1830, the brig "Fawn," James Briant, master, and owned by Robert Brookhouse, was lost at the Feejee Islands, and Capt. Charles Millett, of the ship "Clay," gave captain and crew a passage to Manila. The ship "Glide," in March, 1832, is driven ashore at Tackanova, and lost. Her boat's crew were attacked by the natives at Ovalou, Dec. 26, 1831, and two of them killed. In the same gale which destroyed the "Glide," another Salem vessel, the brig "Niagara," was lost, at an island 140 miles from Tackanova.

The brig "Charles Doggett," owned by Nathaniel L. Rogers & Brothers, and commanded by George Batchelder, was at Kandora, one of the Feejee Islands, in September, 1833, and her crew were curing the beche-de-mer for the East India market. They were attacked by the natives for the sake of plunder, and five of the crew were killed, including Charles Shipman, the mate. The remainder escaped in the boats, but were all more or less injured. James Magoun, of Salem, who had lived among the islanders several years, was dangerously wounded. On the way to Manila, the vessel touched at the Pelew Islands, and the crew were again attacked by the natives, and a boy was killed. The vessel reached Salem, from Manila, in October, 1834.

The story of a previous voyage of the "Charles Doggett," under the command of William Driver, is one of most romantic interest, and deserves a place in history. As an introduction, it may be well to give a brief account of the mutiny of the "Bounty," which, though an oft-repeated tale, is still one of thrilling interest. Capt. William Bligh was sent by the British Government in the "Bounty," in December, 1787, to Tahiti. He reached that island in October of the following year, and remained there six months, collecting bread-fruit plants, with which he started for Jamaica. Twenty-four days out, on the 28th of April, a part of the crew mutinied, and forced Capt. Bligh and eighteen men into the ship's launch, which they cast adrift, turning their own course back to Tahiti. The captain and his companions arrived, on the 14th of June, after suffering almost incredible hardships, at the island of Timor, a distance of 3,600 nautical miles from the place where they were abandoned. The mutineers, after staying at Tahiti for some time, fearing pursuit, sailed eastward, taking with them eighteen natives, six men and twelve women, and leaving part of their comrades at Tahiti. They landed at Pitcairn Island, a solitary island in the Pacific Ocean, lying at the south-east corner of the great Polynesian Archipelago, having an area of only one and a quarter square miles. Here they took up their residence, and burned the "Bounty." From the time they left Tahiti in 1792, nothing was heard of them, until an American, Capt. Folger, touched at the island in 1808. At this time, all the men, save Alexander Smith, and several of the women, were dead. The island was visited by British vessels in 1825 and 1830.

In 1831, their numbers had increased to eighty-seven, and the island was scantily provided with water. At their own request, they were transported by the British Government to Tahiti. All the original settlers were dead, and their descendants had been reared away from contact with the world, and were, despite their wild ancestry, virtuous and religious. Never having looked upon vice, they found themselves among a people where virtue was unknown. Disgusted with the immoralities of the Tahitians, the most loose, voluptuous and unchaste people that exist under the tropic sun, they yearned with a homesick longing for the isolation and quiet of the little island that had so recently been their home.

It was at this time that the brig "Charles Doggett," William Driver, master, and owned by Nathaniel L. Rogers & Brothers, arrived at Tahiti. These poor homesick people besought Capt. Driver to take them back to their native island. For their own sake, but above all for the sake of their children, they desired to leave this land of sensual indulgence. Capt. Driver finally consented to carry them, sixty-five in number, back to the island, fourteen hundred miles away, from whence they had so recently arrived, taking in pay some old copper, twelve blankets, and one hundred and twenty-nine dollars in missionary drafts. They left on the 15th of August, 1831, and were landed on Pitcairn Island on September 3d, after an absence of about nine months. In 1855, finding their numbers again too large for the island, for they now numbered 202, they petitioned the British government, and in 1856 were removed to Norfolk Island. In 1859 two 'families, in all 17, returned to Pitcairn Island. An English writer in speaking of them says, "From their frequent intercourse with Europeans, the

Pitcairn Islanders have, while retaining their virtuous simplicity of character, and cheerful, hospitable disposition, acquired the manners and polish of civilized life, with its education and taste."

May it not well be said that a Salem vessel saved this people from sinking into the immoral life that surrounded them at Tahiti, and that in their strange and romantic history there is no chapter more impor-tant than that which records the assistance rendered them by Salem in their time of need?

South American Trade.—The trade between Salem and South America has been quite extensive. This trade began early and contin-ued to be prosecuted after trade with other foreign countries had been abandoned. On the 25th of August, 1789, the schooner "Lark" ar-rived from Surinam with sugar and cocoa. The brig "Katy," Nathan-iel Brown, master, cleared for Cayenne in April, 1798, with fish, flour, bacon, butter, oil, tobacco, candles and potter's ware. The schooner "Sally," Daniel Procter, master, cleared for Cayenne in March, 1802. For forty years, from 1820 to 1860, there was con-stant commercial intercourse between Salem and the ports of South America.

Para was the port most frequently visited, there having been 435 arrivals at Salem from that port, mainly between the years 1826 and 1860. The largest number of arrivals in a single year was in 1853, when 20 vessels entered. The last entries were in 1861. Rubber, hides, cocoa, coffee and castana nuts were among the articles imported. A few of the entries from Para are given, to indicate the merchants en-gaged in this traffic. The schooner "Betsey," James Meagher, master, entered from Para in March, 1811, with cassia, coffee and cocoa, con-signed to John Howard. The schooner "Four Sisters," Joseph Ervin, master, in August, 1811, with 138,000 pounds of cocoa, to William Orne. The schooner "Resolution," Edward Brown, Jr., master, in July, 1812, consigned to Jeremiah L. Page. The brig "Mercator," Samuel B. Graves, master, in September, 1817, to Robert Upton. The schooner "Cyrus," Benjamin Russell, master, in March, 1820, to Robert Upton. The schooner "Charles," Richard Smith, master, in August, 1822, to Michael Shepard. The schooner "Phœbe," Benj. Upton, master, in December, 1824, to Robert Upton. The schooner "Leader," Nathaniel Griffen, master, in April, 1826, to Richard Sav-ory. The schooner "Dollar," Thomas Holmes, master, in April,

1826, to David Pingree. The schooner "Cepheus," Charles Holland, master, in August, 1826, to Joseph Howard. The brig "Romp," Clarke, master, in December, 1828, to Thomas P. Pingree and Michael Shepard. The schooner "Gazelle," Warren Strickland, master, in August, 1830, to James Brown. The brig "Abby M.," R. Wheatland, master, in October, 1830, to Gideon Tucker. The brig "Amethyst," John Willis, master, in July, 1831, to Robert Upton. The brig "Fredonia," S. K. Appleton, master, in September, 1832, to Benjamin Creamer. The brig "Deposit," G. E. Bailey, master, in January, 1842, to James Upton. This vessel made regular trips between Salem and Para. The brig "Mermaid," C. Conway, master, in April, 1842, to P. I. Farnham. The brig "Eagle," M. S. Wheeler, master, in December, 1842, to Benjamin Upton. The brig "Deposit," under command of Charles Upton, entered in March, 1844, and made several voyages thereafter, consigned to Luther Upton. The brig "Granite," S. Upton, master, entered in October, 1844, and made regular trips to S. F. Upton. The brig "Rattler," C. W. Trumbull, master, entered in July, 1846, and made a number of voyages consigned to John Bertram. The brig "M. Shepard," H. B. Manning, master, entered in March, 1853, and continued for some time in the trade, consigned to John Bertram. Messrs. Phippen & Endicott were the last among the Salem merchants engaged in this trade. There were two entries in the year 1861, and these entries closed the trade of Salem with Para.

There has been a large trade between Salem and Cayenne, beginning in the last century. The whole number of arrivals from this port between the years 1810 and 1877, was about 300. The largest number of entries in a single year was in 1835, when there was eleven entries from that port. From 1835 to 1840 inclusive, there was 58 entries. The Cayenne trade was the last foreign trade engaged in by Salem merchants at the port of Salem.

Among the entries from that port was that of the brig "Trial," Eben Learock, master, in June, 1810, with molasses and coffee, consigned to Francis Quarles. The schooner "Rachel," Mark Knowlton, master, in August, 1812, to John Winn. The brig "Return," Henry King, master, in March, 1813, to Thomas Perkins. The schooner "Essex," Thomas Cloutman, master, in May, 1816, with cocoa, molasses and almonds, to William Fabens. The brig "Rambler," W. D. Shatswell, master, in February, 1821, to William Fabens, and in February, 1828, to Benjamin Fabens. The brig "Cynthia," in July, 1821, to J. H. Andrews, in 1824 to Michael Shepard, and in 1825, to David Pingree. The brig "General Jackson," Shatswell, master, in May, 1826, to P. I. Farnham. The brig "Jeremiah," Joshua F. Safford, master, in June, 1821, to David Pingree. The brig "Rotund," Joseph R. Winn, master, in May, 1825, to Benjamin Fabens. The schooner "Betsey and Eliza," Benj. Pickering, master, in August, 1829, to Joseph Shatswell. The schooner "Numa," D. R. Upton, master, in March, 1833, to Robert Upton. The brig "Romp," Peter Lassen, master, in September, 1851, to Joseph Shatswell. The brig "Esther," W. H. Fabens, master, in February, 1850, to Benjamin Fabens, Jr., and in August, 1850, Peter Lassen, master, to Charles H. Fabens. The bark "Lawrence," Fabens, master, in September, 1851, to Charles H. Fabens.

David Pingree and Joseph Shatswell were largely engaged in this trade. The Fabens family for four generations have carried on the trade between Salem and Cayenne. William Fabens began it about 1816, Benjamin Fabens about 1825, Charles H. Fabens about 1850, and Charles E. and Benjamin H. Fabens about 1869. The successive generations have prosecuted the trade continuously from 1816 to the present day. The last-named removed the business to Boston in 1877, and now carry it on from that port. The last arrival at Salem from a South American port was the schooner "Mattie F.," which was entered from Cayenne, by Messrs. C. E. & B. H. Fabens, March 21, 1877. The entry of the "Mattie F." closed the foreign trade of Salem.

The trade between Salem and Buenos Ayres is the next in importance. From 1816 to 1860, inclusive, there were 121 arrivals at Salem from this port. The period of greatest activity was from 1841 to 1860. Robert Upton, James Upton, David Pingree, and Benjamin A. West were among the merchants principally engaged in this trade. The entries from this port include that of the brig "Nancy Ann," John B. Osgood, master, in April, 1816, to Stephen Phillips. The ship "Diomede," Samuel L. Page, master, in March, 1817, to Philip Chase. The brig "Cambrian," H. G. Bridges, master, in June, 1823, to Joseph Peabody. The brig "Bolivar Liberator," James Garney, master, in January, 1831, to P. I. Farnham. The bark

"Chalcedony," J. E. A. Todd, master, entered in April, 1841, and made several voyages thereafter, commanded by Capt. Todd, and a number after 1849, with George Upton as master. She was consigned on these voyages to James Upton. The bark "Three Brothers," Welch, master, entered in May, 1843, consigned to David Pingree. The brig "Cherokee," Mansfield, master, entered in October, 1843, consigned to Michael Shepard. The brig "Gazelle," Dewing, master, in November, 1843, to John Bertram. The brig "Olinda," S. Hutchinson, master, in December, 1843, to Gideon Tucker. The bark "King Philip," George Upton, master, in June, 1844, to James Upton. The brig "Gambia," G. E. Bailey, master, in September, 1848, to Benjamin A. West. The bark "Maid of Orleans," Charles Upton, master, in September, 1848, and on several subsequent voyages, consigned to James Upton. The bark "Manchester," S. Upton, master, in May, 1853, to Robert Upton. The brig "Russell," in August, 1854, to George Savory. The bark "Salem," in August, 1860, to James Upton. The last entry at Salem from Buenos Ayres was in 1860.

Rio Grande was a place with which Salem merchants traded quite extensively. Hides and horns were the principal articles imported. From 1817 to 1860 there were about 155 arrivals at Salem from that province, and of that number, 100 were during the time from 1845 to 1854, inclusive. The largest number of arrivals in a single year was seventeen, in the year 1851. The Uptons were largely interested in this trade, as they were in most of the Salem trade with the ports on the eastern coast of South America. Robert Upton, James Upton, Benjamin Upton, Luther Upton, and H. P. Upton and David Pingree, George Savory, Thomas P. Pingree, Benjamin Webb and David Moore, were among those engaged in trade with Rio Grande.

From the list of entries from that place at Salem a few are given. A complete list would hardly interest the general reader. The brig "Trader," John Eveleth, master, entered in June, 1817, with tallow, consigned to Edward Lander. The brig "Rotund," John Ingersoll, master, in July, 1822, to Gideon Tucker. The brig "Cynthia," Shillaber, master, in October, 1828, to David Pingree. The brig "Abby M.," R. Wheatland, master, in October, 1829, to Putnam I. Farnham and others. The brig "Quill," Thomas Farley, master, in

November, 1831, to Nathaniel L. Rogers & Bros. The brig "Mermaid," George Savory, master, in May, 1841, to Benjamin Upton. The brig "Northumberland," Kane, master, in November, 1842, to Thomas P. Pingree. The bark "Chalcedony," J. E. A. Todd, master, in October, 1846, to James Upton, and in May, 1847, to Luther Upton. The brig "Russell," R. F. Savory, master, in May, 1847, to H. P. Upton. The bark "Wm. Schroder," J. E. A. Todd, master, in March, 1848, to Robert Upton. The bark "Wyman," J. Madison, master, in July, 1849, to James Upton. This vessel made many trips between Salem and Rio Grande, commanded by George Harrington. The bark "Sophronia," E. A. Emmerton, master, in July, 1849, to Ephraim Emmerton. The schooner "Maria Theresa," O. Baker, Jr., master, in August, 1849, to D. R. Bowker. The brig "Draco," E. S. Johnson, master, in October, 1849, and in April, 1850, to David Moore. The brig "Prairie," E. Upton, master, in November, 1850, to George Savory and others. The bark "Delegate," D. Marshall, master, in January, 1851, to Benjamin Webb and others. The bark "Arrow," in June, 1860, to James Upton. There were two entries from Rio Grande in 1860, and with those entries the Salem trade with that place closed. There was a single entry from Rio Grande in 1870, but neither vessel nor cargo was owned by Salem merchants.

The Salem trade with Montevideo began about 1811, and ended in 1861. There was no entry from this port between 1811 and 1823. The largest number of entries was during the years 1847, 1848, and 1853. Robert Upton, James Upton, and Benjamin A. West were among those engaged in trading with that port. Hides and horns were the principal articles imported. The brig "Hope," Benjamin Jacobs, master, entered in June, 1811, consigned to Thomas Perkins. The ship "Glide," Nathan Endicott, master, entered in November, 1823, consigned to Joseph Peabody. The brig "Dawn,'' C. Davis, master, in April, 1833, to Putnam I. Farnham. The brig "Chalcedony," George Upton, master, in May, 1839, and in October, 1847, to James Upton; and in March, 1848, to Luther Upton. The bark "Zotoff," G. E. Bailey, master, in January, 1853, and again in August, 1853, to Benjamin A. West. The bark "Peacock," Upton, master, in April, 1853, to Robert Upton. The bark "Argentine," George Upton, master, in June, 1853, to James Upton. The bark

23

"Miquelon," S. Hutchinson, in July, 1853, to E. H. Folmer. The brig "Mary A. Jones," in January, 1860, and again in July, 1860, to Benjamin A. West. There was a single entry in 1861, the last entry at Salem from Montevideo.

In the years 1824 and 1825 there were twenty-four entries from Maranham. From 1817 to 1858 there were 110 entries. Joseph Howard and James Brown were among those most largely interested in this trade. The brig "Henry," George Burchmore, master, entered from Maranham in January, 1817, consigned to Stephen White. The brig "Anson," Hasket D. Lang, master, in May, 1819, to P. & A. Chase. The brig "Alonzo," George K. Smith, master, in August, 1819, to Joseph Howard. The brig "Betsey," Timothy Ropes, master, in August, 1819, to George Nichols. The schooner "Mermaid," John Willis, master, in April, 1824, to Pickering Dodge. The schooner "General Brewer," George Gale, master, in August, 1825, to Stephen White. The brig "Stork," Stephen Gale, master, in November, 1825, to James Brown and others. The brig "Calliope," George Creamer, master, in March, 1826, to Robert Upton. The schooner "Spy," Benjamin Russell, master, in April, 1826, to Nathaniel L. Rogers & Bros. The brig "Edward," Thomas C. Whittredge, master, in May, 1826, to Thomas Whittredge. The schooner "Sally Barker," F. Quarles, master, in June, 1826, to Michael Shepard. The brig "Stork," Oliver Thayer, master, in July, 1826, to Joseph Howard. The brig "Cynthia," Benjamin Shillaber, master, in April, 1827, to David Pingree. The brig "Wm. Penn," S. K. Appleton, master, in January, 1836, to John F. Allen. The brig "Amethyst," R. Hill, Jr., master, in February, 1837, to James Upton. The brig "Palm," in September, 1840, to Thomas P. Pingree. The schooner "East Wind," in June, 1858, to Phippen & Endicott; and this entry closed the Salem trade with Maranham.

Surinam was visited early by Salem vessels. The period of the greatest activity in this trade was between the years 1797 and 1810. There were twelve arrivals at Salem from this place in 1799, and the same number in 1804. There were two entries in 1860, the last made at Salem from Surinam. Coffee, cocoa, sugar, cotton, molasses, and distilled spirits were the principal articles imported.

The schooner "St. John," W. Grafton, master, entered from Surinam in October, 1791, consigned to Joseph Waters. The brig "Lydia,"

Eben. Shillaber, master, in August, 1796, to William Gray. The brig "Three Friends, John Endicott, master, in October, 1796, to Jonathan Gardner and Joseph Peabody. The schooner "Cynthia," Hezekiah Flint, master, in December, 1796, to Joseph Peabody and Thomas Perkins. The schooner "Diligent," James Buffington, master, in February, 1797, to Joseph Sprague & Sons. The brig "Katy," Nathaniel Brown, master, in August, 1798, to Benjamin Pickman, Jr. The schooner "Fame," Downing Lee, master, in April, 1798, to Samuel Gray and John Osgood. The brig "Neptune," Robert Barr, master, in May, 1797, to John Barr. The ship "Henry," Stephen Webb, master, in June, 1799, to Elias H. Derby. The ship "Belisarius," Edward Allen, master, in August, 1799, to George Crowninshield & Sons. The schooner "Helen," Samuel King, master, in November, 1799, to Benjamin West. The ship "Atlantic," Eben Learock, in April, 1804, to Joseph Peabody. The bark "Active," John Endicott, master, in July, 1804, to Benjamin Hodges. The schooner "Union," Moses Yell, master, in December, 1807, to Michael Shepard. The brig "Nabby," Hardy Phippen, master, in April, 1808, to Samuel Archer, 3d. The brig "Union," Timothy Ropes, master, in October, 1823, to John H. Andrews. The brig "Rambler," S. Upton, master, in March, 1829, to Benjamin Fabens. The brig "Cynthia," John G. Waters, master, in August, 1829, to David Pingree. The ship "William and Henry," C. H. Fabens, master, in January, 1838, to David Pingree. The brig "Mary Francis," in July, 1855, to Joseph Shatswell. The bark "Lawrence," in April 1857, to Charles H. Fabens. The brig "Elizabeth," in April, 1860, and in August, 1860, to Benjamin Webb. The above mentioned entries are given to show the names of the Salem merchants engaged in trade with Surinam.

There were three entries at Salem for Rio Janeiro in 1810. The largest number of entries in a single year was in 1824, when six vessels entered from that port. The schooner "Mercury," Edward Barnard, Jr., master, entered from that port in June, 1810, consigned to Nathaniel West. The brig "New Hazard," Edward Stanley, master, in July, 1810, to John Gardner, Jr. The ship "Marquis de Somernelas," Thomas Russell, master, in July, 1810, to John Gardner, Jr., and Michael Shepard. The ship "John," Jeremiah Briggs, master, in March, 1811, to George Crowninshield. The brig "Cora,"

P. P. Pinel, master, in December, 1811, to Jerathmael Pierce. The brig " Alonzo," Philemon Putnam, master, in April, 1823, to Joseph Howard. The ship "Friendship," Richard Meek, master, in November, 1823, and again in November, 1824, to George Nichols. The brig " Pioneer," Andrew Ward, master, in April, 1824, to John W. Rogers. The brig " Edward," Thomas C. Whittredge, master, in August, 1824, to Thomas Whitredge. The brig "Roscius," J. Kinsman, master, in November, 1824, to Robert Upton. The brig "Thomas Perkins," B. Shillaber, master, in September, 1832, to Michael Shepard. The bark "Richard," J. Hodges, master, in November, 1832, to Joseph Hodges. The bark "Imaun," Batchelder, master, in April, 1852, to Benjamin A. West. The entry of the "Imaun," closed the Salem trade with Rio Janeiro. The principal articles imported were coffee and sugar.

In August, 1832, the brig " Mexican," of Salem, owned by Joseph Peabody, and commanded by John G. Butman of Beverly, left Salem for Rio Janeiro, having on board $20,000 in specie. On Sept. 20th, between the hours of 8 and 9 A. M., she was hailed by the piratical Spanish schooner "Pinda," Commander Gibert. The pirates came on board the " Mexican," and threatened all hands with instant death unless the specie was immediately produced. They obliged the crew to bring the boxes containing it on deck, when they at once transferred it to the schooner. They then ransacked the cabin and rifled the captain's pockets, taking his watch and money. Not being successful in finding any more specie aboard the brig the pirates returned on board their schooner. In eight or ten minutes they came back, apparently in great haste, shut all the crew below, fastened the companion-way, fore scuttle and after hatchway ; stove the compasses to pieces in the binnacles, and cut away tiller-ropes, halliards, braces and most of the running rigging. They then took a tub of tarred rope-yarn, and what they could find combustible about the deck, put it into the caboose house and set it on fire. As soon as the pirates left, the crew of the " Mexican" reached the deck, through the cabin scuttle, which the pirates had neglected to secure, and extinguished the fire, which in a few moments would have set the main-sail on fire and destroyed the masts. The crew immediately repaired damages, as far as possible, and set sail for home, where they arrived October 12. It was doubtless the intention of the pirates to burn the brig, but seeing another vessel in the distance, and being eager for more plunder, they did not stop to fully accomplish their design, and the crew thus escaped a horrible fate. The " Mexican " had a crew of 13 men all told, and those now living are John Nichols, John Battis, Jacob Anderson and Thomas Fuller, all of Salem, and Benjamin Larcom of Beverly.

Our government ordered a vessel to cruise in pursuit of the pirate, but she soon gave up the chase as hopeless. The piratical vessel was afterwards captured by an English vessel, and on August 27, 1834, H. B. M. brig " Savage," Lt. Com. Loney, from Portsmouth, England, arrived in Salem harbor with sixteen of the pirates as prisoners. They had an examination in Salem, and then were taken to Boston and tried before Chief Justice Story. Five of them were hanged June 11, 1835. Bernardo de Soto, the mate of the "Panda," when master of the Spanish brig "Leon," had in 1831, at great personal risk, rescued seventy-two persons from the burning ship " Minerva," of Salem, Capt. George W. Putnam, and for the bravery and humanity displayed by him on this occasion he was pardoned by President Jackson.

Pernambuco was a port at which many Salem vessels touched for orders. There were not a great many direct entries at Salem from that port. The largest number was in 1826 when there were six entries. Among the entries were the brig " Welcome Return," Jeremiah Briggs, master, in September, 1809, consigned to Josiah Dow. The schooner "Hannah," Edward Briggs, master, in June, 1810, to Josiah Dow. The brig " Alonzo," Isaac Killam, master, in August, 1811, to John Derby. The schooner " Rising States," Samuel Lamson, master, in March 1812, to James Cook. The ship "Endeavour," Nathaniel L. Rogers, master, in May, 1812, to John Forrester. The brig " Levant," Samuel Rea, master, in October, 1812, to Joseph Peabody. The brig " Cora," Philip P. Pinel, in September, 1815, to Jerathmael Pierce. The brig " Eliza," Stephen Gale, master, in November, 1819, to Benjamin Barstow. The brig " Eliza & Mary," S. Benson, master, in November, 1825, to S. White and F. H. Story. The brig " Olinda," R. Wheatland, master, in December, 1825 and in June, 1826, to Gideon Tucker. The brig "Washington," A. Marshall, master, in August, 1826, to William Fettyplace. The brig " Amethyst," R. Hill, Jr., master, in May, 1836, to Robert Upton. The brig " Mermaid," George Savory, master, in May, 1840, to Putnam I.

Farnham. The brig "Gazelle," J. Dewing, master, in March, 1841, to Joseph Shatswell. The entry of the "Gazelle" closed the direct trade between Salem and Pernambuco. The principal article imported thence was sugar.

Bahia, Paraiba, and Patagonia on the eastern coast, and Valpariso, Lima, and Guayaquil on the western coast of South America, were among the places from which vessels entered• at the port of Salem. The trade with these places was not very extensive. The brig "Blakely," Benjamin Fabens, master, entered from Bahia in July, 1819, with molasses consigned to William Fabens. The brig "Lion," J. P. Felt, master, entered from Bahia in June, 1821, consigned to John Dike. The brig "Augusta," Seth Rogers, master, entered from Bahia in March, 1824, consigned to Gideon Tucker. The brig "Mercator," Aaron Miller, master, entered from Bahia in September, 1826, consigned to John F. Andrew. The schooner "Generous," E. B. Hooper, master, made several voyages in 1832 and '33 between Salem and Paraiba, consigned to Michael Shepard. The ship "China," H. Putnam, master, entered from Lima in July, 1828, consigned to Joseph Peabody. The brig "Herald," Aaron W. Williams, master, entered from Guayaquil in August, 1824, consigned to George Nichols. The brig "Phœnix," George Hodges, Jr., master, entered from Guayaquil in December, 1826, with 166,120 pounds of cocoa, consigned to Moses Townsend. The brig "Java," Nathaniel Osgood, master, entered from Guayaquil in January, 1829, and proceeded to New York.

West Coast of Africa Trade.—If the natives on the West Coast of Africa have been temperate, they have been so in spite of the efforts of the Salem merchants to supply them with the materials for intemperance. The trade opened early, and Oct. 6, 1789, the schooner "Sally," and Oct. 8, 1789, the schooner "Polly" cleared for Senegal, each with a cargo of New England rum; and from that time forward, Salem has contributed largely to spread a knowledge of the virtues and good qualities of New England rum, of the astounding effects of gunpowder, and of the consoling influences of Virginia tobacco, among the savage tribes of the West Coast. The Salem trade with this coast has been quite extensive. The period of the greatest activity was between the years 1832 and 1864. During that time, there were 558 arrivals at Salem from the West Coast of Africa. From 1844 to

R Brookhouse   L C Phillips

John Bertram   Daniel A Kimball

1860, only the years 1854 and 1855 show less than twenty entries. Robert Brookhouse, Daniel Abbot, Putnam I. Farnham, David Pingree, William Hunt, Charles Hoffman, Edward D. Kimball, and George West, were among those engaged in this trade. Hides, palm-oil, peanuts, and gum-copal were the principal articles imported. Among the entries, were the brig "St. John," Thomas Bowditch, master, which entered from Sierra Leone in June, 1796, consigned to Henry Gardner & Co.; the brig "Sukey," John Edwards, master, which entered from Senegal in July, 1801, consigned to Henry Prince & Co. The brig "Star," Richard J. Cleveland, master, entered from Goree in July, 1808, consigned to John Derby. The brig "Siren," James Vent, master, entered in March, 1828, consigned to Robert Brookhouse. The schooner "Fredonia," Charles Hoffman, master, in September, 1829, to Daniel Abbot. The brig "Shawmut," J. Emerton, master, in July, 1831, to Robert Brookhouse. The schooner "Complex," J. Burnham, master, in June, 1832, to Richard S. Rogers. The schooner "Dollar," John Stickney, master, in September, 1835, to Putnam I. Farnham. The brig "Selina and Jane," Joseph Rider, master, in August, 1836, to David Pingree. The brig "Elizabeth," N. Frye, master, in March, 1837, and in November, 1837, J. A. Phipps, master, consigned to William Hunt. The brig "Richmond," H. Breed, master, in April, 1837, to Ephraim Emmerton. The brig "Cipher," J. Rider, master, in August, 1839, to Charles Hoffman. The brig "Tigris," N. A. Frye, master, in December, 1840, to Robert Brookhouse. The brig "Richmond," William B. Bates, master, in January, 1842, to Ephraim Emmerton. The brig "Malaga," S. Varney, master, in October, 1844, to E. G. Kimball. The brig "Herald," P. Ayres, master, in February, 1845, to William Hunt. The brig "Hamilton," H. Tufts, master, in March, 1847, to Edward D. Kimball. The brig "Fawn," J. Rider, master, in June, 1847, to George West. The brig "Tam O'Shanter," J. R. Francks, master, in February, 1848, to Benjamin Webb. The brig "Ohio," Josiah Webber, master, in April, 1848, to Edward D. Kimball. After 1848, the trade was largely in the hands of Robert Brookhouse, Edward D. Kimball, and Charles Hoffman. The last arrival at Salem from the West Coast of Africa was the brig "Ann Elizabeth," from Sierra Leone, which was entered by Charles Hoffman, in July, 1873. Salem merchants are still engaged in this trade, but their vessels do not enter the harbor of Salem.

West India Trade. — The early trade of Salem was mainly in the product of her fisheries. The first settlers came hither for the purpose of establishing a fishing and trading post, and among their first acts was the building of stages, on which fish could be dried and prepared for consumption. The islands of the West Indies, offered a market for the exchange of the fish for other products, such as sugar, cotton, and tobacco, and it was natural that a trade between Salem and those islands should commence at a very early period. The island of Barbadoes, one of the Caribbean group, was one of the earliest places at which Salem vessels traded. Salem was trading with Barbadoes as early as 1647. William Hollingworth, then a merchant in Barbadoes, writes to his mother, Mrs. Eleanor Hollingworth, at Salem, under date of Sept. 19, 1687, that "fish now att present bares a good rate by reason ye Newfoundland men are not yet come in but I believe itt will be low anuffe about three months hence. Oyle will be ye principal commodity. Pray lett my brother see this letter I cannot tell what to advise him to send as yett besides oyle but in a short time wee shall see what these Newfoundland men will doe, what quantity of fish they bring in, and then I will advise him further."

The ketch "Providence," John Grafton, master, on her passage from Salem to the West Indies, in September, 1669, was cast away on a rock, in a rainy night, and six of the crew were drowned. The master, mate, and a seaman remained on the rock till morning. They then succeeded, with difficulty, in reaching an island about half a mile away, where they found another of their company. There they remained eight days, sustained by salt fish ; and the last four days by cakes made from a barrel of flour which had been washed ashore. After four days they found a piece of touch-wood and a flint, and with the aid of a small knife, they struck fire. They framed a boat, with a tarred mainsail and some hoops, and then fastened pieces of boards to them. With a boat so made, they sailed ten leagues, to Anguilla and St. Martin's, where they were kindly received. Joshua Ward was one of these sufferers.

The dangers to which these early navigators were exposed we can hardly realize. With no correct charts, and with the rudest instruments, they had no method of fixing their exact location while at sea. The dangers of approaching coasts were also vastly greater, owing to the want of light-houses. Boston light-house was first lit up in 1716; Thatcher's Island light-house, in 1771; and Baker's Island light-house in 1798. It is related that in 1788, a schooner from Bilboa, bound for Marblehead, was only saved from shipwreck by a seaman first seeing the rock in our harbor, called "Satan," close to the bows (there was a snow-storm at the time), and shouting the fact to the crew; the captain being then for the first time aware of his true longitude on the coast.

Salem was trading with the Barbadoes for cotton in 1685, for in September of that year, as the small-pox raged there, the selectmen order "that all cotton-wool imported thence shall be landed on Baker's Island." In 1686, the governor issues a pass to the pink "Speedwell," Thomas Beadle, master, to go to Barbadoes; to the ketch "Hannah," John Ingersoll, master, for Fayal and Barbadoes; to the ketch "Industry," Lewis Hunt, master, for St. Christopher's; and to the ketch "Penelope," Edward Hilliard, master, also for St. Christopher's. In 1688, a similar pass is issued to the ketch "Diligence," Gamaliel Hawkins, master, and the ketch "Virgin," John Allin, master, both bound for Antigua; and in 1689, to the pink "Dove," Zebulon Hill, master, and the ketch "Jas. Bonaventure," Philip Prance, master, both bound for Barbadoes. In 1688, Philip English is trading with St. Christopher's.

The records of our early commerce are vague and fragmentary, but enough is known to indicate that the Salem trade with the West Indies was continued, in a greater or less degree, from the year 1638, when the ship "Desire" made a voyage to New Providence and Tortuga, and returned laden with cotton, tobacco, salt, and negroes (slaves), the latter the first imported into New England, to a very late period in her commercial history. In 1639, the first importation of indigo and sugar seems to have been made, and in 1642 eleven vessels sailed from New England for the West Indies with lumber. The custom-house records prior to the Revolution have disappeared. Tradition tells us that they were carried to Halifax at the breaking out of the war. They have never since been found, and we must content our-selves with such information as can be gleaned from other sources.

In 1736, Richard Derby, the father of Elias Hasket Derby, was trading at the West Indies. He continued to prosecute the trade until 1751, when he relinquished it to his sons. The law imposing a tax on sugar and molasses created great dissatisfaction among the Salem

24

merchants, and there were many forfeitures in consequence. It was upon a petition of James Cockle, Collector at Salem, for a warrant to search for smuggled molasses, heard at the old State House in Boston, February, 1761, that James Otis made his immortal plea against writs of assistance.

While the trade between Salem and the West Indies was probably continuous from 1638 down to quite recent times, the last entry from Havana being in 1854, the period of the greatest activity was from 1798 to 1812. The entries from Havana and Martinico were four each in the year 1797, while in 1798 there were 21 from Havana, and 13 from Martinico. The largest number of arrivals from Havana in a single year was in 1800, when there were 41 entries from that port. During that year there was imported into Salem over eight million pounds of sugar. In 1805, there were 28 entries from Havana, and 44 from Martinico. Between 1798 and 1812 there were 332 entries from Havana, and 232 from Martinico. There was a large trade in the latter part of the last century between Salem and Aux Cayes, Port au Prince, and the other ports of the island of St. Domingo, and with the island of St. Eustatia. But while Salem vessels were found in almost every port in the West Indies, Havana and Martinico were the principal places with which trade was carried on.

A list of the merchants engaged in this trade would include the names of almost every one interested in commerce during the years that the West India trade flourished. Benjamin Pickman was engaged extensively in this trade, and amassed a large fortune in it. In recognition of the service rendered him by the codfish, which was the principal article of export to the West Indies, Mr. Pickman had a carved and gilded effigy of that fish placed on the side of each stair in the principal hall of his house, which he built in 1750 and which still stands on Essex Street, next the East India Marine Building. The front of this house is now hidden by a block of stores.

It is not possible, in the space allotted to this chapter, to give any extended list of the vessels entering from the West Indies. In the palmy days of this trade Salem was a point of distribution for large quantities of sugar and coffee, and the buyers from all parts of the country must have given a bustling and busy aspect to streets now quiet and almost deserted. It was a custom in those days to make up the cargo of a large vessel by inducing various persons to send adventures, the owner of the vessel getting a commission for buying and selling. The brig "Massafuero," Andrew Haraden, master, entered from Havana in September, 1805, with 150,000 pounds of sugar consigned to Joshua Ward, Jr., 9,000 to Timothy Wellman, 6,000 to Eben Seccomb, 62,000 to S. B. Doane, 2,000 to William Monroe, 20,000 to Robert Hooper & Sons, 4,000 to John Jenks, 65,000 to William Gray, 4,000 to Benjamin H. Hathorne, 5,000 to Joshua Pope, 3,000 to Joshua Phippen, Jr., and with a small quantity of merchandise consigned to Benjamin West. Among other entries from Havana, we find the ship "Mount Vernon," Elias H. Derby, Jr., master, which entered in May, 1799, with 500,000 pounds of sugar, consigned to Elias Hasket Derby, and paying a duty of $12,-842.15 and the ship "Martha," Nicholas Thorndike, master, which entered in December, 1799, with 400,000 pounds of sugar; the two vessels landing nearly a million pounds of that commodity. In October, 1809, the schooner "Neutrality," Benjamin Fabens, master, entered from St. Bartholomew's, with sugar and coffee consigned to William Fabens. The Fabens family for several generations have been engaged in trade with the West Indies and Cayenne. The last vessel to enter at Salem from Havana was the brig "Vincennes," on June 29, 1854, consigned to Phillips, Goodhue & Bowker.

Russia Trade.— Salem vessels opened the American trade with St. Petersburg. On the 15th of June, 1784, the bark "Light Horse," Capt. Buffinton, was sent by Elias Hasket Derby with a cargo of sugar, and she was the first American vessel to trade at St. Petersburg.

Salem merchants, in the palmy days of her commerce, were largely engaged in trade with Russia. There have been about 289 arrivals from the ports of Russia at Salem. The period of the greatest activity in this trade was from 1797 to 1811 inclusive, 162 of the 289 entries having been made during that time. The largest number of entries in a single year was in 1811, when there were 31 entries. The war caused a suspension of the trade, and in 1812 there were but three entries, and none in 1813 and 1814. In 1815 there were nine entries, and the trade continued till 1829, when it ceased almost entirely, there having been but about six entries after that year. The last vessel to enter from St. Petersburg was the ship "Eclipse," Johnson, master, to H. L. Williams, in September, 1843. All the

East India merchants carried on more or less trade with Russia, and brought from there duck, hemp and iron, with which to make up their cargoes for the East. Elias Hasket ·Derby, William Gray, Joseph Peabody, Nathaniel West, William Orne, Nathaniel Silsbee, Gideon Barstow, Thomas Perkins, Peirce & Wait, Stephen Phillips, Stephen White, Pickering Dodge, Simon Forrester, William Silsbee, Joseph White, Dudley L. Pickman, John H. Andrews, James Devereux and Samuel Orne were among the Salem merchants engaged in this trade. A few of the earlier entries are given, showing the different ports from which the vessels arrived.

The brig " Ceres," Thomas Simmons, master, entered from Russia, in October, 1789, with 1,546 pieces of sail-cloth and sheeting, 180 bundles of hemp, 948 bars of iron, and 359 cwt. cordage. The brig " Iris," Benjamin Ives, master, entered from St. Petersburg, in October, 1790. The brig " Hind," John Bickford, master, cleared for the Baltic, June 17, 1790, with 600 barrels of tar, 10 barrels of turpentine, 4 hhds. tobacco, 27 casks of rice, 21 hhds. N. E. rum and 73 chests Hyson tea, and entered from St. Petersburg, on her return, in November, 1790. The ship " Commerce," John Osgood, master, entered from St. Petersburg in December, 1790, again in November, 1791, and again in September, 1792. All these vessels were owned by William Gray. The brig " Good Intent," M. Haskell, master, entered from Russia in December, 1791, again in November, 1792, and again in November, 1793, consigned to Simon Forrester. The brig " Polly & Betsey," Gamaliel Hodges, master, entered from ·St. Petersburg in November, 1794, consigned to Joseph White. The bark " Essex," John Green, master, entered from Russia in January, 1795, and again in October, 1795, consigned to William Orne. The bark " Vigilant," Richard Wheatland, master, entered from Russia in October, 1795, consigned to Simon Forrester. The brig " Hopewell," James Dowling, master, entered from St. Petersburg in September, 1797, consigned to Nathaniel West. The bark " William," Benjamin Beckford, Jr., master, entered from St. Petersburg in January, 1798, and again in August, 1798, consigned to William Gray. The brig " Neptune," Robert Barr, master, entered from Russia in October, 1798, consigned to John Barr.

The first entry from Archangel appears to be that of the ship " Perseverance," Richard Wheatland, master, in October, 1798. She proceeded to Boston with her cargo. The brig "Fanny," Jesse Smith, master, entered from Archangel in November, 1798, with hemp, cordage, candles and soap, consigned to John Derby, Jr. The ship "Cincinnatus," Samuel Endicott, master, entered from St. Petersburg in November, 1799, consigned to Joseph Peabody. The brig "Good Hope," Nicholas Thorndike, master, entered from St. Petersburg in October, 1801, consigned to Nathaniel West. The ship "Mount Vernon," Samuel Endicott, master, entered from St. Petersburg in September, 1804, consigned to Joseph Peabody. The brig "Admittance," C. Sampson, master, entered from St. Petersburg in September, 1805, consigned to John Osgood. The brig "Augusta," Timothy Haraden, master, entered from Archangel in September, 1810, consigned to Joseph Peabody. The ship "Friendship," Edward Stanley, master, entered from this same port in September, 1811, consigned to Jerathmael Peirce. The ship "America," Samuel Briggs, master, entered from Riga in April, 1812, consigned to Benjamin W. Crowninshield. The ship "Herald,"[*] Eleazer Graves, master, entered from Archangel in August, 1815, consigned to Nathaniel Silsbee. The brig "Saucy Jack," Nathaniel Osgood, master, entered from Archangel in November, 1815, consigned to Pickering Dodge.

Among the later arrivals was the brig "Niagara," Oliver Thayer, master, which entered from Cronstadt in September, 1828, consigned to Joseph Peabody.

The two last arrivals from Archangel appear to have been the ship "Diomede," Samuel L. Page, master, which entered from that port in October, 1820, and the schooner "Regulus," George Chin, master, which entered in November, 1820, consigned to Edward Lander and others. The last arrival from Cronstadt was the brig "Mexican," H. Johnson, master, which entered in August, 1836, consigned to Joseph Peabody. There was no other arrival from Russia until September, 1843, when the ship "Eclipse," Johnson, master, entered from St. Petersburg, the last vessel to arrive at Salem from that port.

Trade with Spain and Portugal. — Among the earliest ports to which Salem sent the product of her fisheries for a market, were those of Spain and Portugal. This trade began before the year 1700, in which year Higginson speaks of the foreign trade of Salem as being in "dry merchantable codfish for the markets of Spain and Portugal." Bilboa and Lisbon were among the ports earliest visited. In 1710, the ship "Macklesfield," a frigate of 300 tons, belonging to London, and from Lisbon, was cast away outside of Baker's Island and lost. In February, 1715, the ship "Hopewell," loaded with fish for Bilboa, and anchored in the harbor, was driven ashore on the rocks in South Field. Most of her cargo was unloaded before she was got off. Bilboa and Lisbon are mentioned as ports with which Salem vessels traded from 1714 to 1718. Philip English was trading at Spanish ports from 1694 to 1720; and Richard Derby from 1732 to 1757. The last entry from Bilboa was in 1809. The years 1803 and 1807 show each eight entries from Lisbon. From 1800 to 1808 the trade with Spain and Portugal was at its height. Bilboa, Cadiz, Barcelona, Malaga, Tarragona, Alicant, Lisbon, and Oporto were among the ports from which Salem vessels brought cargoes. After the war of 1812 there were but few entries from either of those ports, saving that of an occasional cargo of salt from Cadiz.

The ship "Astrea," Henry Prince, master, entered from Alicant in April, 1799, with 58,003 gallons of brandy and 4,446 gallons of wine, consigned to Elias H. Derby, and paying a duty of $20,930.59. The brig "Favorite," Henry Rust, Jr., master, entered from Bilboa in December, 1800, consigned to Peter Lander & Co. The schooner " Willard," from Alicant, in July 1800, with red wine and brandy to Willard Peele & Co. The brig "Essex," Joseph Orne, master, from Barcelona, in July, 1800, with red wine and soap to William Orne. The brig "Nancy," Thomas Barker, master, from Tarragona, in October, 1801, with brandy to Samuel Gray. The brig "Minerva," Archelaus Rea, master, from Alicant, in May, 1802, with brandy and salt to William Gray. The snow "Concord," William Leech, Jr., master, from Oporto, in September, 1802, with port wine, &c., to William Gray. The brig "Hannah," Clifford C. Byrne, master, from Malaga, in November, 1802, with wine, &c., to Joseph White. The ship "Restitution," John Derby, 3d, master, from Lisbon, in April, 1805, with wine, figs, and salt to Simon Forrester. The bark "Active," William P. Richardson, master, from Malaga, in June, 1807, with 23,746 gallons of Malaga wine to Timothy Wellman, Jr. The brig "Washington," Nathan Story, master, from Barcelona, in July, 1807, with red wine, brandy, and soap consigned to Stephen Phillips. The brig "Sukey and Betsey," Caleb Cook, master, from Malaga, in November, 1807, with wine and raisins to Edward Allen.

The ship "Sally," Nathan Cook, master, from Lisbon, in September, 1824, with salt, &c., to James Cook. The last entry from Lisbon was in 1829. The principal articles imported from Spain and Portugal were salt, wine, brandy, and soap.

Trade with other European Ports. — Prior to the war of 1812 Salem vessels were to be found in all the principal ports of Europe, and Salem merchants were trading with Copenhagen, Gottenburg, Stockholm, Amsterdam, Antwerp, Hamburg, Rotterdam, London, Liverpool, and Bordeaux. The principal trade with Copenhagen was between 1796 and 1807; there were 8 entries in 1799; with Gottenburg, from 1809 to 1812, and from 1820 to 1823, there being 13 entries from that port in 1810; with Antwerp, from 1817 to 1830, there being 9 entries from that port in 1827; with Hamburg, from 1798 to 1802, there being 5 entries in the last-named year; with Amsterdam, from 1802 to 1806, there being 5 entries in the first-named year; and with Bordeaux, from 1794 to 1807, there being 12 entries in 1804 and the same number in 1805, the whole period showing 69 entries. There were only occasional entries from the other ports. The last entry from Copenhagen was in 1816; from Amsterdam, in 1823; from Antwerp, in 1836; from Hamburg, in 1828; from Gottenburg, in 1837; from Rotterdam, in 1834; and from Bordeaux, in 1815.

From Copenhagen the brig "Francis," J. Wallace, master, entered in March, 1792, and again in November, 1792, with iron and glass consigned to William Gray. The early trade with Copenhagen seems to have been carried on largely by Mr. Gray. John Fisk, Ezekiel H. Derby, Joseph Peabody, Thomas Perkins, and George Crowninshield & Sons were also engaged in this trade. The whole number of entries from Copenhagen was 45. The last entry was the schooner "Rover," Josiah Dewing, master, in August, 1816, consigned to Pickering Dodge.

From Gottenburg, the schooner "Nancy," Richard Derby, master, entered in August, 1791, with iron consigned to E. H. Derby, Jr., & Co., and John Fisk. The ship "Nancy," J. Devereux, master, entered in August, 1792, consigned to John Fisk. From 1794 to 1804 there were no entries from this port. The ship "Rising States," Benjamin Beckford, Jr., master, entered in February, 1804, with hemp to William Gray. The schooner "Saucy Jack," Benjamin

Upton, master, in September, 1809, with glass to Timothy Wellman, Jr. The brig "Neptune," Henry King, master, in December, 1810, with cordage, steel, and sheet-iron to John Saunders. The ship "China," Hiram Putnam, master, in October, 1820, with iron to Joseph Peabody. The brig "Jane," Thomas Saul, master, in July, 1820, with iron to Willard Peele. The brig "Roscoe," J. Briggs, master; in October, 1825, with iron to Charles Saunders. The brig "Cynthia," Benjamin Shillaber, master, in October, 1826, to David Pingree. The ship "Borneo," I. Nichols, master, in September, 1835, with iron consigned to Z. F. Silsbee. The brig "Leander," J. S. Kimball, master, in August, 1836, to Joseph Peabody. The whole number of entries from Gottenburg was 61. The last entry was the brig "Mexican," in July, 1837, consigned to Joseph Peabody.

From Antwerp, the ship "Messenger," Edward Stanley, master, entered in June, 1817, consigned to John Forrester. The brig "Nancy Ann," John B. Osgood, master, in August, 1817, to Stephen Phillips. The brig "Naiad," Nathaniel Osgood, master, in July, 1823, to Gideon Barstow and others. The brig "Indus," Thomas Moriarty, master, in April, 1826, to Pickering Dodge. The brig "Centurion," William Duncan, master, in May, 1826, with linseed oil to Nathaniel West, Jr. The ship "Friendship," Nathaniel Osgood, master, in May, 1827. The brig "Niagara," Oliver Thayer, master, in August, 1829, to Joseph Peabody. The whole number of entries from Antwerp was 55. The last entry was the brig "Curlew," J. Cheever, master, in October, 1836, consigned to Edward Allen.

From Amsterdam, the brig "Peggy," Jonathan Derby, master, entered in September, 1794, with glassware, paint, iron, steel, and ribbons, consigned to Benjamin Pickman, Jr. The ship "Essex," Solomon Stanwood, master, in September, 1800, with 42,871 pounds of cheese, 5,000 pounds of nails, and 8,000 gallons of gin to Nathaniel West and William Gray. The ship "Minerva," Matthew Folger, master, in September, 1802, with gin, steel, and cheese to West, Williams & Crowninshield. The whole number of entries from Amsterdam was 23. The last entry was the ship "Endeavour," James D. Gillis, master, in October, 1823.

From Hamburg, the schooner "John," Benjamin Webb, master, entered in December, 1792, with steel, glass, and spirits, consigned to John Fisk. The schooner "Patty," Edward Allen, Jr., master, in October, 1794, with gin, brandy, hemp, and bohea tea to Nathaniel West. The brig "Hope," Benjamin Shillaber, master, in October, 1794, to John Norris. The brig "Salem," Oliver Obear, master, in June, 1799, with gin and hemp to William Gray. The ship "Friendship," Israel Williams, master, in July, 1799, to Peirce & Wait. The brig "Thetis," John Fairfield, master, in November, 1799, to Jonathan Gardner. The schooner "Cynthia," John H. Andrews, master, in November, 1801, to Pickering Dodge and others. The brig "Helen," Samuel C. Martin, master, in December, 1816, with iron to Humphrey Devereux. The brig "Roscoe," Benjamin Vanderford, master, in September, 1823. The whole number of entries from Hamburg was 36. The last entry was the brig "Texel," Samuel Wells, master, in January, 1828.

From Rotterdam, the ship "Peggy," James Very, master, entered in August, 1791. The ship "Active," George Nichols, master, in August, 1803, with gin to Benjamin Hodges & Co. The bark "Georgetown," Joshua Safford, master, in September, 1806, to Pickering Dodge. The brig "Indus," John Day, master, in November, 1823, with white lead, nutmegs, and mace to Henry Prince. The whole number of entries from Rotterdam was 16. The last entry was the ship "Borneo," C. Prescott, master, in May, 1834.

From Bordeaux, the brig "Essex," John Green, master, entered in November, 1790, consigned to Orne & Saunders. The brig "Columbia," Henry Rust, master, in April, 1792, to William Gray. The brig "Nancy," Edward West, master, in July, 1794, with wine and sweetmeats to John Derby, Jr. The brig "Favorite," Peter Lander, master, in October, 1795, to John Norris & Co. The schooner "Betsey," Israel Williams, master, in November, 1796, with brandy, wine, and cheese, to Peirce & Wait. The brig "Exchange," William Richardson, master, in May, 1797, with claret wine and brandy to Ezekiel H. Derby. The schooner "Jason," Benjamin West, Jr., master, in June, 1797, to Benjamin West & Son. The brig "Nancy," Jonathan Neal, master, in August, 1797, to William Gray. The brig "Catherine," Daniel Gould, master, in May, 1803, to Joseph Peabody. The brig "Pompey," James Gilchrist, master, in March, 1804, with wine and 21,772 gallons of brandy to Joshua Ward. The ship "Prudent," Edward Ford, master, in July, 1804, to Nathaniel West. The brig "Edwin," Penn Townsend, master, in October, 1804, with wine and prunes to

Moses Townsend. The brig "Industry," J. Cook, master, in February, 1805, to William Orne. The ship "Algol," Thomas Folinsbie, master, in October, 1807, with wine to Nathan Robinson. The whole number of entries from Bordeaux was 75. The last entry was the schooner "Cyrus," Benjamin Upton, master, in November, 1815, with brandy, yellow ochre, and prunes to Robert Upton.

From Stockholm the ship "China," H. Putnam, master, entered in August, 1823, consigned to Joseph Peabody. The brig "Centurion," Samuel Hutchinson, master, in October, 1829, with iron, consigned to Gideon Tucker.

From Christiania, the brig "Industry," Samuel Smith, master, in March, 1812, with iron hoops and window-glass to William Orne. The brig "Cuba," Josiah B. Andrew, master, in November, 1816, with iron, steel and glass, to John Andrew.

On the 7th of January, 1796, the ship "Margaret," of Boston, John Mackay, master, with a valuable cargo from Amsterdam, went ashore in Salem harbor on the eastern Gooseberry, during a snow-storm. The captain and three others perished on the wreck. The rest were saved by men from Marblehead. On the 11th of the same month, the brig "John," Ebenezer B. Ward, master, from London, was lost on the Great Misery, during a snow-storm. There was, at this time, no light on Baker's Island, and these shipwrecks led the Salem Marine Society to send a memorial to Congress, dated in February, 1796, in which it is stated that "much of the property, and many of the lives of their fellow-citizens are almost every year lost in coming into the harbor of Salem, for want of proper lights to direct their course. No less than three vessels, with their cargoes and sixteen seamen have been lost the present season." The Act authorizing the erection of a light-house on Baker's Island, was approved April 8, 1796, and the lights were shown for the first time January 3, 1798.

Mediterranean Trade.—Besides the Spanish ports on the Mediterranean, Salem vessels visited Marseilles, Genoa, Naples, Leghorn, Messina, Palermo, Smyrna and Trieste. Salt, wine, brandy, figs, raisins, almonds, candles and soap were among the articles imported from those ports. Leghorn and Marseilles were the ports most frequently visited. From 1804 to 1808 there were 46 entries from the former and 20 from the latter port. From 1821 to 1829 there were

41 entries from Leghorn and 17 from Marseilles. The last entry from Leghorn was in 1841, and from Marseilles, in 1833. The principal trade with the Mediterranean ports was from 1800 to 1808.

From Leghorn, the ship "Martha," John Prince, Jr., master, entered in July, 1799, with 40,893 gallons of wine, 18,490 gallons of brandy, and 6,744 pounds of soap, consigned to Elias H. Derby, and paying a duty of $12,840.12. The ship "Lucia," Thomas Meek, master, in July, 1800, with brandy, soap, &c., to William Gray, and paying a duty of $20,301. The brig "Sukey," Samuel Sweet, master, in August, 1800, to Simon Forrester. The ship "Friendship," Israel Williams, master, in September, 1805, to Peirce & Wait. The brig "Betsey," Andrew Tucker, master, in June, 1806, with soap, tallow, figs, currants, raisins, almonds and candles, to Joseph Peabody and Gideon Tucker. The ship "America," Joseph Ropes, master, in June, 1807, to Nathaniel Silsbee. The ship "Hope," James Barr, master, in November, 1807. The brig "William and Charles," Isaac Killam, master, in November, 1807, with soap, candles, currants and wine, to Michael Shepard. There were no entries from Leghorn from 1808 to 1816. The ship "Sophia," Jonathan P. Felt, master, entered in April, 1816, consigned to Charles H. Orne. The ship "Eliza," William Osgood, master, in January, 1821, to Stephen Phillips. The brig "Essex," William Fairfield, master, in January, 1822, with candles, soap, raisins, &c., to Nathaniel Silsbee. The ship "Two Brothers," William Messervy, master, in February, 1823, to Holten J. Breed. The brig "Gov. Endicott," H. C. Mackay, master, in October, 1823, to Pickering Dodge. The brig "Malay," J. Richardson, master, in May, 1825, with lead and currants to Nathaniel Silsbee. The bark "Patriot," John Marshall, master, in August, 1826, to John H. Andrew. The ship "Janus," Henry G. Bridges, master, in August, 1829, with salt, wine, and letter paper, to Gideon Tucker. The brig "Amazon," Oliver Thayer, master, in March, 1832, with salt, &c., to Joseph Peabody. The last vessel to arrive from Leghorn was the brig "Mexican," H. Johnson, master. She entered in September, 1839, in March, 1840, and in September, 1841, consigned on each voyage to Joseph Peabody. The whole number of entries from Leghorn was one hundred and thirteen.

From Marseilles, the schooner "Union," Stephen Field, master, entered in October, 1802, consigned to Edward Allen. The ship

"Ulysses," William Mugford, master, in August, 1804, with prunes, almonds, 18,199 pounds of soap, 48,233 gallons of wine, and 1,571 gallons of brandy, consigned to William Gray. The ship "Endeavour," James Buffinton, master, in July, 1805, with 44,902 gallons of claret wine, &c., to Simon Forrester. The brig "Industry," Jonathan Cook, master, in March, 1806, to William Orne. The brig "Sukey," Samuel B. Graves, master, in November, 1807, to Nathan Pierce. The schooner "Agawam," Francis Boardman, master, in June, 1816, to John Dodge. The ship "Perseverance," James Silver, master, in October, 1816, with salt, brandy and claret wine, to Willard Peele and William Fettyplace. The brig "Cygnet," Samuel Kennedy, master, in July, 1823, with wine, to Stephen White, The brig "Java," William H. Neal, master, in September, 1823, with 35,295 gallous of red wine, 1,045 gallons of oil, and 9,708 pounds of soap, to Jonathau Neal. The ship "Endeavour," J. Kinsman, master, in December, 1827, to Dudley L. Pickman. The ship "Messenger," James Buffinton, master, in January, 1828, to John Forrester. The ship "Bengal," J. Richardson, master, in August, 1830, to Pickering Dodge. The whole number of entries from Marseilles was fifty-three. The last entry was the brig "Roque," T. Seaver, master, in February, 1833, with salt, &c., to Joseph Peabody.

From Naples, the ketch "John," Stephen Phillips, master, entered in March, 1799, with 25,000 gallons of brandy and 46,417 pounds of soap, consigned to Elias H. Derby, and paying a duty of $11,299. The brig "Cruger," John Barton, master, in July, 1800, with soap and wine, to John & Richard Derby. The ship "John," Daniel Bray, master, in May, 1804, with 32,437 gallons of wine, to Benjamin Pickman, Jr. The brig "Belleisle," Samuel Leech, master, in August, 1805, to Pickering Dodge and Nathan Robinson. The ship "Hercules," Edward West, master, was seized in Naples in 1809, but Capt. West had the good fortune to obtain her release in order to transport Lucien Bonaparte and family to Malta, thus saving his ship from confiscation. The "Hercules" was owned by Nathaniel West. The schooner "Joanna," Jonathan Hassam, master, entered in January, 1810, with brandy, &c., to Samuel Gray. The last entry from Naples was the ship "Francis," William Haskell, master, in August, 1810. This vessel was purchased of the Neapolitan government by the American consul, to bring home the crews of American vessels confiscated by order of that government. She brought 214 persons, a large number of whom belonged in Salem. The Salem vessels and cargoes condemned at Naples were valued at $783,000.

The ship "Margaret," of Salem, William Fairfield, master, left Naples April 10, 1810, with a crew fifteen in number, and thirty-one passengers. On Sunday, May 20, a squall struck the ship, and she was thrown on her beam-ends. As every person on board was on deck at the time, they all reached either the bottom or side of the ship, the waves at the time making a continual breach over her. Monday morning the sea was tolerably smooth, and one of the boats having been repaired, Capt. Fairfield and fourteen men left the ship in her, and were picked up on Saturday, May 26, by the brig "Poacher," of Boston. The sufferings of those left on the wreck can hardly be imagined. After the long-boat had departed, they raised a signal of distress. On the 28th, a gale swept away the stage they had erected, and the provisions they had gathered, except a small quantity of wine and salt meat. On the 30th, they made another stage over the fore-castle, and so kept themselves out of the water. June 3d, one of the number died of fatigue and famine. For seven days they had nothing to drink each day but an allowance of three gallons of wine for all, and a glass of vinegar for each man. Many could not resist the temptation to quench their thirst from a pipe of brandy which had been saved from the cargo. On the 5th, twelve of their number, overcome by their hardships and privations, died; and another on the next day. By the 6th, the whole of the upper deck had gone, and no food was left but beef and pork, which could not be eaten, because there was no fresh water. Since the time of the disaster, May 20, four vessels had passed in sight of the sufferers on the wreck, and added the pangs of disappointed hope to their other trials.

On the 7th, five of the number left the wreck in a small yawl. These were John C. Very, E. A. Irvin, and Jeptha Layth, of Salem; Henry Larcom, of Beverly; and John Treadwell, of Ipswich. They left about ten survivors on the wreck, and from these no tidings ever came. Who can imagine their agony, as hope gradually faded out, and they died one by one in mid-ocean. The escape of those in the small boat is a remarkable instance of human endurance amid sufferings and hardships almost incredible. For sixteen days after leaving the wreck they had nothing to sustain them but brandy, a gill in twenty-four hours; and to quench their thirst were obliged to resort to most revolting means. On the night of June 22d there was a fall of rain, and water was caught in handkerchiefs sufficient to partially allay their thirst. June 23d, Treadwell, worn out with fatigue, hunger, and thirst, died without a struggle. The same day they caught some rudder fish, which was the first food they had eaten since they left the wreck. On the 28th, Layth died, leaving three survivors in the boat. The next day, with a heavy sea running, they lost their oars and mast, and having nothing to steer by they gave themselves up for lost. They had already been passed by three vessels, when on the 30th they saw another in the distance, and strained every nerve to get in her track. In this they were successful, and Capt. Stephen L. Davis, of Gloucester, the master of the vessel, received them and treated them with great care and kindness. Tossed about in a small and shattered boat for twenty-three days, with scarcely any food or water to sustain them, exposed to storms and gales in which it seemed hardly possible that such a craft could keep afloat, their escape from such extraordinary perils and privations is hardly paralleled in the history of marine disasters.

From Messina, the ship "Prudent," Benjamin Crowninshield, master, entered in December 1803, with 11,406 gallons of red wine, 6,413 gallons of white wine, 4,303 gallons of brandy, and 9,810 pounds of soap, consigned to Nathaniel West. The ship "Two Brothers," John Holman, master, in October, 1804, to Israel Williams. The brig "Louisa," Richard Ward, Jr., master, in August, 1810, to James Cook. The brig "Harriot," Samuel Becket, master, in October, 1811, with soap, raisins, almonds and wine, to Nathaniel Silsbee. The brig "Eliza and Mary," Thorndike Procter, master, in August, 1818, to Stephen White. The last entry was the brig "Centurion," Samuel Hutchinson, master, in June, 1831, with currants, oil, &c., to Gideon Tucker.

From Smyrna, the brig "Independence," Nathaniel L. Rogers, master, entered in April, 1810, to Dudley L. Pickman. The brig "Reward," James Hayes, Jr., master, in July, 1810, with almonds, raisins and figs, consigned to Charles H. Orne and Dudley L. Pickman. The brig "Resolution," Samuel Rea, master, in April, 1812, to Joseph Peabody. The brig "Hope," John Beckford, master, in December, 1829, with 125,000 pounds of figs, to Daniel Abbot and

Robert Stone. The last entry was the brig "Leander," James Silver, master, in January, 1831, with salt, figs, raisins and wool, to Joseph Peabody.

From Trieste, the brig "Texel," Charles Hill, master, entered in December, 1825, with olive oil and lead, consigned to John W. Rogers. The bark "Eliza," Samuel Benson, master, in July, 1829, with hemp and glass, to Stephen White.

The brig "Persia," John Thistle, master, from Trieste for Salem, belonging to Silsbee, Stone & Pickman, and having a cargo of rags and sumac, was wrecked in the storm of March 5, 1829, on a rocky shore near Brace's Cove, about a mile and a half below Eastern Point, Gloucester, and all on board perished.

From Genoa, the brig "Nereus," David A. Neal, master, in March, 1822, with raisins, &c., to John W. Rogers. The brig "Rebecca," J. P. Andrews, master, in July, 1831, to John H. Andrew.

Among other entries was that of the brig "Telemachus," Penn Townsend, master, from Constantinople, in May, 1810, with cordage, figs, raisins and currants, to David Burditt.

Nova Scotia Trade. — About the year 1840 the trade between Salem and Nova Scotia, and the other British provinces on the eastern coast of North America, began to be vigorously prosecuted, mainly by English vessels, whose captains often owned both ship and cargo. This trade increased very rapidly. Wood, coal, and plaster were among the principal articles of import. In 1840, there were fifteen entries; in 1845, 107; in 1850, 391; in 1855, 328; in 1860, 215; in 1865, 118; in 1870, 117; in 1875, 59; in 1878, 53. During the thirty·years from 1841 to 1870, inclusive, there were 5,724 entries. The period of the greatest activity was from 1848 to 1857, inclusive, when there were 3,253 entries, or an average of 325 for each year.

California Trade. — A letter giving definite information of the discovery of gold in California, reached Salem in October, 1848. The brig "Mary and Ellen" was then fitting for sea. A cargo suitable for the California trade was at once put on board, by Stephen C. Phillips and others, and the brig, under command of Capt. J. H. Eagleston, was cleared Oct. 27, 1848, for the Sandwich Islands via California. Salem again takes the lead, for this was the first vessel to sail for California from Massachusetts after the gold discovery.

Both vessel and cargo were sold in California. The first vessel that cleared from Massachusetts for San Francisco direct, with an assorted cargo and passengers, was the barque "Eliza," of Salem, loaded by John Bertram and others, and commanded by Capt. A. S. Perkins. She left Salem, Dec. 23, 1848, and arrived at San Francisco, June 1, 1849. Alfred Peabody, of Salem, was among the passengers, and upon his arrival he found that Capt. Eagleston had already sold the "Mary and Ellen," and her cargo. John Beadle, Jr., Dennis Rideout, George P. Buffum, George W. Kenney, and Jonathan Nichols, all of Salem, were passengers with Mr. Peabody.

The bark "Lagrange," Joseph Dewing, master, sailed from Salem for San Francisco March 17, 1849, taking as passengers the "Salem and California Trading Company," among whom were Joseph Dewing, Anthony Francis, Nicholas Bovey, J. K. Vincent, P. Gilman, John H. Pitman, H. B. Bogardus, H. A. Tuttle, C. R. Story, A. Robbins, John McCloy, George Harris, C. C. Teele, Joseph L. Bartlett, William P. Leavitt, Thomas B. Flowers, Eben Chapman, Charles E. Brown, William H. Sibley, O. A. Gordon, John H. Dakin, Daniel Couch, D. A. Nichols, Moses Prime, Edward Fuller, William Brown, B. F. Symonds, William Sinclair, and James Stewart, of the Trading Company, and Nathaniel Osgood, and Richard H. Austin, all of Salem. On board the same vessel were twelve passengers from Danvers, four from Lynn, two each from Manchester and Beverly, four from Gloucester, and about ten from other places.

The ship "Elizabeth," J. S. Kimball, master, was cleared for San Francisco April 3, 1849, by W. P. Phillips. Brackley R. Peabody and Robert M. Copeland, of Salem, went as passengers. The bark "Ann Parry," William M. Harron, master, was cleared June 20, 1849, for San Francisco, by Benjamin Webb. James C. Briggs and William H. Clark, of Salem, passengers. The ship "Talma," William B. Davis, master, cleared Sept. 11, 1849, and the bark "Backus," A. D. Caulfield, Jr., master, cleared Nov. 28, 1849, for San Francisco. In the "Backus," Joseph Allen, Charles R. Julyn, Thomas W. Taylor, William Stafford and William H. Brown, went as passengers.

The ship "Crescent," John Madison, master, cleared for Benecia, California, Dec. 3, 1849. She had been purchased by the Salem Mechanics' Trading and Mining Association, and was loaded with

130,000 feet of lumber, framed, and made ready for erection into houses; and the framework of a small steamboat. On the 6th of December the "Crescent" left Salem with the following-named members of the association as passengers: Albert Lackey, Thomas J. Gifford, Dean C. Symonds, John Madison, Thomas Dickson, Jr., John H. Newton, Jonathan Davis, Eben Waters, Nathaniel Jenkins, John D. Chapple, Edward A. Wheeler, George S. Nichols, John P. Dickson, Joshua Pope, Gilman Andrews, Israel Herrick, Charles L. Hardy, William Graves, William P. Buffum, Asa A. Whitney, William H. Searles, James Gardner, Payne Morse, Benjamin S. Boardman, Samuel H. Larrabee, and John Nichols, all of Salem, and a number from Lawrence, Fitchburg, Lynn, Newton, in all numbering about sixty-one. She arrived at her destination, May 26, 1850, and was sold, with her cargo, very soon after arrival.

During the gold excitement a large number of Salem residents went to California, sailing from other ports. Stephen C. Phillips and John Bertram were among those engaged in the California trade.

Salem Tonnage. — In 1793, twelve ships were owned in Salem; in 1807, sixty; and in 1833, only twenty-nine. In 1825, there were thirty-two ships, five barks, ninety-five brigs, sixty schooners, and six sloops owned in Salem, measuring 34,224 tons—the ship "Nile," of 400 tons, was the largest; and in 1828, thirty ships, 102 brigs, eight barks, and thirty schooners—the largest being the ship "Arabella," of 404 tons. In 1833, there were 111 Salem vessels engaged in the foreign trade.

For some time after Salem ceased to be a port to which vessels from foreign countries brought their cargoes, Salem merchants continued to own a large amount of tonnage, but they transacted their business mainly in Boston and New York. At the present time (1879), there are scarcely more than a dozen vessels hailing from Salem engaged in the foreign trade. The ships "Sumatra," 1,073 tons, and "Highlander," 1,352 tons, owned by Benjamin W. Stone; the ships "Sooloo," 963 tons, "Mindoro," 1,021 tons, "Formosa," 1,253 tons, and "Panay," 1,190 tons, owned by Silsbee & Pickman; the barks "Glide," 493 tons, and "Taria Topan," 631 tons, owned by John Bertram; the ship "Cultivator," 1,508 tons, owned by Paul Upton and others; the brigs "Mary E. Dana," 219 tons, and "Lizzie J. Bigelow,"

130 tons, and the schooners "Cayenne," 88 tons, and "Charles H. Fabens," 301 tons, owned by C. E. & B. H. Fabens, are all that are left to carry the name of Salem to foreign lands.

Where once vessels were arriving, sometimes two in a single day, from India or other remote ports, but a solitary schooner found her way into Salem harbor from a foreign port, other than those from the British provinces, during the year ending June 30, 1878, and she brought a cargo of coal from England. At the custom-house, where in the *week* ending Sept. 15, 1798, seven Salem vessels, three ships, one bark, and three brigs cleared for Copenhagen, there was cleared during the *year* ending June 30, 1878, one vessel to the West Indies, and one to Liverpool; the single entry and the two clearances being in the month of December. The whole number of foreign entries for that year was seventy-nine, of which eight were American vessels, and the total tonnage was 8,183. The number of foreign clearances was ninety-six, of which nine were American vessels, the total tonnage being 10,090.

Whale Fishery. — After the decline of the foreign commerce of Salem it was hoped that the whale fishery might be successfully prosecuted, and for a short time there was quite a fleet of whalers hailing from this port. Stephen C. Phillips was agent in 1841 for the ships "Elizabeth," 398 tons, and "Sapphire," 365 tons; and the barks "Emerald," 271 tons, "Eliza," 240 tons, "Henry," 262 tons, and "Malay," 268 tons. John B. Osgood was agent in the same year for the ships "Bengal," 300 tons, "Izette," 280 tons, "Jas. Maury," 395 tons, and "Mount Wollaston," 325 tons; and the barks "Reaper," 230 tons, and "Statesman," 258 tons. Nathaniel Weston was agent for the bark "Palestine," 248 tons. The "Malay" was lost July 27, 1842, on Europa Rocks in Mozambique Channel. The "Eliza" was condemned at Tahiti June 15, 1843, and the "Statesman" at Talcahuana, Nov. 3, 1844.

During the year ending April 1, 1837, sperm oil to the value of $124,440, and 108,065 gallons of whale oil, valued at $40,866, were landed at Salem. There were 432 hands employed in this business. During the year ending April 1, 1845, there was landed at Salem 45,705 gallons of sperm oil, valued at $39,306, and 18,345 gallons of whale oil, valued at $5,686; the number of hands employed being 110. The hopes entertained at the outset in regard to the whale fishery were destined never to be realized. Felt says, in 1847, "there are two whalers from Salem. The prospect is that this perilous employment, recommenced in hope as to its increase, continuance and profit, will soon terminate in disappointment." Benjamin Webb had some vessels engaged in this fishery, and John C. Osgood was agent of the last whalers that hailed from the port of Salem. This business was abandoned several years ago and to-day (1879) no whalers are owned in Salem.

Coasting Trade. — While Salem has lost her foreign trade, the harbor of Salem is not entirely barren of vessels; for a large amount of tonnage, larger even than when she was at the height of her commercial prosperity, engaged in the coasting trade, brings coal to Salem for distribution to the mills of Lowell and Lawrence. In 1870, there entered the harbor, 1,812 coasting vessels, having an aggregate tonnage of 213,514; and 1,237 vessels, measuring 203,798 tons, entered during the year ending June 30, 1878. The Salem and New York Steamship Company maintained a line of steam packets between Salem and New York from July, 1871, to June, 1872.

The "Massachusetts," the first steamboat to enter Salem harbor, arrived from New York in July, 1817, and was employed for a short time in making excursions in the bay. She was regarded at the time as a great curiosity and attracted considerable notice from the towns-people.

The Custom-House. — Hand in hand with commerce come the collectors and officers of the customs revenue. Before 1819, and during the palmy days of Salem commerce, there was no government building for the accommodation of such officers. Salem has been established as a port of entry at least since 1658. In 1663, Hilliard Veren was collector; and in 1683, Marblehead, Beverly, Gloucester, Ipswich, Rowley, Newbury, and Salisbury are annexed to the port of Salem by order of the Court of Assistants, and it is decreed that this port and Boston shall be lawful ports in this Colony, where "all ships and other vessels shall lade or unlade, any of the plantations enumerated goods, or other goods from foreign ports, and nowhere else, on penalty of the confiscation of such ship or vessel, with her goods and tackle, as shall lade or unlade elsewhere."

At an early period, commerce seems to have centred about

Creek Street and the locality of the present Eastern Railroad Station. This is the supposed location of the "Port House on the South river" mentioned in an order of the Quarterly Court in 1636. All the "cannowes of the South Syde, are to be brought before the Port House att the same time to be viewed by the Surveiors." These "cannowes" were used for transporting passengers to North and South Salem before the days of bridges, and in them they sometimes went fowling "two leagues to sea." There was another port house on North River, and much business was done in former years on that side of the town.

The Custom-House for thirty-four years was in a building on the corner of Gedney Court, erected in 1645, and known as the French house, having been tenanted by French families. In 1789, it was on the site of the present bank building in Central Street. Maj. Hiller was the collector. In 1805, it was removed, under Col. Lee, to the Central Building on the opposite side of the street, where a carved eagle and shield, lately restored, still mark the spot. In 1807, it was in Essex Street for a time, opposite Plummer Hall; in 1811, it was on the corner of Essex and Newbury streets; and in 1813, in the Central Building again, where Col. Lee resided, and whence, in 1819, it was removed to the government building erected for the purpose at the head of Derby Wharf, where it now remains. This building stands upon land bought of the heirs of George Crowninshield, and was the site of the Crowninshield mansion-house, which was removed to make way for the present structure. It was "intended to accommodate a hoped-for increase in the commercial prosperity of the place— hopes destined never to be realized—and was built a world too large for any necessary purpose, even at the time when India was a new region, and only Salem knew the way thither." This custom-house is a substantial, two-story brick building, with a large warehouse in the rear, the whole surmounted by a cupola, from which the inspectors can watch for incoming vessels. It is now out of all proportion to the business of the port, and the time is not far distant when it will be abandoned for some smaller quarters.

There has been collected in imposts at the port of Salem, since the organization of the Union in 1789, more than twenty-five millions of dollars. From August 15, 1789, to 1791, the amount collected was $108,064.48, and the number of foreign entries was 205.

From 1791 to 1800, inclusive, the duties were $2,949,817.19, and the foreign entries 1,508. From 1801 to 1810, inclusive, the duties were $7,272,633.31, and the foreign entries 1,758. From 1811 to 1820, inclusive, the duties were $3,832,894.81, and the foreign entries 835. From 1821 to 1830, inclusive, the duties were $4,685,139.58, and the foreign entries 1,226. From 1831 to 1840, the duties were $1,987,509.12, and the foreign entries, 903. From 1841 to 1850, the duties were $1,534,558.58, and the foreign entries 2,327. From 1851 to 1860, inclusive, the duties were $1,816,676.42, and the foreign entries 3,693. From 1861 to 1870, inclusive, the duties were $846,741.74, and the foreign entries, 1,420. The large increase in the number of foreign entries since 1841 is due to the large trade then carried on between Salem and Nova Scotia. From 1871 to 1878, inclusive, the duties were about $223,911.96. The duties for the quarter, ending December 31, 1807, when the embargo was officially announced in Salem, were $511,000, which is the largest amount ever collected at Salem in a single quarter. The goods were imported in 22 ships, 3 barks, 19 brigs and 23 schooners. In 1868 there was collected in duties $118,114.37, of which $30,000 was paid in a single month. In 1878 the whole amount collected was only about $11,000, of which only about $3,600 was for direct imports.

Foreign Arrivals. — As an indication of the changes that took place in the foreign trade of Salem it will be interesting to note at periods of ten years the different ports from which vessels arrived.

In 1790, the foreign entries at the custom-house were : from Cadiz 4, St. Martin's 15, St. Eustatia 14, Bristol 2, Cape of Good Hope 2, Aux Cayes 10, St. Lucia 6, Corinna 2, Guadaloupe 9, Cape Francois 11, Isle of May 3, Lisbon 7, Port au Prince 15, Bilboa 4, Canton 4, Cape de Verde 2, Malaga 2, Martinico 5, St. Ubes 2, St. Petersburg 4, and one each from St. Mark's, New Brunswick, Nantes, Gottenburg, Bordeaux, St. Domingo, Gibralter, St. Croix, Turk's Island, Isle of France, Hispaniola, St. Sebastian, Oporto, Ireland, Antigua and Trinidad.

In 1800, the foreign entries were : from Cape Francois 8, Curacoa 3, Port au Paix 2, Hamburg 3, Martinico 13, Havana 41, Cadiz 4, Surinam 2, Trinidad 5, St. Thomas 2, La Guayra 3, Bilboa 7, Corunna 2, Gibralter 3, Lisbon 4, Alicant 5, St. Christopher's 3, St. Lucia 3, Port Republican 4, Barcelona 2, Leghorn 4, Naples 2, St. Petersburg

3, Copenhagen 2, and one each from Honduras, Jamaica, Tobago, Turk's Island, Isle of May, Demerara, Cumana, Calcutta, Port Danphin, L'Archahaye, Nova Scotia, St. Bartholomew's, Port Liberty, Russia, Canton, Liverpool, Parimaribo, St. Ubes, Bombay, Cayenne, Madras, Amsterdam, London, Sumatra, Halifax, Genoa, Malaga, Nassau and Batavia.

In 1810, the foreign entries were : from St. Bart's 10, Tonningen 12, Sumatra 10, Malaga 2, Naples 2, Liverpool 3, St. Domingo 4, Baracoa 2, Cadiz 4, Cayenne 2, Gottenburg 13, La Guayra 2, Havana 26, Canton 2, Smyrna 2, Matanzas 8, Valencia 2, Turk's Island 2, Pernambuco 2, Rio Janeiro 3, Messina, 3, St. Pierre's. 3, Point Petre 3, Martinique 2, Cronstadt 2, Archangel 7, St. Lucia 2, Trinidad 2, Surinam 2, St. Petersburg 3, and one each from Calcutta, Porto Rico, Palermo, Algesiras, Constantinople, Cumana, Kiel, Angostura, Jacquemel, Gustavia, Malta, Gibralter, Exuma, Buenos Ayres, Christiana, Stralsund, St. Ubes, Cape Henry, Guadaloupe, Nevis, Riga, Madras, St. Vincent's and Pillau.

In 1820, the foreign entries were : from Cape Henry 3, Port au Prince 4, Havana 5, Canton 2, St. Pierre's 8, Sumatra 6, Amsterdam 3, Maranham 3, Para 3, Leghorn 4, Calcutta 6, Batavia 7, St. Salvador 3, Surinam 3, St. Jago 2, Matanzas 3, Manila 3, Isle of May 2, Gottenburg 5, West Indies 2, Bermuda 2, St. Andrew's 5, Antwerp 2, St. Petersburg 6, Archangel 2, Cayenne 3, and one each from Samarang, Martinico, Java, St. Thomas, Mocha, South Sea Islands, Jeremie, Liverpool, Malaga, Marseilles, Africa, Cronstadt, St. Lucia, Havre de Grace, Point Petre, St. Michael's, Pernambuco, Padang, Cape Haytien, Port au Prince and St. John's.

In 1830, the foreign entries were : from Maranham 5, Para 11, Cayenne 7, Sumatra 4, Calcutta 2, Manila 4, Matanzas 4, Port Royal 2, St. Jago 5, Marseilles 3, Porto Rico 3, Cape de Verde 2, Africa 3, Havana 5, Point Petre 3, Buenos Ayres 4, Montevideo 3, Rio Grande 3, Paraiba 2, Antwerp 3, St. Andrew's 2, and one each from Martinico, Surinam, Crooked Island, Siam, Cadiz, Majunga, Bombay, Smyrna, St. Thomas, Canton, Trieste, Halifax, Pernambuco, St. Salvador, Madagascar, St. Pierre's, Girgenti, Campo Bello, Cronstadt and Liverpool.

In 1840, the foreign entries were : from Surinam 2, Cayenne 10, Para 11, Africa 15, Zanzibar 7, Montevideo 3, Sumatra 3, Indian

Ocean 3, Pernambuco 3, St. Jago 4, Manila 2, Maranham 3, Windsor, N. S., 8, Cadiz 3, Pictou 2, Sidney, N. S., 4, and one each from Pulo Penang, Cardiff, Leghorn, Porto Rico, Calcutta, St. John's, St. Ubes, Rio Grande, Glasgow, Bridgeport, Ceylon and Martinico.

In 1850, the foreign entries were: from Nova Scotia 391, Para 15, Africa 22, Rio Grande 13, Zanzibar 9, Cayenne 6, New Brunswick 2, St. Martin's 2, Buenos Ayres 6, Surinam 2, Newport, Eng., 3, and one each from Penang, Havana, Matanzas, Manila, Turk's Island, Prince Edward Island and Aquilla.

In 1860, the foreign entries were: from Nova Scotia 215, Para 7, Africa 25, Cayenne 10, Montevideo 2, Zanzibar 4, Surinam 2, Rio Grande 2, Buenos Ayres 2, and one each from Mozambique, Shields, Eng., Sunderland, Eng., Port Praya, Newcastle, Eng., and Trapani.

In 1870, the foreign entries were: from the British Provinces 117, Cayenne 3, Newcastle, Eng., 2, an done each from Zanzibar, Africa, Rio Grande, Cape Verde Islands and Sunderland, Eng.

In 1878, the foreign entries were: from the British Provinces 53, and none from any other ports.

Collectors of Customs.—The successive collectors since the Revolution have been Warwick Palfray (born, Oct., 1715; died, Oct. 10, 1797), from 1776 to 1784; Joseph Hiller (born, March 26, 1748; died, Feb. 9, 1814), 1784 to 1802; William R. Lee (born, 1744; died in office, Oct. 26, 1824), 1802 to 1824; James Miller, 1825 to 1849; Ephraim F. Miller, 1849 to 1857; William B. Pike, 1857 to 1861; Willard P. Phillips, 1861 to 1865; Robert S. Rantoul, 1865 to 1869; Charles W. Palfray, 1869 to 1873; Charles H. Odell, 1873 to the present time.

Deputy Collectors.—The deputy collectors, under the present organization, have been: Charles Cleveland, from 1789 to 1802; William W. Oliver, 1803 to 1839; John B. Knight, 1839 to 1843; Ephraim F. Miller, 1843 to 1849; J. Linton Waters, 1849 to 1854; Henry E. Jenks, 1854 to 1857; Chipman Ward, 1857 to 1859; Henry Derby, 1859 to 1861; Ephraim F. Miller, 1861 to 1864; Charles S. Osgood, 1864 to 1873; J. Frank Dalton, 1873 to the present time.

Surveyors.—The surveyors during the same period have been, Bartholomew Putnam, from 1789 to 1809; George Hodges, 1809 to 1817; John Saunders, 1818 to 1830; James Dalrymple, 1830 to 1834;

Joseph Noble, 1834 to 1838; Edward Palfray, 1838 to 1841; Stephen Daniels, 1841 to 1843; Nehemiah Brown, 1843 to 1846; Nathaniel Hawthorne, 1846 to 1849; Allen Putnam, 1849 to 1854; Lewis Josselyn, 1854 to 1857; Ebenezer Dodge, 1857 to 1861; William C. Waters, 1861 to 1863; Charles F. Williams, 1863 to 1865; Joseph Moseley, 1865 to 1871; Charles D. Howard, 1871 to 1875, when the office was abolished.

Naval Officers.— The naval officers have been William Pickman, from 1789 to 1803; Samuel Ward, 1803 to 1812; Henry Elkins, 1812 to 1829; John Swasey, 1829 to 1842; Abraham True, 1842 to 1846; John D. Howard, 1846 to 1849; William Brown, 1849 to 1853; Charles Millett, 1853 to 1858; John Ryan, 1858 to 1860; Joseph A. Dalton, 1861 to 1865, when the office was abolished.

Nathaniel Hawthorne.— The two most prominent names in this list are those of Nathaniel Hawthorne and James Miller. The one, the unequalled master of romance; the other, "New England's most distinguished soldier." Nathaniel Hawthorne was born in Salem, July 4, 1804, in the house now numbered twenty-one on Union Street. He was a descendant of Maj. William Hathorne, who came with Gov. Winthrop in the "Arbella." The name is an old and honored one in Salem, and prominently connected with its early history. On the death of his father, in 1808, he lived for a time with his maternal grandfather, Richard Manning, on Herbert Street. For a year he lived in Raymond, Maine, and then returned to Salem. He graduated at Bowdoin College in 1825, in the same class with the poet Longfellow. He was appointed weigher and gauger at Boston in 1838, and was removed in 1841 for political reasons; he was surveyor at Salem from 1846 to 1849; and consul of the United States at Liverpool from 1852 to 1856.

The fame of Hawthorne as a writer was of very slow growth. In 1828, he published anonymously the romance, "Fanshawe," and in 1837, "Twice-told Tales." In 1840, after having been a resident of Lenox, as well as of Concord, he drifted back to the old family mansion in Union Street, where, writing in the solitude of his chamber, he says: "Here I sit, in my old accustomed chamber, where I used to sit in days gone by. Here I have written many tales. If ever I have a biographer he ought to make mention of this chamber in my memoirs, because here my mind and character were formed; and here I sat a long, long time, waiting patiently for the world to know me, and sometimes wondering why it did not know me sooner, or whether it would ever know me at all — at least till I were in my grave." Some years later he published "The Scarlet Letter," and there was no longer any doubt whether the world would ever know him. This romance has become one of the classics of our language, and the subtle genius of the great story-teller has reflected a halo of interest around the custom-house which brings curious travellers from far and wide to visit it. The room he occupied; the desk on which he wrote; the stencil-plate with which he put his name on packages; the room in which he tells us he found the manuscript, telling the sad, strange story of Hester Prynne, were, until a few years, preserved and examined with interest by tourists. The custom-house was refurnished in 1873, and his desk was deposited by his successor in office with the Essex Institute.

About 1849 he removed to Lenox, and there wrote "The House of the Seven Gables." The scene is located in Salem. The work added to his growing fame as an author. Among his later works are "The Blithedale Romance," and "The Marble Faun,"—the one a reminiscence of his residence at Brook Farm, the other of his abode in Italy. He died in Plymouth, N. H., May 19, 1864, while making a short journey, in the company of his friend and class-mate, President Franklin Pierce.

James Miller was born in Peterboro, N. H., in 1776. He was bred to the law, and left the courts for the camp, on being appointed by Jefferson, in 1808, a major in the 4th U. S. Infantry. He was with Gen. Harrison throughout his famous western campaign of 1811; then followed Brownstown, Chippewa, and Lundy's Lane, and from the last dates his national fame and his brigadier's commission. At that battle Maj. Gen. Brown was in command, and was disabled, and Scott of the First Brigade was also disabled. It was plain that a certain hill, whose frowning front bristled with artillery, was the key to victory. At this juncture Col. Miller was called on to storm the work. "I'll try, sir!" was Miller's reply, and as he says, with his regiment reduced to less than three hundred men, he at once obeyed the order. Two regiments ordered to his support quailed and turned back. "Col. Miller," says the official records, "without regard to this occurrence, advanced steadily and carried the height." "Not one man at the cannon," says he, in writing to his wife, "was left to put

27

fire to them." The memorable words, "I'll try sir!" were at once embossed upon the buttons of his shattered regiment, which was presented with a captured gun for distinguished gallantry. On the following November Congress voted him a gold medal bearing his likeness, his famous words, and the names of Chippewa, Niagara, and Fort Erie. He was also presented with a sword by the State of New York. Gen. Miller was governor of Arkansas Territory in 1819. He died July 7, 1851, in Temple, N. H.

Mr. Cleveland and Mr. Oliver are remarkable among the deputy collectors. The former was born in Norwich, Conn., June 21, 1772, and died June 5, 1872, coming within sixteen days of living out the century. At the age of ninety-eight he attended Mr. Oliver's funeral, who died at ninety-one. Mr. Oliver was connected with the custom-house forty-six years. He was born in Salem, December 10, 1778, and died December 29, 1869.

Jonathan Pue, now immortalized in "The Scarlet Letter," became "searcher and surveyor" in 1752, and died suddenly in office, March 24, 1760. In 1734 William Fairfax, whose name was afterwards pleasantly associated with that of Washington, left the collectorship of this port and removed to Virginia.

Marine Insurance Companies.—The rapid increase in the shipping at this port which took place after trade was opened between Salem and the East Indies, led to the organization of a number of insurance companies where the merchant could insure ship and cargo. At the different offices of these companies the merchants assembled in the evening to transact their business, to read the papers, and to hear the general gossip of the day. Here the shipmasters recounted the perils they had encountered, and compared notes with each other regarding the voyages from which they had just returned; and here, in the busy days of Salem's commerce, all was bustle and activity and life. Many of the offices were retained long after the business had greatly diminished, and became a place where the retired shipmasters of Salem resorted to discuss the news of the day, and recount the departed glories of the past.

The Essex Fire and Marine Insurance Company was incorporated March 7, 1803, William Gray and others incorporators, and was located in the building on Essex Street, facing Central Street; Nathaniel Bowditch was its President for many years; the Merchants' Insurance Company, Peter Lander, President, was located in the store now occupied by Asa Hood, on the west side of Essex House yard; the Salem Commercial Insurance Company was incorporated in 1818, N. Silsbee, Joseph Story and others incorporators; George Cleveland, for many years, President. The Mercantile Insurance Company, incorporated in 1825, John Winn, Jr., President, was located on the western corner of Essex and St. Peter's streets. After that company gave up business, the Essex Insurance Company was formed and occupied the same location. The Oriental Insurance Company, incorporated in 1824, was located in the East India Marine building, and subsequently removed to Asiatic Bank building. The Social Insurance Company was incorporated March 1, 1808, and revived June 5, 1830, for ten years, to settle old claims. The Salem Marine Insurance Company, which was incorporated in February, 1856, and commenced business in February, 1857, is the only marine insurance company now doing business in Salem. William Northey is President, and F. P. Richardson, Secretary.

Ship-Building.—It was natural that early attention should have been given to ship-building, in a settlement where the staple article of trade was the product of the fisheries. In 1629 the Home Company sent six ship-builders to Salem, of whom Robert Moulton was chief. Salem Neck was used for ship-building from the very earliest period. So many people were located in that vicinity in 1679 that John Clifford was licensed to keep a victualling house for their convenience. In 1636, Richard Hollingworth, a ship-builder, who came to Salem in 1635, gets a grant of land on the neck from the town, and builds a ship of 300 tons there in 1641. It is most probable that prior to 1637, Robert Moulton and his shipwrights built several small decked vessels for the fisheries and for trading. The Home Company order three shallops to be built in Salem in 1629, doubtless for fishing purposes. From 1629 to 1640, Salem had not much shipping of her own; but in the latter year, the Rev. Hugh Peters, of the First Church, a man of great energy and sagacity, interested the people in ship-building, and in a few years an abundant supply of vessels were built. Salem became noted as one of the principal places in the Colony for building vessels.

From 1659 to 1677, there appear to be four noted ship-builders in Salem, one of whom, Jonathan Pickering, gets a grant of land about

Hardy's Cove from the town, to himself and heirs forever, to build vessels upon. From 1692 to 1718, seven ship-builders appear prominent in Salem, among whom are Joseph Hardy and William Becket. In 1662 the town authorities endeavor to accommodate, at Burying Point, near the foot of Liberty Street, those desirous of graving vessels. In 1676 Salem is said to be one of the principal places for building vessels, at £4 per ton. Of the 26 vessels belonging to Salem in 1698–99, seventeen were built here. From 1700 to 1714 inclusive, 'registers were granted to 4 ships, 3 barks, 9 brigs, 24 sloops and 19 ketches belonging to Salem. They ranged from 15 to 90 tons, and 40 of them were built here. In 1705 the ship "Unity," of 270 tons, was built in Salem, for Boston and London merchants, and in 1709 Joseph Hardy built the brig "American Merchant," of 160 tons burden. In 1712 a sale is recorded by Ebenezer Lambert, shipwright, of Salem, of ye good sloop "Betty," lately built, of about 80 tons burden, to Benjamin Marston, of Salem, for £240, or £3 per ton.

Vessels were built or repaired in Salem on the neck, including Winter Island; on the creek running into South River, near the foot of Norman Street; at the Burying Point near the foot of Liberty Street, and at other places on the South River; at Frye's Mills on the North River; and at Hardy's Cove. Referring to the creek running into the South River, Felt says, writing in 1842, that "its course was from the South River, below the mills, and up between Norman and High streets. A century since boys would go in boats from its waters to a swamp in Crombie Street, and collect eggs from blackbirds' nests. Britton's Hill, running from Summer Street, formerly had a ship-yard, whence vessels were launched into the creek. An octogenarian vividly remembers a brig of 150 tons, which was built on the margin of the same waters." It seems hardly credible that the principal commerce and shipbuilding of the town was at one time carried on in this locality, for scarcely a vestige remains to-day of the creek or cove, and the South River is gradually disappearing from view, and at this point runs through a covered culvert.

The Beckets have been famous as ship-builders in Salem. The ship-yard of the Beckets was situated between Phillips Wharf and Webb's Wharf. This place has been known as Becket's Beach, and is directly in front of the old mansion-house built by John Becket about 1655. It was occupied by the Beckets as a shipyard from 1655 to 1800, a period of 145 years.   After 1800, Retire Becket built his vessels on land further to the eastward.

The most famous vessel built by Retire Becket, was the yacht "Cleopatra's Barge," of 191 tons burden, whose owner, Capt. George Crowninshield, spared no expense in her construction or in her appointments.   She was built for a pleasure-trip to the Mediterranean, and excited wonder, even at Genoa, for her beauty, luxury and magnificence.   She was launched October 21, 1816, in the presence of an immense concourse of people.   During the winter of 1817 the harbor was frozen over to the Haste and Coney Island, and this vessel having returned from her voyage, a great many people drove over the ice in sleighs to visit her.   Retire Becket also built, in 1799, the brig "Active," of 206 tons, in which William P. Richardson made the first trading voyage from Salem to the Feejee Islands, in 1810; in 1800, the ship "Margaret," of 295 tons, which made the first voyage from Salem to Japan, leaving Salem November 10, 1800, under command of Samuel Derby; and in 1794, for Elias H. Derby, the ship "Recovery," of 284 tons, which, under command of Joseph Ropes first displayed the stars and stripes at Mocha.   He also built for Elias H. Derby in 1798, the ship "Mount Vernon," of 356 tons; for George Crowninshield & Sons, in 1804, the ship "America," of 473 tons, famous as a privateer in the war of 1812; for Z. F. Silsbee and James Devereux, in 1807, the ship "Herald," of 274 tons.   The last vessel built by Mr. Becket was the brig "Becket," of 128 tons, for John Crowninshield in 1818.

Ebenezer Mann came to Salem from Pembroke in 1783, and in the same year commenced building vessels in a yard near Frye's Mills on North River, and continued in the business until about the year 1800. Among the vessels built by Mr. Mann was the brig "William," of 182 tons, in 1784, for William Gray; the brig "Fanny," of 152 tons, in 1785, for Benjamin Goodhue; the bark "Good Intent," of 171 tons, in 1790, for Simon Forrester; the schooner "Betsey," of 108 tons, in 1792, for Jerathmael Peirce; the brig "Hind," of 157 tons, in 1795, for William Orne; the ship "Good Hope," of 188 tons, in 1795, for Nathaniel West; the bark "Eliza," of 187 tons in 1796, for Joseph White; and the ship "Prudent," of 214 tons, in 1799, for Nathaniel West.

Christopher Turner, who came to Salem from Pembroke, where he was born in 1767, continued the business of ship-building at Frye's Mills after Mr. Mann retired. He built, among others, the schoone· "Essex," of 114 tons, in 1800, for William Fabens, for the West India and Cayenne trade. The ship "Pompey," of 188 tons, in 1802, for William Orne. She was afterwards sold to Joshua Ward, made into a brig, and commanded by James Gilchrist. The ship "Hope," of 282 tons, in 1805, for J. & J. Barr. The ship "Hunter," of 296 tons, in 1807, for Jerathmael Peirce. The brig "Romp," of 232 tons in 1809, for Nathaniel Silsbee. She was commanded by William Lander, and was confiscated at Naples, in 1809, on her first voyage. The ship "Rambler," of 286 tons, in 1811, for George Nichols. She was captured by the British in 1812, while commanded by Timothy Bryant. Mr. Turner built, at Union Wharf, for George Crowninshield, the sloop "Jefferson," of 22 tons, for a pleasure-yacht. She was launched in March, 1801, and is believed to have been the first regular yacht built in the United States.

David Magoun built, on the neck, between the gate and Col. John Hathorne's house, in 1805, the ship "Alfred," 200 tons, for Joseph White.

Barker & Magoun built, at the same place, the schooner "Enterprize," 200 tons, in 1812, and the schooner "Gen. Stark" in 1813.

Enos Briggs was one of the most noted ship-builders in Salem. He came here from Pembroke in 1790, and built the ship "Grand Turk," of 560 tons, for Elias Hasket Derby. She was built on the lot of land next east of Isaac P. Foster's store, and was launched March 10, 1791, and replaced the ship "Grand Turk," of 300 tons, which was sold at the Isle of France in 1788. Having built the "Grand Turk," Mr. Briggs returned to Pembroke for his family. They arrived at Salem July 4, 1791, and the sloop in which they came brought, also, the frame of a dwelling-house, which he erected on Harbor Street, and which, for many years after his decease, was occupied by the family of his daughter, Mrs. Nathan Cook. Mr. Briggs was born in Pembroke July 29, 1746, and died in Salem Oct. 10, 1819. His shipyard in Salem was located between Peabody and Harbor streets, west of the Naumkeag Cotton Mills. Here he built, for Elias Hasket Derby, in 1792, the ship "Benjamin," of 161 tons, which was afterwards commanded by Nathaniel Silsbee; in 1794, the ketch "Eliza," of 184 tons, which, under command of Stephen Phillips, made some of the early voyages to Calcutta and the Isle of France; in 1795, the ketch "John," of 258 tons, and the ketch "Brothers," of 148 tons; and, in 1796, the ship "Martha," of 340 tons. For George Crowninshield & Sons, he built, in 1794, the ship "Belisarius," of 261 tons. For Peirce & Wait, in 1797, the ship "Friendship," of 342 tons, afterwards commanded by Israel Williams. For Joseph Peabody, in 1798, the schooner "Sally," 104 tons; in 1798, the brig "Neptune," 160 tons; in 1801, the brig "Catherine," 158 tons; in 1803, the ship "Mount Vernon," 254 tons; in 1804, the ship "Janus," 277 tons; in 1805, the ship "Augustus," 246 tons; in 1807, the ship "Francis," 297 tons; in 1811, the ship "Glide," 306 tons; in 1812, the brig "Levant," 265 tons; and in 1816, the ship "China," of 370 tons. For Nathaniel West, in 1794, the schooner "Patty," 111 tons, which, under command of Edward West, made one of the earliest voyages from Salem to Batavia; and in 1801, the ship "Commerce," 239 tons. For Benjamin Pickman, in 1803, the ship "Derby," of 300 tons. For Simon Forrester, in 1805, the ship "Messenger," 277 tons. For William Gray, in 1806, the ship "Pactolus," 288 tons. Mr. Briggs built, while in Salem, fifty-one vessels of 11,500 tons, among them the famous frigate "Essex," of 850 tons, built in 1799, and referred to elsewhere.

Elijah Briggs, on the death of his cousin Enos, continued the business of ship-building at the yard in South Salem. He built for Pickering Dodge, in 1819, the ship "Gov. Endicott," 279 tons; in 1828, the ship "Lotos," 296 tons; in 1828, the ship "Mandarin," 295 tons; and in 1829, the ship "Rome," 344 tons. For Jonathan Neal, in 1820, the brig "Java," 225 tons. For John Forrester, in 1823, the ship "Emerald," 271 tons. For Joseph Peabody, in 1824, the brig "Mexican," 227 tons, and the brig "Amazon," 202 tons. For Gideon Tucker, in 1825, the brig "Olinda," 182 tons. Mr. Briggs was born in Scituate July 17, 1762, and died in Salem May 29, 1847.

Elias Jenks and Ichabod R. Hoyt continued the business of ship-building in South Salem down to 1843, and built their vessels a little to the westward of the spot occupied by Enos Briggs. They built for Joseph Peabody, in 1827, the ship "Sumatra," 287 tons; in 1831, the ship "Eclipse," 326 tons; in 1833, the ship "Naples," 309 tons; and in 1837, the ship "Carthage," 426 tons. For Nathaniel L.

Rogers & Brothers, in 1828, the ship "Crusoe," 350 tons. For the Messrs. Silsbee, in 1831, the ship "Borneo," 297 tons ; and in 1840, the ship "Sooloo," 400 tons. For Thorndike Deland, in 1836, the schooner "William Penn," 125 tons. For David Pingree, in 1843, the bark "Three Brothers," 350 tons.

In 1834, there had been built in Salem for the foreign trade since 1789, sixty-one ships, four barks, fifty-three brigs, three ketches, and sixteen schooners, measuring 30,557 tons.

On the 1st of December, 1825, there was launched from the ship-yard of Mr. Cottle, in North Salem, near Orne's Point, a schooner of 40 tons, built for the use of the American missionaries at the Sandwich Islands. She was called the "Missionary Packet," and sailed from Boston Jan. 17, 1826, for the Sandwich Islands.

Samuel Lewis built, in 1849, the bark "Argentine," for Robert Upton, and in 1850 the brig "M. Shepard," 160 tons, for John Bertram.

Justin Carter built, in 1854, under the superintendence of A. H. Gardner, and on the eastern side of Phillips Wharf, for Edward D. Kimball, the bark "Witch," 417 tons ; and subsequently, at the same place, for other parties, the ship "Europa," 846 tons.

Edward F. Miller, whose shipyard was at the point of land in South Salem opposite the end of Derby Wharf, built for R. W. Ropes & Co., in 1855, the brig "Mary Wilkins," 266 tons ; and in 1859 the bark "La Plata," 496 tons. For Benjamin A. West, in 1857, the bark "Arabia," 380 tons. She was lost at the Cape of Good Hope on her first voyage. For John Bertram, in 1856, the bark "Guide"; in 1861, the bark "Glide," 493 tons ; in 1869, the bark "Jersey," 599 tons, which was lost at Madagascar on her first voyage ; and, in 1870, the bark "Taria Topan," 631 tons. For John C. Osgood and others, in 1862, the brig "Star," 250 tons.

Joshua Brown built, near Miller's shipyard, the schooner "Prairie Flower," 106 tons. This vessel was launched on the 27th of April, 1858. She sailed from Salem Tuesday, June 8, 1858, for Boston, to obtain a part of her fishing outfit. A large party of young men were on board, invited by the owners to make the trip to Boston. About 2 P. M., when in the Broad Sound and entering Boston Harbor, the schooner was struck by a sudden gust of wind and capsized. The water rushed into the cabin, filling it, and of those there at the time, seven were drowned. They were all under thirty years of age, and all of Salem. Osgood Sanborn was 28 ; Daniel R. Fitz, 24 ; George C. Clark, 24 ; Francis Donaldson, 21 ; William H. Russell, 20 ; William H. Newcomb, 20, and Lewis B. Smith, 14. The remainder of the party were rescued by vessels that chanced to be near the scene of the accident. No such calamity had occurred in Salem since the 17th of June, 1773, when the king's boat, belonging to the customhouse, was capsized in Salem Harbor during a squall, and three men and seven women, all of Salem, were drowned.

Mr. Brown built a number of other vessels, among them the schooner "David B. Newcomb," 92 tons, in 1860, and the brig "Albert," 325 tons, in 1862.

Salem Privateers in the Revolution. — The colonists in the War of the Revolution were almost destitute of ships of war. They were engaged in a struggle with one of the most powerful maritime nations, without the means to cope with their enemy on the high seas. Their own commerce was ruined, and it was essential to their success that provision be made for making the commerce of Great Britain suffer, in common with them, the fortunes and vicissitudes of war. Boston and New York were occupied and nearly ruined by the enemy, and Newport, Philadelphia, Savannah, and Charleston soon shared their fate. The main reliance of the country to preserve its intercourse with Europe, and for supplies of arms and military stores, was on the shipping of Salem, and a cluster of small ports around it, including Marblehead and Beverly.

Salem at this crisis showed the same patriotic spirit which she has always exhibited when the country in its need and distress has called on her for assistance. The merchants and mariners of Salem turned their vessels into men of war, equipped them with cannon, manned them with gallant seamen, and sent them out to meet Great Britain on the deep. During this contest there were equipped and sent out from this port at least 158 vessels, manned by several thousand brave sailors from Salem. They mounted more than 2,000 guns, carrying on an average twelve or fourteen each. The number of prizes taken by Salem armed vessels during the Revolution was about 445. About fifty-four of the privateers and letters-of-marque were captured. Among the gallant officers who commanded the privateers of Salem, were Jonathan Haraden, Thomas Benson, John Carnes, Benjamin

28

Crowninshield, John Derby, John Felt, Simon Forrester, William Gray, Thomas Perkins, S. Tucker, and Joseph Waters.

Jonathan Haraden. — The daring deeds performed by these men deserve a more extended notice than history accords them. A type of the character of the Salem commanders may be found in Jonathan Haraden. He was one of the bravest officers and best seamen who sailed from Salem in the Revolution. His desperate actions and wonderful triumphs, his consummate courage and serene intrepidity, entitle him to a place in history by the side of Paul Jones and Decater, and Farragut and Cushing. The equal of these in bravery and daring, his memory should be cherished as one of the dauntless heroes of the Revolution. He was born in Gloucester, and died in Salem, in 1803, in his fifty-ninth year. He came to Salem when a boy. Soon after hostilities commenced between Great Britain and her Colonies, Captain Haraden was appointed a lieutenant in the "Tyrannicide," Capt. Fiske, of Salem, which vessel captured a royal cutter, bound from Halifax to New York, and carried her in triumph into Salem. Lieut. Haraden soon rose to the post of captain, and took command of the "Gen. Pickering," a Salem ship of 180 tons, carrying fourteen six-pounders and a crew of forty-five men and boys. In this ship he sailed from Salem in the spring of 1780, with a cargo of sugar for Bilboa, then a famous resort for American privateers. On his passage, May 29, 1780, he was attacked by a British cutter of twenty guns, and beat her off after a contest of about two hours. Upon entering the Bay of Biscay, he fell in with a British privateer of twenty-two guns and sixty men. Having approached in the night, unobserved, he ran alongside and commanded her through his trumpet to strike to an American frigate or he would sink her. The privateer struck her flag, and the captain, when he came on board the "Pickering," was mortified to think he had submitted to such inferior force. Mr. John Carnes, of Salem, was put in charge of the prize.

As the vessels approached Bilboa they met a sail coming out, which the captured captain said was the "Achilles," a privateer from London, of forty-two guns and 140 men, and added that he knew her force. Capt. Haraden coolly replied, "I shan't run from her." The British ship first retook the prize and placed a crew on board, and, night coming on, deferred her attack on Capt. Haraden till morning. As the day dawned, June 4, 1780, the "Achilles" bore down upon the

"Pickering," and Capt. Haraden placed his vessel in condition for action. After a desperate contest of about three hours' duration, the British ship was obliged to seek safety in flight, notwithstanding her greatly superior force. Capt. Haraden gave chase, but the "Achilles" was light, outsailed the "Pickering," and escaped. He then returned, coolly recaptured his prize, and carried her in safety into Bilboa.

The battle was fought so near the Spanish coast that an immense concourse of spectators, amounting, as was supposed, to nearly one hundred thousand, assembled along the shore, in boats, and on the hillsides, during the action, and before Capt. Haraden with his prize had been at anchor half an hour, one could walk a mile from his ship by stepping from one boat to another. So great was the admiration with which the battle and victory were witnessed, that when the captain landed he was surrounded by this vast throng of strangers and borne in triumph into the city, where he was welcomed with public and unbounded honors. The late venerable Robert Cowan, who was with him, in this action, said that the "Gen. Pickering," in comparison with her antagonist, "looked like a long-boat by the side of a ship," and "that he fought with a determination that seemed superhuman," and that although in the most exposed positions, "where the shot flew around him in thousands, he was all the while as calm and steady as amidst a shower of snowflakes."

On one of the subsequent cruises of this gallant officer in the "Pickering," he fell in with a king's mail-packet, from one of the West India isles, homeward bound, which gave him a very warm reception. After an action which lasted four hours, Capt. Haraden found it necessary to haul off and repair damages. Having done so, he went again alongside the packet, with all the powder he had left in his cannon. He then hailed the enemy, and told him he would give him five minutes to haul down his colors, and if they were not down at the expiration of that time he would sink him. At the end of three minutes the colors came down. The boat, on going alongside the prize, found the blood running from her scuppers, while the deck appeared more like the floor of a slaughter-house than the deck of a ship.

Space will not permit the recital of the numerous other conflicts, sometimes against great odds, in which this intrepid commander engaged. During the war he captured more than a thousand guns from the ships of the enemy. Amid the din of battle he was calm and cool and self-possessed. The more deadly the strife, the more imminent the peril, the more terrific the scene, the more perfect seemed his self-command and serene intrepidity. He was a hero. among heroes and his name should live in honored and affectionate remembrance.

The armed ships of Salem performed valiant service to the country; they intercepted the transport and supply ships sent from England and Nova Scotia to the troops in Boston and New York. They resorted to the French islands for munitions of war, and captured the ships engaged in the sugar trade. They cruised in the Bay of Biscay, in the English and Irish channels; raised the rate of insurance on British ships to twenty-three per cent., and compelled England to employ most of her navy in convoying merchantmen; and, although a large number were captured, they rarely yielded to an equal force.

Salem Privateers in the War of 1812.— When this country was once more engaged in a war with Great Britain in 1812, Salem again did her part in harassing the commerce of the enemy. She sent out forty privateers, with an aggregate tonnage of 3,405 tons, mounting 189 cannon, and manned by 2,142 men. Some of these privateers were very successful in capturing prizes from the enemy. The whole number of privateers and private armed ships that were commissioned as cruising vessels during the war of 1812 was 250. Baltimore sent out fifty-eight; New York, fifty-five; Salem, forty; Boston, thirty-one; Philadelphia, fourteen; Portsmouth, eleven; and Charleston, ten. The schooner "Fame," of Salem, was a fishing-boat of thirty tons and carried two guns and thirty men. She received her commission July 1, 1812, at noon, sailed in the afternoon, and sent the first prize into Salem. Robert Brookhouse, Jr., was one of her commanders. The sloop "Jefferson," a pleasure-boat of fourteen tons, belonging to George Crowninshield, sailed the same day as the "Fame," and sent the second prize into Salem. She carried only one gun and twenty men.

The ship "America," of Salem, belonging to George Crowninshield & Sons, was the fastest-sailing vessel afloat during the war of 1812, and the most fortunate. She was of 350 tons burden, and carried twenty guns and 150 men. She made four cruises, commanded on the first by Joseph Ropes, and on the third and fourth by James Chever, Jr. She arrived in Salem from her third cruise with fifty prisoners on board, having taken twelve prizes. She captured in her first three cruises twenty-six prizes, and the property taken and safely got into port amounted to about $1,100,000.

From the journal of the "America" on her first cruise, commanded by Joseph Ropes, the following extracts are made.

Monday, Sept. 7, 1812, at half-past 11 o'clock weighed anchor and beat out of the harbor. At noon passed Baker's Island.

Friday, Sept. 11, carried away the main-top-mast with five men aloft, but none of them were injured. All hands employed clearing the wreck.

Wednesday, Sept. 23, at half-past 5 A. M., captured the British brig "James and Charlotte," Lavitt, master, from Liverpool bound to St. John's. Cargo,—coal, hats, dry-goods, etc. Put Mr. Tibbetts, prize master, and six men on board, and ordered her for the first port she could make.

Monday, Oct. 5, all hands employed in exercising the guns. Saw the island of St. Michael's bearing W. S. W. ½ W., 24 leagues.

Friday, Nov. 6, at 4 P. M., saw a sail to the southward. Wore round after her and made all necessary sail in chase. At 9 A. M. brought her to and boarded her. She proved to be the British brig "Benjamin," James Collins, master, from Newfoundland to England.

Saturday, Nov. 7, manned the brig with Joseph Dixon, prize master, and eight men and ordered her for the first port to northward of Nantucket in North America. Took the mate and seven men from the brig and left the captain, one man and a boy on board.

Wednesday, Nov. 18, at 7.30 A. M., saw a sail bearing N. W. by W. Let two reefs from the topsails and set the main-top-gallant sail in chase.

Thursday, Nov. 19, at 1 P. M., came up with the chase and boarded her. She proved to be the ship "Ralph Nickerson," from Quebec, bound and belonging to London, with a cargo of lumber. Put on board John Procter as prize master, and eleven men, and ordered her for America.

Tuesday, Nov. 24, at 7.30 A. M., saw a sail bearing S. W. by S.

and made all necessary sail in chase. At 9 A. M. brought her to and boarded her. She proved to be the British ship "Hope," from St. Thomas bound to Glasgow. Cargo, sugar, rum and cotton. The captain informed us he left a fleet three days previous, consisting of 45 sail of vessels under convoy of the "Ring Dove" and "Scorpion," sloops of war. Put on board Joseph Valpey as prize master, and twelve men, and ordered her for America.

Wednesday, Nov. 25, at 3.45 P. M., saw a sail bearing south, standing easterly. Gave chase and at 4.45 P. M. fired and brought her to and boarded her. She proved to be the British brig "Dart," from St. Thomas bound to Glasgow. Cargo, principally rum and cotton. The boat left the brig with Mr. Sparhawk, Thomas Fuller and five prisoners, but unfortunately the boat got under the ship's counter and foundered. Mr. Sparhawk, Thomas Fuller and three of the prisoners were saved, the other two prisoners were drowned.

Thursday, Nov. 26, at 3 P. M., bent the foresail and set it. Brig in company, bearing down occasionally to keep in sight of us.

Friday, Nov. 27, at 3.30 P. M., made a signal for the brig to bear down under our lee. Boarded her and put on board Anthony D. Caulfield as prize master, and eight men, and took out all the brig's company except the captain, a passenger and one man, and ordered her for America.

Sunday, Dec. 6, begins with a hard gale and squally with rain. Several of the officers and crew attacked with a very troublesome inflammation of the eyes, which disorder cannot be accounted for. Curtailed the allowance of water to $3\frac{1}{2}$ pints per 24 hours.

Wednesday, Dec. 16, at 7.30 A. M., saw a sail to the south-east and made all necessary sail in chase. At 8 perceived she was a brig steering to the eastward. At 11 brought her to and boarded her. She proved to be the British brig "Euphemia" of Glasgow, from La Guayra bound to Gibraltar, John Gray, master, mounting ten guns and navigated by twenty-five men.

Thursday, Dec. 17, took eight guns from the prize and put on board Archibald S. Dennis as prize master, and eleven men, and took from her the first and second officers and twenty-one men. At 5 P. M. parted from her and made sail.

Thursday, Jan. 7, 1813, at 3 P. M., saw the land about Marblehead, and at 8 o'clock came to anchor in Salem harbor.

The six prizes captured by the "America" on this cruise were valued at $158,000. After her return from her last cruise in 1815, she lay at Crowninshield's wharf until she was sold at auction in June, 1831, and broken up, being 27 years old.

The brig "Grand Turk" was one of the finest vessels of her class in the United States. She was fortunate as a cruiser, and as famous for her good qualities as the "America." She was of 310 tons burden, carried eighteen guns and 150 men, and was commanded at first by Holten J. Breed and afterwards by Nathan Green. She arrived at Salem, after a cruise of 103 days, with forty-four of her original crew (the rest being on board her prizes) and fifty prisoners. She captured seven or eight vessels, one with an invoice of £30,000 sterling. She had on board goods to the value of $20,000.

From the journal of the "Grand Turk" while on her last cruise, commanded by Nathan Green, the following extracts are made.

Sunday, Jan. 1, 1815, at 12.30, got under way, stowed the anchor and cleared the decks. At 2 P. M. passed Baker's Island.

Friday, Feb. 17, at 3.30 P. M., boarded a catamaran for the purpose of gaining information. She proved to be from Pernambuco, and informed us of there being eight British vessels at said port. At 6 P. M. saw Pernambuco.

Sunday, Feb. 19, at 5.30 P. M., saw a sail in the north. At 9 A. M. boarded the brig "Joven Francisco," under Spanish colors, from Pernambuco for London, with a cargo of tea, coffee, sugar and cinnamon, consigned to British merchants. By examination of one of the crew, who states the cargo to be British property, and some letters and invoices, I have every reason to believe the property to be *bona fide* British. Accordingly, manned her with Nathaniel Archer, as prize master, and ordered her for the United States.

Tuesday, Feb. 21, at 5 P. M. saw a sail in the south, standing to the northward. Lay by for her. At 6.30 boarded her. She proved to be the British ship "Active Jane," of Liverpool, bound from Rio Janeiro to Maranham, in ballast. Took from her seven bags of specie, containing 14,000 mill rees, equal to 17,500 dollars and manned her out to keep company during the night. At daylight, boarded, dismantled and scuttled her.

Friday, Mar. 10, at daylight, the man at the mast-head descried a sail in the eastern quarter. Called all hands immediately and made sail in chase. Soon after saw another sail on the weather bow. Still in pursuit of the chase and approaching her fast. At 6.30 passed very near the second sail, which was a Portuguese schooner standing W. S. W. At 7 saw the third sail three points on our lee bow, the chase a ship. At 8 discovered the third to be a large ship by the wind to the north and westward. At 10, being ¾ of a mile to windward, discovered the chase to be a frigate, endeavoring to decoy us. Tacked ship and she immediately tacked and made all sail in pursuit of us. Soon perceived we had the superiority of sailing, displayed the American flag and fired a shot in defiance. At 11, the wind hauled suddenly to the westward. The frigate received a favorable breeze which caused her to lay across and nearing us fast. At 11.30 the frigate within gunshot, got out our sweeps and made considerable progress although calm and a short head sea. Frigate commenced firing, got out her boats and attempted to tack four different times but did not succeed. Hoisted our colors and gave her a number of shot. A ship to leeward, a frigate also. At noon swept our brig round with her head to the northward, and having the sea more favorable, left the chaser considerably. The day ends with extreme sultry weather, all hands to the sweeps and both ships in pursuit of us.

Saturday, Mar. 11, at dark, frigates using every exertion to near us.

Sunday, Mar 12, at 1.30 P. M., saw two sail two points on our lee bow, soon discovered them to be the two frigates still in pursuit of us and much favored by the breeze. At 5 P. M. light, variable winds with us, and the enemy still holding the breeze. Took to our sweeps. At dark the enemy's ships bore S. S. W.

Monday Mar. 13, at 2 P. M., the enemy having been out of sight 4½ hours, concluded to get down the fore-topmast and replace it with a new one. All hands busily employed. At 3 saw a sail in the northwest quarter. At 4 descried a second sail ahead standing for us. At 5.30 got the new fore-topmast and top-gallant-mast in place, rigging secured, yards aloft and made sail in pursuit of the latter. At 7 came up and boarded her; she proved to be a Portuguese brig bound from Bahia to Le Grande, with a cargo of salt. Finding ourselves discovered by the British cruisers and being greatly incumbered with prisoners, concluded to release them and accordingly paroled five British prisoners and discharged ten Spaniards and put them on board the brig, after giving a necessary supply of provisions.

Saturday, Mar. 18, at 2 P. M., came up and spoke a Portuguese brig from Africa bound to Rio Janeiro with a cargo of slaves. Filled away in pursuit of a second sail in the N. W. At 4.30 she hoisted English colors and commenced firing her stern guns. At 5.20 took in the steering sails, at the same time she fired a broadside. We opened a fire from our larboard battery and at 5.30 she struck her colors. Got out the boats and boarded her. She proved to be the British brig "Acorn," from Liverpool for Rio Janeiro, mounting fourteen cannon and having a cargo of dry-goods. At 5.50 we received the first boat-load of goods on board. Employed all night in discharging her.

Sunday, Mar. 19, at daylight saw two frigates and a brig on the lee beam in chase of us. Took a very full boat-load of goods on board, manned out the prize with Joseph Phippen and eleven men and ordered her for the United States. As the prize was in a good plight for sailing I have great reason to think she escaped. One of the frigates pursued us for three-quarters of an hour, but finding that she had her old antagonist, gave over the pursuit. Having on board one hundred and sixty odd bales, boxes, cases and trunks of goods, which I conceive is very valuable, and the brig's copper and rigging being very much out of repair and the water scant, conclude to return home with all possible dispatch. As another inducement I have information of a treaty of peace being signed at Ghent between the United State and Great Britain and only remains to be ratified by the former.

Wednesday, Mar. 29, at 4 A. M., saw a sail to windward very near us, and tacked in pursuit of her. At 8.30 came up with and boarded her. She proved to be a Portuguese ship from Africa bound to Maranham with 474 slaves on board. Paroled and put on board said ship eleven British prisoners.

Saturday, April 15, boarded the American schooner "Commit," of and from Alexandria, for Barbadoes, with a cargo of flour. They gave us the joyful tidings of peace between America and England, which produced the greatest rejoicing throughout the ship's company.

Saturday, April 29, 1815, at 7.30 A. M., saw Thatcher's Island bearing N. W. At 8 saw Baker's Island bearing west. At 9.30 came to anchor in Salem harbor, cleared decks and saluted the town. Thus ends the cruise of 118 days.

The "Grand Turk" was sold to William Gray May 30, 1815.

29

The schooner "Helen" was a merchant vessel, loaned by her owners, the Messrs. White and J. J. Knapp, for the purpose of capturing the English privateer "Liverpool Packet," which for months had rendered herself a terror to all vessels entering the bay. Her cruising-ground was in the vicinity of Cape Cod, although she once was seen inside Half-Way Rock. Capt. John Upton originated the project of fitting out the "Helen," and going to capture the "Liverpool Packet." He spoke to others about it on the morning of Nov. 12, 1812, and the "Helen" was got ready, and seventy volunteers raised, in about four hours. Before the next morning she was at sea. Those who started the expedition formed a procession, preceded by the American flag, and by James McCarthy with his drum, and Henry Hubon with his fife, and marched through the streets of Salem, led off by Capt. James Fairfield. Before night, on the day the expedition was first talked of, the vessel was prepared with stores, ammunition, and cannon, and at nine o'clock that night she was off Naugus Head. They found the English vessel they sought had sailed the previous day for St. John, and thus the object of their expedition failed.

Of the forty private armed vessels belonging to. Salem during the war of 1812, three were ships, three brigs, twenty-three schooners, four sloops, two launches, and five boats. Twenty-three of the number were built in Salem. Twenty-six were captured by the enemy.

This account is necessarily brief, but the extracts from the journals of the "America" and "Grand Turk," two of the most famous vessels that sailed from Salem during the war, will serve to show the manner of life led on board a Salem privateer, and will further show that even by the crews of these vessels the news of peace was hailed as "joyful tidings."

Conclusion.—The sketch of Salem's commerce and matters connected therewith, contained in this chapter, is sufficiently extended to give the reader an insight into that interesting period of her history. The younger readers will find it hard to realize that Salem led the way from New England round the Cape of Good Hope to the Isle of France, and India, and China; that her vessels were the first from this country to display the American flag and open trade with St. Petersburg, and Zanzibar, and Sumatra; with Calcutta and Bombay; with Batavia and Arabia; with Madagascar and Australia: and yet such is the plain story of her achievements. The adventures of her brave officers in unknown seas; their encounters with pirates and savage tribes; their hairbreadth escapes; their tales of shipwreck, and of imprisonment among the Algerines, and in the prisons of France and Spain; and the strange and thrilling incidents of their early voyages,—would make a tale which even the imaginings of romance could hardly parallel.

But the commercial prosperity of Salem is a thing of the past. Her triumphs on the seas have passed into history, and the record is closed. Derby Street no longer presents a scene of bustle and activity,—of sailors greeting friends on their arrival from the far East, and of others preparing for departure; the shop windows no longer display curious trinkets and odd ventures gathered from all quarters of the world; the boarding-houses where the returning sailor found a home, with the inevitable clothing-shop attached, where he was invited to spend his hard-earned wages, have been a long time closed; and the rope-walks, the sail-lofts, and the ship chandlers' shops are deserted and abandoned. The foreign commerce of Salem, once her pride and glory, has spread its white wings and sailed away forever. But the traditions of the past will always make a bright page in her history, and the motto on her municipal seal, "To the furthest port of the rich East," scattered far and wide as she each year sends forth her official documents, will serve to perpetuate and hand down to posterity her brilliant commercial record.

CHAPTER IX.

SKETCH OF THE MANUFACTURING AND BUSINESS INTERESTS OF SALEM.

Proceeding from the commercial to other business interests of Salem, the manufacture and trade in leather first demand consideration, as these two branches form by far the largest single interest.

The Leather Interest.—A brief retrospect of the foundation and growth of this business may be interesting. The exact date of the beginning of the manufacture of leather in Salem is not attainable, neither are any very definite facts regarding the location of the first tanning and currying shops. There appears to have been a tannery near the present lower end of Liberty Street, at a very early date. This is shown by the records, and has been corroborated by the excavation there of remains of tan and of horns of cattle. The common, and the territory eastward of it, previous to 1800, was a more or less swampy locality, and on the north and east sides of it had been located, for many years, a number of tanneries. Within a dozen years, evidences of the location of tan yards have been found in digging to lay sewers in the lower end of Forrester Street. The business finally located on the North River, and extended up towards Peabody, along the line of the water-course, and this valley is to-day the greatest tanning district in the country. The trade hereabouts suffered a decline about forty years ago; but during the last thirty years it has grown rapidly, and all attempts to divert it to other places have failed to check its increase in this its original *habitat.* Salem is as famous for its tanneries as Lynn is for its shoe-shops.

In 1639, Philemon Dickerson was granted land "to make tan pits and to dress goat skins and hides." Afterwards, tanners were occasionally mentioned, and in 1642, "Ould Thomas Eabourne" was "prosecuted" for "wronging the country by insufficient tanning." For the offence he was "admonished" and fined a small sum. The same year the General Court passed an order "that no person using the feat and mistery" of currier, butcher or shoemaker, "shall exercise the feat or mistery of a tanner." It seems to have been not un-common in those days for families to tan their own leather and make their own shoes. For this purpose they used a trough hollowed out of a pine log. The hides were cut into strips of a suitable width for the soles of shoes, and alternated in the trough with layers of oak bark pounded up with a mallet.

In a century after the first beginnings, or in 1750, an old Quaker preacher in Danvers, named Joseph Southwick, had so far improved the method as to grind the bark with a circular stone revolved by horse-power. This was the first bark-mill. Another and much greater advance in the art of tanning was made in the early part of this cen-tury, when steam and water-power were brought into use in the more laborious parts of the process. This, together with some improve-ments in the methods of working, led to a great improvement in the business.

There were four tanneries in 1768; eight in 1791; seven in 1801; twelve in 1811; thirteen in 1821; twenty-three in 1831; twenty-four in 1836; eighteen in 1840. In 1836 there were tanned 68,677 hides; the value of leather tanned and curried was $398,897; hands em-ployed, 194; capital used, $299,170. In 1844 there were forty-one tanneries, employing 280 hands; value of leather tanned and curried, $642,671; capital invested, $401,668. In 1850 there were thirty-four tanners, the same number of curriers, fifteen who followed both trades, and two leather and morocco dressers and colorers,—total, eighty-five. Then 550 hands were employed in the business, and the value of the leather tanned and curried was $869,047.70. It has been found extremely difficult to obtain even an estimate of the aver-age business for the last five years, as a fair statement to pass into history; but careful investigation and consultation with leading man-ufacturers and dealers place the figures at the following estimate: Capital employed, $1,250,000; annual production, $4,000,000; num-ber of men employed, about 1,000. Most of the capital employed is home capital, and the Salem banks discount a large proportion of all the "leather paper" passed in the transaction of this great business.

Cotton Manufacture. — The next industry in order of importance is the manufacture of cotton cloth, carried on by the Naumkeag Steam Cotton Company, which was incorporated April 5, 1839, with a capi-tal of $200,000. The first mill erected was completed in 1847, the capital stock having been meanwhile increased to $700,000. It was then the largest and best appointed mill in the United States. The building was 400 feet long by 60 feet wide, contained 32,768 mule spindles, and 643 looms, and its weekly production was 94,000 yards of cloth, weighing 22,000 pounds, made from No. 30 yarn, 72 picks to the inch.

The mill was successful from the start; and, after twelve years of uninterrupted prosperity, the capital stock was increased to $1,200,-000, and a second mill, 428 feet long by 64 feet wide, containing 35,000 spindles and 700 looms, was built, and successfully operated in connection with the first mill.

In 1865 the capital stock was further increased to $1,500,000, and a third mill built. This building is 189 feet long and 95 feet wide, and contains 15,000 spindles, and 350 looms. The three mills at this time (1879) contain 90,000 spindles and 1,900 looms, driven by two pair of Corliss steam-engines, of 2,000 horse-power in the aggregate. The mills employ 1,200 operatives, and consume 11,500 bales of cotton per annum, in the production of 14,700,000 yards of cloth, weighing 4,730,000 pounds, and varying from 28 to 108 inches wide.

Manufacture of Jute.—The manufacture of jute bagging was commenced in 1865 by the late Francis Peabody, who built a mill at the foot of Skerry Street, and commenced to weave the first cloth in the fall of that year. In 1867, a second mill was built on Webb Street, and a company was formed under the name of the India Manufacturing Company. About the year 1870, Mr. Peabody transferred the original mill to a company organized as the Bengal Bagging Company. In June, 1875, David Nevins & Co., of Boston, purchased the interest of the Bengal Bagging Company; and in June, 1877, acquired the property of the India Manufacturing Company. The mills are now known as the Nevins Bagging Mills. Each contains about 500 spindles, and the annual production is upwards of 1,000,000 yards. The business is conducted on private capital. The source of supply for raw material is Bengal. The cloth manufactured is used chiefly for baling cotton.

Boots and Shoes. — The manufacture of boots and shoes is an industry of considerable importance in Salem. There are about forty establishments, employing over 600 hands. The capital invested is about $130,000, and the annual production is over $600,000.

Lead Manufacture.—This business has been carried on in Salem since 1826, when the Salem Lead Company, formed in 1823, commenced operations on the site of the Naumkeag Mills. The company was incorporated Feb. 7, 1824, with a capital of about $200,000, which was afterwards increased. In 1835, the works were sold at auction for $20,500. The total cost to the date of sale had been $120,000.

About 1826, Col. Francis Peabody commenced the white lead business in South Salem, where La Grange Street now is. In 1830, he purchased Wyman's Grist Mills, on Forest River, and the grinding and mixing of the lead was done there, the corroding being done at the old works. In 1843 these mills were sold to the Forest River Lead Company, which became an incorporated company three years later. The works on the site of La Grange Street were torn down, and a number of dwellings located near them were moved to lots adjoining the Forest River Mills. The Forest River Company now manufactures white and sheet lead, its capacity for the former being about 1,000 tons annually.

The Salem Lead Company (the second of that name), was incorporated Feb. 7, 1868. Its manufactures are white lead and lead pipe, the capacity of the works for white lead being 1,500 tons per annum. Its works are at the foot of Saunders Street.

The manufactures of the Forest River and Salem companies are known throughout the country as among the best productions now in the market.

The Salem Gas-Light Company was organized in April, 1850. Its works are at the foot of Northey Street, though premises have been secured and a large "holder" built on the "Peirce and Wait Lot," Bridge Street. The stores were first lighted with gas Dec. 17, 1850, and the street-lamps Dec. 25, 1850.

Car Manufacture. — The Salem Car Company was formed in 1863, for the manufacture of horse-cars. Not meeting with the necessary degree of success, the works, on Bridge Street, were sold to Mr. John Kinsman, who closed out the stock on hand, then built a few railway passenger-cars, and in turn sold the works to the Eastern Railroad. The shops are still continued for the manufacture and repairing of cars for that corporation.

The Atlantic Car Company was organized in 1872, and a factory

for the manufacture of railway passenger coaches and freight cars was
built on Broadway, South Salem.   The depression in business the
following year caused a suspension of work, and car building has
never been revived there.   The buildings were sold, and after remaining unoccupied for about four years, were started up as a factory for
the manufacture of furniture, an industry that was prosecuted there
for a time, but this business has been suspended.

The Salem Laboratory Company was incorporated Feb. 1, 1819,
and is the oldest manufacturing company in the city.   This company
was formed to enlarge and develop the manufacture of chemicals,
commenced a few years previously on Lynde Street.   Its manufactures at the present time include a number of chemicals, of which
blue vitriol is the principal.

Oil and Candle Manufacture. — About 1836 Mr. Francis Peabody
commenced, in South Salem, the refining of sperm and whale oil, and
the manufacture of sperm candles.   In one year he purchased $100,-
000 worth of sperm oil, and $50,000 worth of whale oil.   His
candles had a great reputation, at home and abroad.   He imported the
first braiding machines, and made the first candles with the braided
wick.   In 1837, or thereabouts, Mr. Peabody commenced the manufacture of linseed oil at Middleton, where he had established, four
years previously, a paper mill ; and for this business, he imported to
Salem large quantities of flaxseed from Europe and Calcutta.   In
order to procure larger quantities of seed, he chartered, in 1841, the
ship "Gen. Harrison," and purchased the same year the ship "Isaac
Hicks," and in 1842 the ship "New Jersey."   When the latter
returned to Salem from Calcutta, in December, 1842, it was said to
be the largest ship that ever discharged in Salem.   She registered
between 600 and 700 tons.   Mr. Peabody shipped to London large
quantities of linseed cake, used for the feeding of cattle.

The Seccomb Oil Manufacturing Company, engaged in the manu-.
facture of lubricating and curriers' oils, was organized in 1865.   This
company is the successor of Ebenezer Seccomb, who had occupied the
same factory, at the foot of Harbor Street, for several years in the
manufacture of oils, and previous to that in making candles.   Mr.
Seccomb was a successor in business of Caleb Smith & Sons, successors of Caleb Smith, who had been engaged in candle manufacture on
the same premises from 1835.

The Salem and South Danvers Oil Company was organized in 1855, and manufactures kerosene oil, at works on Mason Street.

Miscellaneous Manufacturing Business. — Numerous smaller manufacturing occupations and trades employ a great number of people, and a large aggregate capital is employed, with reasonable financial results. The State Census of 1875 gives the number of manufacturing establishments in Salem as 550; the capital employed as $4,230,008; the value of manufactured goods and work done as $8,512,693, and the number of persons employed as 4,045. These are all considered low figures.

Railroads. — The business of the Eastern Railroad in Salem is to be counted by the hundreds of thousands yearly. The receipts annually from the passenger business are about $150,000; and the freight department contributes about $250,000 yearly to the income of the road.* Nineteen passenger trains now leave Salem for Boston daily (except Sunday—two on Sunday), against five or six when the road was opened, in August, 1838. The depot in those days was a small wooden structure, very insignificant as compared with the commodious granite and brick one of to-day. When the tunnel was built, in 1839, and the road opened to Newburyport in 1840, the business of Salem received a fresh impetus; and from that day to this the Eastern Railroad has contributed much to the substantial prosperity of the city; the branches to Marblehead, Gloucester, Lawrence, and South Reading (now Wakefield), all adding new outlets and inlets for trade. The Lowell road has also done its share; and with its tracks and those of the Lawrence Branch of the Eastern road, extending to tide-water at Phillips Wharf and Pennsylvania Pier, Salem has had unlimited railroad facilities for transporting coal and merchandise to the inland cities of Lowell and Lawrence. With these iron bands extending in all directions, Salem has been favored with railroad facilities hardly surpassed by any city, however fortunate in its railroad accommodations.

Horse Railroad. — In 1862, an Act of incorporation was obtained, and a horse railroad built from Salem to South Danvers, now Peabody. The first car to the latter town was run July 8, 1863. The road was extended to Beverly, and was opened to that town Oct. 28,

---

* These figures do not represent the *earnings* of the station, but the gross amount of business transacted.

1863. A branch was built to South Salem (Ward V.) in 1864, and was opened May 10. A branch to North Salem (Ward VI.) was opened June 4, 1869. An extension of the main line to Salem Neck and the "Willows" was opened June 10, 1877. The entire road is now operated by the Naumkeag Street Railway Company, which was incorporated in 1875, and which assumed the lease of the Salem Street Railway, the company previously controlling the road, March 1, 1875. The capital of the Naumkeag Street Railway Company is $70,000, and of the Salem, $150,000.

Coal Business. — In 1850, upon the completion of the Salem and Lowell Railroad, a coal business was begun at Phillips Wharf, with Lowell and Lawrence, which amounted to 1,000 tons that year. This became the leading wharf in the city. It was built about 1800, and was owned by the India Wharf Corporation. In 1836, it was rebuilt by Stephen C. Phillips. The coal business here grew steadily and rapidly, and in 1872, when the wharf was leased to the Boston, Lowell, and Nashua Railroad, it had reached 200,000 tons annually. Since the lease to the Lowell road, the business has diminished, the road having transferred a considerable proportion of its business to Boston, but the Wilkesbarre Coal Company still lands large quantities of coal for transportation to the manufacturing cities of Lowell and Lawrence.

Pennsylvania Pier, built in 1873, is the scene of an immense coal business, conducted by the Philadelphia and Reading Coal and Iron Company. This company's steamers land there about 90,000 tons of coal annually, for transportation into the interior, — mainly to Lowell. The "coal pockets" here have a capacity of 8,000 tons.

Express and Freight Business. — Before the days of railroading, "baggage-wagons" transported goods to supply the business wants of the community. In 1804, a wagon was run to Boston and back twice a week. It was called a "stage-wagon" by its proprietor, John L. Matthews. A wagon designated by this name was run to Boston as early as 1792, and one from Gloucester to Salem before that date. In 1815, a daily wagon was run to Boston, and from that time till 1838, when the Eastern Railroad was opened, the business grew steadily, but was not considered very remunerative. With the advent of the railroad came a greatly increased express and freighting business. This has grown to immense proportions ; and J. H. Moulton, and Merritt & Co., to-day do a thriving and enterprising business in the freight-ing and express lines, while Savory & Co's Express, founded by the late Benjamin Savory, a driver of the old Boston Stage Company, and numerous smaller parcel expresses, are doing a large business.

Banks. — The business interests of the city are accommodated by seven national banks ; and two savings banks serve as depositories for the earnings of the working people.

The Essex Bank, the first bank established in Salem, began busi-ness July 2, 1792, with a capital of about $300,000. It occupied the building on Central Street used for the custom house for a series of years. Central Street was then known as "Bank Street." The Essex Bank was incorporated June 18, 1799, when it was allowed a capital of $400,000. It expired in 1819, although its affairs were not fully wound up until 1822.

The Salem Bank, now the "Salem National," was incorporated March 8, 1803, with a capital of $200,000. This was increased Feb. 8, 1823, to $250,000 ; reduced Feb. 14, 1859, to $187,500 ; restored April 1, 1865, to $200,000 ; increased Feb. 12, 1873, to the present amount, $300,000. Its presidents have been Benjamin Pickman, 1803 ; Joseph Peabody, 1814 ; George Peabody, 1833 ; Benjamin Mer-rill, 1842 ; George Peabody, 1847 ; William C. Endicott, 1858 ; Augustus Story, 1875. Its cashiers : Jonathan Hodges, 1803 ; John Moriarty, 1810 ; Charles M. Endicott, 1835 ; George D. Phippen, 1858. The bank was originally located in a brick building on the south side of Essex Street, next west of the Benjamin Pickman es-tate, nearly opposite St. Peter's Street. It stood in from the street. The bank adopted the national system in 1864 ; and removed to its present location, Holyoke building, November, 1866.

The Merchants' Bank was organized in 1811, and incorporated June 26th of that year, with a capital of $200,000 ; which was afterwards increased to $400,000, and reduced in 1845 to its present figure, $200,-000. The first banking rooms were in the Union building, on the corner of Union and Essex streets. Afterwards the bank occupied rooms in the Bowker building, and in 1855 removed to its present lo-cation in the Asiatic building. Its presidents have been Benj. W. Crowninshield, Joseph Story, John W. Treadwell, and Benjamin H. Silsbee. Its cashiers, John Saunders, John W. Treadwell, Francis H. Silsbee, Benj. H. Silsbee, and Nathl. B. Perkins. It became a national bank Jan. 19, 1865.

The Commercial (now First National) Bank was organized April 19, 1819, with a capital of $300,000. This was reduced to $200,000 in 1830, and restored in 1851. It has always occupied its present quarters in the Central Street bank building. Its presidents have been Willard Peele and William Sutton; cashiers, N. L. Rogers, Z. F. Silsbee, and E. H. Payson. The bank entered the national system, as the First National Bank, in June, 1864.

The Exchange Bank was incorporated Jan. 31, 1823, with a capital of $300,000; which was afterwards reduced to its present amount, — $200,000. The bank commenced business at No. 172 Essex Street, on the site of William Gray's garden, next below the Essex House; and continued there until it was removed to its location in the First Church building, Dec. 8, 1864. It originally faced Essex Street, but now occupies the opposite corner of the building on Washington Street. Its presidents have been Gideon Tucker, John Webster, Henry L. Williams. Its cashiers, John Chadwick, Joseph H. Webb. It adopted the national system, Feb. 18, 1865.

The Asiatic Bank was incorporated June 12, 1824, with a capital of $200,000. It commenced business in July, 1824, with a capital of $315,000, in the old bank building on Central Street. From thence it removed to the East India Marine building; and from there to the Asiatic building, on Washington Street, in 1855. Its presidents have been Joseph S. Cabot and Leonard B. Harrington. Its cashier, William H. Foster, has been fifty-three years in the bank's employ, fifty of which as cashier. There is but one older bank officer in the United States. The Asiatic became a national bank Feb. 1, 1865.

The Mercantile Bank was organized May 8, 1826, with a capital of $200,000, which has never been changed. It first occupied a room with Mr. John W. Fenno, a broker, in the Central building, Central Street, the room now occupied by J. B. Osborn as a barber-shop. The bank was moved into its present rooms early in 1827. Its presidents have been Nathaniel L. Rogers, David Putnam, John Dwyer, Aaron Perkins; and Charles Harrington, the present holder of the office. The cashiers have been John A. Southwick; Stephen Webb; and Joseph H. Phippen, the present cashier. The bank entered the national system Jan. 10, 1865.

The Mechanics' and Traders' Bank was incorporated March 10, 1827, and allowed a capital of $200,000. It, however, never commenced business.

The Naumkeag Bank was incorporated March 17, 1831, with a capital of $200,000, which was subsequently increased to $500,000. It commenced business in the store of Benjamin Dodge ; thence removed to the Manning building, now Bowker Place ; from there to the East India Marine Building ; and then to its present location in the Asiatic building, Washington Street. It became a national bank in December, 1864. Its presidents have been David Pingree, Edward D. Kimball, Charles H. Fabens, William B. Parker, and David Pingree, (Jr.) ; its cashiers, Joseph G. Sprague and Joseph H. Towne.

The Bank of General Interest was incorporated March 17, 1831, with a capital of $200,000. It ceased business in 1842.

The North American Bank was incorporated March 31, 1836, and was allowed a capital of $300,000. It never went into operation.

The Salem Savings Bank was incorporated Jan. 29, 1818, and was the second institution of its kind in the State. It commenced business April 18th, in the old bank building, on Essex Street, originally occupied by the Salem Bank in 1803. Its presidents have been Dr. Edward A. Holyoke, 1818 ; Joseph Peabody, 1830 ; Nathaniel Silsbee, 1844 ; Daniel A. White, 1851 ; Zach. F. Silsbee, 1861 ; John Bertram, 1864 ; Joseph S. Cabot, 1865 ; Benjamin H. Silsbee, 1875 : its treasurers, William P. Richardson, 1818 ; William Gibbs, 1820 ; William Dean, 1821 ; Peter Lander, Jr., 1822 ; Daniel Bray, 1823 ; Benjamin Shreve, 1837 ; Henry Ropes, 1839 ; William Wallis, 1861 ; Charles E. Symonds, 1865. In 1855 the bank removed to its present location, on Washington Street, in the Asiatic building, of which it is now the owner. In 1846 over $900,000 was on deposit in this bank. In 1878 the number of depositors was 15,095, and the assets were $6,011,440.36.

The Salem Five Cents Savings Bank was incorporated in 1855. Its presidents have been Edward D. Kimball, 1855 ; Edmund Smith, 1861 ; Henry L. Williams, 1862 : its treasurers, J. Vincent Browne, 1855 ; Charles H. Henderson, 1868. The bank was originally located on Essex Street, opposite St. Peter's ; then, in the second story of Downing block ; from which it removed to its present location in the Northey building, corner of Essex and Washington streets. The number of its depositors is 7,049 ; amount of assets, $2,139,160.48.

The Salem Board of Trade was organized in 1866, and opened a reading-room. Meetings were held for several years ; but in 1876 the interest in the association had so far abated that it was deemed inexpedient to longer continue the reading-room, though an organization is maintained.

Insurance Companies. — The Essex Mutual Fire Insurance Company was incorporated June 11, 1829. Its risks are confined to buildings, dwellings, and furniture. "The Mutual Fire Insurance Company in Salem" was incorporated April 16, 1838. Its risks are buildings, dwellings, household furniture, and stocks of goods. The Holyoke Mutual Fire Insurance Company was incorporated in 1843, and is to-day the leading insurance company of Essex County. The Hamilton Insurance Company was organized in 1852. Its business was closed up in 1864. The Marine Insurance Companies have been mentioned in the preceding chapter.

CHAPTER X.

BIOGRAPHICAL SKETCHES OF SOME OF THE NOTED MEN OF SALEM.

In tho preceding chapters there have been given brief notices of some of the noted men connected with the history of Salem. Short sketches of those not finding an appropriate place heretofore have been introduced into this chapter. With ample space the list might be easily extended, and names equally deserving of notice be added. What follows is but a chance selection and but a sample of- a complete list.

William Hathorne. — Hathorne was a noted name in the early annals of Salem. Major William Hathorne came over in the " Arbella " with Winthrop. He went first to Dorchester, having had land granted him there in 1634. In 1636 Salem tendered him grants of land if he would remove hither. He came in that or the year following. From that time his name appears on our records as holding important positions : commissioner, speaker of the house of representatives, counsel in cases before the courts, judge on the bench, and soldier commanding important and difficult expeditions. Johnson, in his " Wonder Working Providence," thus says of him : " Yet through the Lord's mercy we still retaine among our Democracy the Godly Captaine William Hathorn, whom the Lord has indued with a quick apprehension, strong memory, and Rhetorick, volubility of speech, which has caused the people to make use of him often in Public Service, especially when they have had to do with any foreign government." Major Hathorne was the emigrant ancestor of Nathaniel Hawthorne, the famous author and novelist. He died in 1681.

John Hathorne was a son of Major William Hathorne, and seems to have inherited many of his father's prominent traits of character and to have succeeded him in his public honors. He was made freeman in 1677, representative in 1683, assistant or counsellor from 1684 to 1712, except the years of Andros' government; a magistrate in the prosecution of the witchcraft trials, afterwards of the Superior

Court; colonel of a regiment and commander of the forces in the expedition of 1696, on the retirement of Church. He died in 1717. There seems to have been no noted name in the line thereafter until the birth of Nathaniel Hawthorne, July 4, 1804.

Benjamin Lynde was born Sept. 22, 1666. He graduated at Harvard in 1686. He was appointed chief justice of the superior court of judicature of the Province of Massachusetts Bay in 1729; and died in office Jan. 28, 1745. Benjamin Lynde, his son, was appointed chief justice of the same court in 1769, and left the bench in 1771. He was born in Salem Oct. 5, 1700; graduated at Harvard in 1718; and died in 1781.

Timothy Pickering was one of the most distinguished citizens of Salem. He was born in Salem, July 17, 1745; and graduated at Harvard in 1763. In 1774 he wrote the address of the people of Salem in regard to the closing of the port of Boston. In 1775 he was chosen colonel of the first regiment of militia; and was present with part of his command at North Bridge, Feb. 26, 1775, where Col. Leslie was successfully prevented from seizing the Provincial cannon. He was about this time a clerk in the office of the registry of deeds for Essex County. Later in the same year, he was appointed a judge of the court of common pleas, and judge of the prize court for Suffolk, Middlesex, and Essex counties. In the fall of 1776, he commanded a regiment of 700 men. He was adjutant-general at the battles of Germantown and Brandywine; member of the Continental board of war, in 1777; and a quartermaster-general in 1780. At the close of the Revolutionary War he settled in Philadelphia, and went into business as a commission merchant. When the convention was held for remodelling the Constitution of the State of Pennsylvania in 1790, Mr. Pickering was present as a member. Washington appointed him postmaster-general in 1791; and he held the office till 1795, when he was transferred to the position of secretary of state.

Upon his retirement from the latter office in 1800, or soon thereafter, he returned to Massachusetts, and in 1803 was elected to the senate of the United States. Retiring from that position in 1811, he turned his attention to horticulture and agriculture, in which he took a great interest. He was again called to participate in public affairs, and was chosen in 1814 the member of Congress from this district. In 1817 he again retired to his farm, and devoted the rest of his life

Nathl Bowditch

N^h^l Hawthorne

Joseph Story

D^r E White

to rural pursuits. He was the founder and first president of the Essex
Agricultural Society. His death occurred in Salem Jan. 29, 1829.
Energetic and faithful in public office, plain and simple in private life,
pure and unblemished in character, he was a man whom his native
Salem and the nation delighted to honor.

Daniel A. White was born in Methuen June 7, 1776, and graduated
at Harvard in 1797. He commenced the practice of law at Newburyport in 1804; was a State senator from 1810 to 1814; and was chosen
a representative to Congress in 1814, but resigned in 1815, before taking his seat, to accept the office of judge of probate for Essex County.
He made an admirable judicial officer, and continued to hold the position till July, 1853, when he resigned. He came to Salem to reside
in 1817; and from that time till his death he contributed largely to
build up the literary and charitable institutions of the city. Harvard
conferred upon him the degree of LL. D. in 1837. He was president
of the Salem Lyceum; of the Essex Historical Society; of the Salem
Athenæum; of the Salem Dispensary, and of the Salem Savings
Bank. When the Essex Institute was established, he was its first
president; and his interest in that society never wavered nor grew
cold. He donated to the Institute, at different times, a library of
8,000 volumes, and contributed money freely to advance the work of
the institution. His death occurred in Salem, March 30, 1861.

Joseph Story, the distinguished jurist, was born at Marblehead,
Sept. 18, 1779. He graduated from Harvard College in 1798, and
studied law in his native town, where he delivered a eulogy on the
life of Washington, Jan. 2, 1800. He located in Salem in 1801, and
was admitted to the bar the same year. His public life began as a
representative to the general court, where he served from 1805 to 1808,
and again in 1810–11, the last time as speaker of the house. In 1808
he was chosen to represent the Essex district in the national congress.
Here he exerted his efforts to secure a repeal of the embargo act,
which he had advocated on its passage as the only measure short of a
declaration of war, but which he now believed had accomplished its
full purpose. On Nov. 11, 1811, Mr. Story was appointed an associate justice of the United States supreme court. In 1820 he distinguished himself as a member of the convention for revising the
State constitution, in which his services were valuable in considering
the tenure and compensation of the judiciary. In 1829, Judge Story

removed from Salem to Cambridge, having been appointed professor of law at Harvard University,   He died Sept. 10, 1845.

Rufus Choate, the eminent lawyer and statesman, was born in Ipswich (now Essex), Oct. 1, 1799. He graduated at Dartmouth College in 1819, and became a tutor there. He studied law at Cambridge, and also in the office of William Wirt, and commenced legal practice in Danvers, in 1824, removing soon afterwards to Salem. He was a member of the State legislature in 1825, a State senator two years later, and in 1832 a representative in Congress. He removed to Boston in 1834. He was elected to Daniel Webster's seat in the United States senate in 1841, Webster entering the cabinet of President Harrison as secretary of state.   On the death of Mr. Webster in 1852, Mr Choate became the acknowleged leader of the Massachusetts bar. In 1853 he was appointed attorney-general for the State. He delivered, while in Congress, eulogies on the death of President Harrison and Daniel Webster. He died at Halifax, N. S., July 13, 1859, while on his way to Europe, whither he was making a trip to recruit his impaired health.

Edward Augustus Holyoke was the son of Pres. Edward Holyoke, of Harvard College, and was born in Marblehead, Aug. 1, 1728, old style, and died in Salem, March 31, 1829. He graduated at Harvard in 1746, and in July, 1747, commenced the study of medicine with Dr. Thomas Berry, of Ipswich. He finished his studies in April, 1749, and came to Salem in June of the same year.   For the remainder of his life he scarcely left the town, and never wandered so far as fifty miles from the spot on which he was born. His longest journey was to Portsmouth, in 1749. In 1755 he was married to Judith Pickman, daughter of Col. Benj. Pickman. She died in 1756, and in 1759 he was married to Mary Viall, daughter of Nathaniel Viall, merchant, of Boston. Dr. Holyoke retained the full possession of his mental faculties until his death. After he attained his hundredth year he passed an hour in the study of one of his medical acquaintances, examining the results of a new operation for a dangerous disease. Cases of longevity are not rare among persons not distinguished for their mental powers, and the close of life with such, is frequently a state of mere existence, "sans everything." Dr. Holyoke used his intellect with vigor and energy to the last of his days.

A public dinner was tendered to him, by his associate physicians of Salem and Boston, on his hundredth birthday. He was still so vigorous at that extreme age that, when the morning came, he rose, dressed and shaved himself without assistance, and walked to the Essex House, where the dinner was given. On being called on for a toast he presented, in his own handwriting, the following sentiment: "The Massachusetts Medical Society: May it continue to improve the art for which it was instituted, to the utmost of its wishes, and be the means, under Providence, of alleviating the pains and evils of life, and promoting the happiness of society by suppressing quackery and rendering the business of the profession as perfect as the nature of things admits; and may each member of the society, and every other gentleman here present, enjoy health and prosperity and the pleasing consciousness that he has contributed somewhat to the advancement and improvement of the public welfare."

After he had passed his hundredth birthday he wrote to a gentleman, who asked him in reference to his mode of life, that "as to my diet, having been taught to eat of anything that was provided for me, and having always a good appetite, I am never anxious about my food. As to the quantity, I am no great eater, and I find my appetite sooner satisfied now than formerly. There is one peculiarity in my diet which, as it may perhaps have contributed to health, I would mention: I am fond of fruit, and have this thirty or more years daily indulged in eating freely of those of the season, as strawberries, currants, peaches, plums, apples, &c., which, in summer and winter, I eat just before dinner, and seldom at any other time; and, indeed, very seldom eat anything whatever between meals. My breakfast I vary continually; coffee, tea, chocolate, with toasted bread and butter, but never any meat in my life. Bread, of flour, makes a large portion of my food, perhaps near one-half. After dinner I most commonly drink one glass of wine; plain boiled rice I am fond of — it makes nearly one-half of my dinner. I rarely eat any high seasoned food. As to drinks, I seldom take any but at meal-times and with my pipe. For the last 40 or 50 years my most usual drink has been a mixture — a little singular, indeed, but as for me it is still palatable and agreeable, I still prefer it. The mixture is this, viz.: good West India rum, 2 spoonfuls, good cider, 3 spoonfuls, of water 9 or 10 spoonfuls; of this mixture I drink about ½ a pint with my dinner, and about the same quantity with my pipe after dinner and my pipe in the evening, never exceeding a pint the whole day. I generally take one pipe after dinner and another in the evening, and hold a small piece of pigtail tobacco in my mouth from breakfast till near dinner, and again in the afternoon till tea; this has been my practice for 80 years. I drink tea about sunset and eat with it a small slice of bread, toasted, with butter. I never eat anything more till breakfast. As to my clothing, it is what my friends call thin; I never wear flannel next my skin, tho' often advised to it, and am less liable to take cold, as it is called, than most people; a good, warm, double-breasted waistcoat and a cloth coat answers me for winter, and as the season grows warmer I gradually conform my covering to it. As to the passions, I need not tell you that when indulged they injure the health; that a calm, quiet self-possession, and a moderation in our expectations and pursuits, contribute much to our health, as well as our happiness, and that anxiety is injurious to both. I have always taken care to have a full proportion of sleep, which, I suppose, has contributed to my longevity."

Dr. Holyoke was the first person on whom the degree of doctor of medicine was conferred by Harvard College, and he afterwards received the degree of doctor of laws. He was the first President of the Massachusetts Medical Society, and was among the original members of the American Academy of Arts and Sciences, and at one time its president. He was at the time of his death the president of the Salem Athenæum, of the Essex Historical Society, of the Salem Savings Bank, and of the Salem Dispensary.

B. Lynde Oliver was born in 1760, and died in Salem, May 14, 1835. He was a distinguished physician and learned theologian. He was noted for his acquirements in several branches of natural philosophy, particularly in that of optics.

Charles Osgood was born in Salem, Feb. 25, 1809. At the age of sixteen he entered the Asiatic Bank as a clerk, and continued there about a year. He early developed a taste for painting, and in 1827 he opened a studio in Boston. In 1828 he came to Salem, where he has resided ever since, with the exception of the year 1840, when he was established in New York City. His portraits hang upon the walls of the historical societies of Boston and Worcester, the Memorial Hall at Cambridge, the Peabody Institute at Peabody, and the City

Hall, East India Marine Hall, Essex Institute, and Athenæum at Salem. Felt, in his "Annals of Salem," writing in 1849, says of him : "His labors have been extensive and his success unsurpassed. He is deservedly ranked among the first painters of our republic."

George Southward was born in Salem, and died Feb. 19, 1876, at the age of seventy-two years. While pursuing his studies in Rome he contracted a severe cold, and his health was feeble ever after. He possessed considerable merit as an artist, but his extreme modesty and love of retirement prevented him from becoming as well known as his merits deserved. The coloring of his pictures was especially good, and his copy of Guido's "Aurora" was an admirable piece of work, and much admired.

William W. Story was born in Salem, Feb. 12, 1819, and was a son of the Hon. Joseph Story. He graduated at Harvard in 1838, and was admitted to the bar in Boston. He soon turned his attention to sculpture, and has given the world some fine specimens of his talent in this direction. Among his prominent works may be mentioned his statues of "Cleopatra" and "Semiramis." He has also made some famous portrait busts. He is an author of note, and wrote the ode on the occasion of the celebration, at Salem, of the 250th anniversary of the landing of Endicott.

John Rogers, the famous modeller of the small character groups which are now so deservedly popular, was born in Salem, Oct. 30, 1829, and was in early life a machinist.

Benjamin Goodhue was born in Salem, Oct. 1, 1748, and died July 28, 1814. He graduated from Harvard in 1766 ; was State senator from 1784 to 1789 ; was elected representative to Congress in 1789 ; and was United States senator in 1796. While in the National House of Representatives he was one of a committee who formed the code of revenue laws, and as senator was chairman of the Committee on Commerce. He resigned his seat in the Senate in 1800, and retired to private life.

Nathan Reed was born in Western, now Warren, Mass., July 2, 1759. He was a graduate of Harvard in the class of 1781, and was a tutor there from 1783 to 1787. He studied medicine with Dr. E. A. Holyoke till October, 1788, when he established himself in the drug business. He constructed the first steamboat with paddle-wheels in this country, and a trial trip took place in 1789. He was a representative in Congress in 1801–3. He died at Belfast, Me., Jan. 20, 1849.

Jacob Crowninshield was born in Salem May 31, 1770, and died at Washington, April 15, 1808. He was a representative to Congress from 1803 to 1805, and at the close of his term was offered a seat in the Cabinet of President Jefferson, a position which he declined, preferring the comforts of private life to the toils and trials of office.

Benjamin Pickman was born in Salem, Sept. 30, 1763, and graduated at Harvard in 1784. He was a merchant, and represented the town in the Legislature in 1800, and was State senator in 1802, '3, '4, and '5. After a number of years' service in the executive council, he was chosen a representative to Congress in 1809, serving till 1811. He was president of the board of directors of the Theological School at Cambridge, and died Aug. 16, 1843.

Nathaniel Silsbee was born in Salem, Jan. 14, 1773. He was first a master-mariner, commanding the ships of E. H. Derby, and afterwards a successful merchant. He was chosen a member of Congress in 1816, served in the House until 1821, and in the Senate from 1826 to 1835. In 1823, '24, and '25, he was president of the Massachusetts Senate. He died in Salem, July 14, 1850.

Gideon Barstow was born in Mattapoisett, Sept. 7, 1783. He died at St. Augustine, Fla., where he had gone to recruit his health, March 26, 1852. He was a member of both branches of the State Legislature, and representative in Congress from 1821 to 1823.

Benjamin W. Crowninshield was born in Salem, Dec. 27, 1772. He was secretary of the navy, under President Madison, from 1814 to 1818, and a member of the State Senate for several years, beginning in 1811. He was a representative in Congress from 1823 to 1831. He built and lived in the house which is now the Home for Aged Women, on Derby Street. He died in Boston, Feb. 8, 1851.

George B. Loring was born in North Andover, Nov. 8, 1817, and graduated at Harvard in 1838. He received the degree of M. D. at the Harvard Medical School in 1842; was surgeon of the Marine Hospital at Chelsea in 1843, and of the 7th Regiment, M. V. M., in 1842, '43, and '44; was postmaster of Salem, 1853–58; was a member of the Massachusetts House of Representatives in 1866–67; was president of the Massachusetts Senate in 1873, '74, '75, and '76; was

United States Centennial Commissioner for Massachusetts in 1876; and was elected a representative to Congress in 1876, and re-elected in 1878, being the present member from this district.

Nathaniel Bowditch was born in Salem, March 26, 1773. His early life was spent in Danvers and Salem, in which latter place he was for several years employed in the ship-chandler stores of Ropes & Hodges, and S. C. Ward. At the age of twenty-one, he made his first voyage to sea. Having a natural taste for scientific research, he early devoted much time to the study of scientific works, and in 1788, at the age of fifteen, he made all the calculations of an almanac for the year 1790. He translated Newton's "Principia" from Latin into English, while in the merchant office of S. C. Ward. His first voyage was in the ship "Henry," Capt. Prince, to the Isle of Bourbon. He made four other voyages, the last in the "Putnam," of which he was master and part owner. His sea-voyages covered a period of nine years. Before the close of his nautical career, he had received the degree of Master of Arts from Harvard University, and had been chosen a member of the American Academy of Arts and Sciences. Immediately after the close of his seafaring life, he was elected president of the Essex Fire and Marine Insurance Company, and held the office about twenty years, till his removal to Boston in 1823. He was a member of the Salem Marine Society, and also of the East India Marine Society, a proprietor in the Social and Philosophical libraries, and a trustee of the Salem Athenæum. He declined a professorship in Harvard College, also one in the University of Virginia, a third at West Point, and the presidency of a Boston insurance company, preferring to remain in Salem; but in 1823, he was persuaded to become the actuary of the Massachusetts Hospital Life Insurance Company, in Boston. After his removal there, he completed and published a translation and commentary on "Mécanique Céleste." This was in four volumes, and it fixed his fame on a most substantial basis, at home and abroad. The "London Quarterly Review" gave it a flattering notice, and it became at once a standard work. Bowditch produced a fine chart of the harbors of Salem, Marblehead, Beverly, and Manchester; contributed largely on astronomical subjects to the "Transactions" of the American Academy; published (1802) "The New American Navigator," and contributed many articles to the "North American Review" and "Rees' Cyclopædia."

While at Boston he became a trustee of the Boston Athenæum, president of the American Academy, and a member of the corporation of Harvard College. He died March 16, 1838.

Robert Cowan was a man whose rare inventive genius has seldom been equalled. Born in Glasgow, Scotland, about 1762, he was brought to this country in a prize vessel during the Revolutionary War. When Capt. Joseph Peabody, afterwards an eminent Salem merchant, was engaged in privateering, Mr. Cowan made several cruises with him; and he was present with that distinguished naval hero of the Revolution, Jonathan Haraden, also of Salem, in the privateer "General Pickering," in his memorable fight with an English privateer near the coast of Spain, on June 4, 1780. After the war he settled in Salem, and became distinguished for shrewdness, industry, and ingenuity. He either invented or introduced the art of varnishing carriages and furniture, and in 1796 articles of furniture were sent from Boston to Mr. Cowan to be varnished. He also manufactured, without assistance from others, organs, pianofortes, and drawing pencils, among the first to be made in this country. His establishment was on the corner of Essex and Beckford streets. He died in Salem, Aug. 24, 1846, at the age of eighty-four years.

Francis Peabody was born in Salem, Dec. 7, 1801. He was the founder of the Forest River Lead Company, and built the paper-mills at Middleton. He was one of the founders of the Salem Lyceum and of the Harmony Grove Cemetery Corporation, and was president of the Essex Institute. He was colonel of the 1st Regiment of the State militia, and was one of the leaders in organizing a famous sham-fight that took place, Oct. 6, 1826, in Danvers. Col. Peabody introduced in Salem the system of miscellaneous courses of public lectures. It was largely through the instrumentality of Mr. Peabody that the old First Church structure was removed from the place of its discovery, near Witch Hill, to the grounds in the rear of Plummer Hall. Mr. Peabody died Oct. 31, 1867.

CHAPTER XI.

SHORT SKETCHES OF MATTERS OF INTEREST CONNECTED WITH THE
HISTORY OF SALEM.

There are many interesting facts relating to the history of Salem
and its surroundings which are not mentioned in the preceding chapters and which should find some place in this sketch.

The Common. — In the year 1714 the commoners voted that the
spot "where the trainings are generally kept before Nathaniel Higginson's house shall be forever a training field for the use of Salem." This
common was for a long time unenclosed, and was little else than a
swamp where the townspeople gathered berries and cut flags and
hoops. The surface of the land was very uneven, and there were
several small ponds included within its limits. Portions of the common were at various times leased by the town to individuals, and in
1770 the town voted to build an almshouse on the north-eastern portion of it, which was opened for occupancy about 1772. The common
remained in this condition till 1801, when Elias Hasket Derby,
having been chosen colonel of the militia, raised a subscription of
about $2,500 for levelling the common and filling up the ponds. This
was done, and rows of trees, chiefly poplar, were planted along the
walks, and in 1802 the selectmen changed the name to Washington
Square. In 1817 the poplar-trees gave place to the present elms, and
a substantial wooden railing was built to enclose the mall. In 1850
the present iron fence was substituted for the wooden railing.

First Houses in Salem. — The four meeting-houses of the First
Church have all occupied nearly the same spot; the first was built in
1634, and the "unfinished building of one story," which had been previously used for worship, was no doubt in the same vicinity. The dwelling-
house of the Rev. Francis Higginson, who died in 1630, was on ground
now covered by the Asiatic Building, and faced towards the South
River. The Rev. Samuel Skelton's house was near where the police
station now stands, on Front Street. Skelton died in 1634. Samuel

22

Sharpe, who was sent over from England in 1629 to take charge of military affairs, lived in a house where is now the corner of Washington and Lynde streets. Next south of Mr. Sharpe's house stood one once owned by the Rev. Nicholas Noyes. This was just south of the present residence of Robert Brookhouse, Esq. Where the new Price Block now stands was a house owned by the Rev. Hugh Peters, pastor of the First Church from 1636 to 1641. South and west of this stood a house which was the homestead of Ralph Fogg, the first town clerk, and afterwards owned by John Hathorne, one of the judges in the witchcraft trials. South of that was a house occupied for a time by Lady Deborah Moody, and next south was the homestead of the Rev. Hugh Peters, afterwards occupied by Judge Corwin,* another justice in the witchcraft trials. On the corner of Norman Street lived Dr. George Emory, here as early as 1637. South of Sweet's Cove (now Creek Street) was a lot of land laid out to the Rev. Samuel Skelton in 1630.† Next south of this was the "Broadfield," originally owned by Gov. Endicott. The almshouse stood on the present site of the State Normal School.

The first Quaker meeting-house was built by Thomas Maule in 1688. "The town bridge," on Boston Street, was built probably about 1640. Next east of the bridge, and north-east of Boston Street, were two houses owned in 1659 by Giles Corey, who was crushed to death in witchcraft days for refusing to confess. Robert Moulton, the "chief" ship-builder, sent over to Gov. Endicott in 1629, lived near the head of the North River, where possibly was built the first vessel constructed in the Colony.

The homestead of Gov. Endicott was "east of Washington Street, and south of the North River." A house that formerly stood on the northern corner of Washington and Church streets, the frame of which is now incorporated in a building used by the Water Department, is said by tradition to have been the original house of Gov.

* Spelled Corwin at that time, but now spelled Curwen.

† In 1651, this and contiguous land became the property of John Ruck, by purchase from his father, Thomas Ruck, of Boston, and this locality, about ten years later, began to be a settlement of shipwrights. It was called "Ruck's Village," and here was carried on all the principal ship-building for several years. The vessels were launched into the creek that made up from the South River. The locality received the appellation "Knockers' Hole," from the knocking and pounding done by the ship carpenters in their work, and was so known up to within a few years.

OLD BAKERY, ST. PETER'S ST.

BIRTHPLACE OF TIMOTHY PICKERING.

Heliotype Printing Co., Boston.

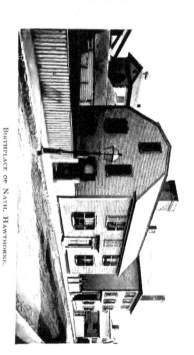

BIRTHPLACE OF NATH. HAWTHORNE.

NARBONNE HOUSE.

Endicott. The story runs that it was built in England, brought to America by the Dorchester Company, and erected at Cape Ann for Roger Conant, in 1624, and removed to Salem when Endicott arrived in 1628. From the best evidence that can be found, it appears probable that the Governor's house did not originally stand on this spot, but about ten rods north of it, where Federal street enters Washington from the east. There is a theory that the original house was moved about 1679, from there to the corner of Washington and Church streets, and that it stood there till moved back on the latter street, and incorporated in the city building above mentioned. Small tack nails, claimed to form the initials "I. E.," have been found in a timber of this old structure. Many doubt the tradition, and a sentence in the preface of Thomas Maule's book, "Truth Held Forth and Maintained," published in 1694, as previously stated, is adduced as evidence that the house could not be placed, even at that time. The sentence is as follows : " One can hardly find where his (Endicott's) fair dwelling in Salem stood." This may refer to the cellar on the original site above referred to, in which case the tradition may be true. At any rate it is an interesting one.

Where Dr. S. M. Cate now lives on, the southern corner of Washington and Church streets, was the house of Thomas Oliver, whose wife, Mary, was a noted character in early colonial history. Thomas Oliver's second wife, Bridget, who afterwards married Edward Bishop, was the first victim of the witchcraft delusion. Where the West Block now stands, the site of the late Mansion House, was the old Ship Tavern, kept for many years by John Gedney. Between that and St. Peter's Street was the homestead of Peter Palfray, one of the old planters. On the north corner of Essex and Washington streets lived Walter Price, and next east, John Woodbury, another of the old planters.

The Bradstreet house, torn down in 1750, stood on the site of the late Francis Peabody's residence, next west of Plummer Hall. It was built by Emanuel Downing, the father of Sir George Downing. The date of its erection is not known, but it was conveyed to Emanuel Downing's daughter Anne, the wife of Capt. Joseph Gardner, in 1656. After the death of Capt. Gardner, who was killed at the Great Swamp fight in the Narraganset war, in 1675, his wife married Gov. Simon Bradstreet, and thus the house became known as the Bradstreet house. Gov. Bradstreet, the last of the colonial governors, died there March 27, 1697.

The exact location of the house of Roger Conant, the first built in Salem, has never been settled ; but the strongest evidence is that it stood on the site of the present Maynes Block, opposite the market, on Essex Street. The house on the north-west corner of Essex and North streets, known as the "Witch House," was originally owned by Roger Williams in 1635 and 1636, and afterwards by Capt. Richard Davenport, whose administrators sold it to Jonathan Corwin in 1674. Judge Corwin lived here, and tradition says that one of the rooms was used for preliminary examinations of those charged with witchcraft in 1692. Hence its name of "old witch house." This is the oldest house standing in Salem, or in this section.*

Other Salem Houses.—The house on Essex Street, in which Dr. E. A. Holyoke lived is now occupied by Israel Fellows as a furniture warehouse. William H. Prescott, the historian, was born May 4, 1796, in a house which stood on the site of Plummer Hall. This house was built by Nathan Reed, member of Congress from this district, and was afterwards occupied by Joseph Peabody. The house in which Joshua Ward lived when he entertained President George Washington on his visit to Salem, in 1789, still stands on Washington Street, and is now occupied by Dr. J. E. Fiske. Nathaniel Bowditch was born in the house formerly numbered fourteen on Brown Street, and which has recently been moved back into the garden formerly attached to the house. The house numbered twenty-one on Union Street was the birth-place of Nathaniel Hawthorne. On Broad Street, in the house now occupied by his grandson, John Pickering, Col. Timothy Pickering was born.

Taverns.—Early provision was made "of taverns or ordinaries." They who kept them were required to be licensed, and were not to suffer "any to be drunk," nor to tipple "after nine of the clock at night." In 1637 John Holgrave, at the earnest request of the town, "has undertaken to keepe an ordinary for the entertaynment of strangers." In 1646 Mrs. Catherine Clarke, having a family of children, is licensed for £10 per annum, if "she provide a fitt man, that is godly to manage the businesse." A house was erected for John

---

* These notes in reference to the first houses of Salem are taken, mainly, from Mr. W. P Upham's contributions to the "Essex Institute Bulletin" in 1869.

Massey in 1661, and became noted as a tavern. It was situated at the Salem end of the Beverly ferry, and was called "The old Ferry Tavern." It was demolished in 1819. The "Great Tavern" stood on the site of the present Stearns Building in 1727. It was known as "the great tavern with many peaks," and for a time as the Ship Tavern. It was here that the Social Library was formed, in 1760. The land was once owned by Hugh Peters. The Stearns Building was erected about 1791. A tavern near the northern corner of Washington and Church streets was also once known as the "Ship Tavern."

The veritable "Old Ship Tavern," noted of that name, was on the site of the present West Block, Essex Street. It was in later years the site of the Mansion House. In this immediate vicinity,—Essex Street, between the present head of Central Street and St. Peter's Street,— stood many taverns : "Mr. Stacey's Tavern," "Mr. Pratt's Tavern," "Mr. Goodhue's Tavern," "Mr. Robinson's Tavern," "Benjamin Webb's Tavern," the "King's Arms Tavern," later, the "Sun Tavern," the "Essex Coffee House," the "Lafayette Coffee House," and the present "Essex House." The last three were the same building, with different names, as above. The "King's Arms Tavern" was a building erected in 1652, by William Browne, as a mansion. It was about 1768 that it was known as the "King's Arms Tavern," and, on the breaking out of the Revolution, as the "Sun Tavern." It was taken down, in 1800, by William Gray, who built a brick house just east of its site. The tavern was next kept in Mr. Gray's former residence, on the site of the present Bowker Block. In 1814 Mr. Gray's new house became a tavern, and was called the "Essex Coffee House." It became the "Lafayette Coffee House" when the Marquis de Lafayette visited Salem the last time, in 1824, and stopped there. It next became the "Essex House," and is thus known now. In 1774 the "Salem Coffee House" was kept in a building near the site of the present St. Peter's Church. "Thomas Beadle's Tavern" stood on Essex Street, nearly opposite the present junction of Pleasant Street. At the time of the witchcraft trials, in 1692, preliminary examinations of accused persons were held there. The "Blue Anchor Tavern," was probably near the site of the Philip English mansion, on English Street. This was in 1678. A third "Ship Tavern" was once kept on or near the present corner of Essex and Crombie streets. In 1803, this was known as the "City Hotel." The Gov. Bradstreet house was known as the "Globe Tavern" in the early part of the 18th century. The "South Fields" residence of E. Hersey Derby is now a public house, known as the "Lafayette House."

Stages and Stage Companies.—The first record of a vehicle for carrying passengers is in 1761, when "a large stage chair," drawn by two horses, passed through Salem from Portsmouth, on its way to Boston, and returned, once a week. In 1766, a stage began to run between Salem and Boston, and one between Salem and Gloucester in 1796. Four years before, a "stage wagon" had run to Gloucester. Stages began to run to Haverhill in 1810; to South Andover, in 1819; to Lowell, in 1826; to Beverly (special) and to Danvers, in 1828; to Essex, in 1833; and to Ipswich about the same year. As early as 1774 a stage ran to Marblehead, occasionally, and in 1794 one was run from that town to Salem. A stage commenced running to Lynn, separate from the Boston stages, in 1832. The Salem and Boston Stage Company (a Salem institution) was incorporated in 1821, and, up to the time of the advent of the Eastern Railroad, in 1838, was a very successful concern, and was considered decidedly progressive. It was as well run and as well equipped as any line in the country, and was the first to introduce the "swing-rack and foot-board," and later, the steel-spring stages. Most of its coaches were built in its own shops in Salem, among the mechanics employed being Osgood Bradley, since the day of railroads a large and successful passenger-car builder in Worcester, and Joseph Smith and Daniel C. Manning, the present livery firm of Smith & Manning. William H. Foster, the present cashier of the Asiatic National Bank, was one of the clerks of the company. On the gradual dissolution of the concern, several of the drivers of the old stage company became in some way connected with the railroad company, a business nearer akin than any other to their "profession."

The Turnpike.—The Salem Turnpike and Chelsea Bridge Corporation was incorporated March 6, 1802. The road was opened for travel Sept. 22, 1803. It extended from Salem to the Charles River, and was twelve miles and 256 poles long. Tolls were abolished and the turnpike became a free public way Nov. 6, 1869.

Railroads.—The Eastern Railroad was opened from Boston to Salem Aug. 27, 1838. The first station building was of wood, and quite small. The present granite and brick structure was commenced in the spring of 1847. The Eastern road was opened to Marblehead Dec. 10, 1839; to Ipswich, Dec. 18, 1839; to Newburyport, June 19, 1840; to the New Hampshire line, Nov. 9, 1840. The tunnel under Washington and Essex streets was built in 1839. The Essex Railroad, Salem to Lawrence, was opened Sept. 5, 1848; the South Reading road, to South Reading (now Wakefield), in September, 1850; and the Salem and Lowell road, Aug. 1, 1850. Of the last three, the Lowell road is operated by the Boston, Lowell, and Nashua Railroad, and the other two by the Eastern road.

Newspapers.—Salem followed closely behind Cambridge and Boston in introducing the printing-press, Samuel Hall, a native of Medford, opening an office here in April, 1768. In the following July he established a paper, the " Essex Gazette," to be issued on each Tuesday. The first number appeared Aug. 2d, and was a folio ten by sixteen inches. In May, 1775, Mr. Hall removed to Cambridge and published his paper there till 1781, when he returned to Salem and started the "Salem Gazette." This paper he published for a little more than four years, removing to Boston and publishing the " Massachusetts Gazette " there. This removal from Salem was on account of heavy taxes levied on advertisements, which sadly reduced his income.

Before Mr. Hall's removal from Salem a paper was started, July 1, 1774, by Ezekiel Russell, and was called the " Salem Gazette and Newbury and Newburyport Advertiser." It terminated in a few months. " The American Gazette or Constitutional Journal," was published by Mr. Russell for a few weeks, commencing June 19, 1776. " The Salem Gazette and General Advertiser " was published by Mrs. Mary Crouch & Co., from Jan. 2, 1781, to October 11 of the same year. " The Salem Chronicle and Essex Advertiser " was published by George Roulstone, for something less than year, commencing March 30, 1786. The present " Salem Gazette " was commenced Oct. 14, 1786, John Dabney and Thomas C. Cushing issuing the first number under the title of the " Salem Mercury." It assumed the name of the " Salem Gazette " Jan. 5, 1790. The present " Gazette " is traced back in a direct line to Mr. Hall's first venture, and the " Gazette " of to-day bears, at the head of its column, the words, " Established, weekly, 1768; semi-weekly, 1796"; and its claim, as a continuation of Mr. Hall's paper, is founded upon the judgment of local antiquarians who were contemporary with Mr. Cushing. He had served his apprenticeship with Mr. Hall, and took his materials and revived the paper, after a break, in 1786. Mr. Caleb Foote, the present senior partner, served as an apprentice with Mr. Cushing,— so the line is traced down, connecting the first issue with that of the present day. Mr. Dabney withdrew in 1789, leaving Mr. Cushing sole proprietor. In 1794 William Carlton assumed the publication, and, in 1797, transferred it back to Mr. Cushing. On account of ill-health, the latter withdrew from the paper, and his son, Caleb Cushing, succeeded him. He published the paper for six months, with Ferdinand Andrews, who then took it alone. He sold one-half the establishment, in 1825, to Caleb Foote, and the other half in 1826 to William Brown. Jan. 1, 1833, Mr. Foote became sole proprietor, and is now the senior partner of the firm of Foote & Horton (N. A. Horton), who are the present publishers, the latter entering the firm in 1854, after a regular apprenticeship in the same office. It is now published as a semi-weekly, on each Tuesday and Friday morning. A weekly edition, the "Essex County Mercury," is issued on each Wednesday. This was started June 8, 1831.

The "Salem Register" was commenced May 12, 1800, as a semi-weekly. William Carlton was its publisher, and it was originally called the "Impartial Register," then the "Salem Register," the "Essex Register," and finally the "Salem Register" again. Mr. Carlton died July 24, 1805, and the paper was published for his widow, then "for the proprietors" for awhile, next by Haven Poole and Warwick Palfray, Jr. Mr. Poole died and the paper was continued by Mr. Palfray, and later by Mr. Palfray and Mr. John Chapman. On the death of Mr. Warwick Palfray, Jr., his son, Charles W., formed a partnership with Mr. Chapman. The latter died in 1873, and Mr. Eben N. Walton was admitted to the firm, which became Palfray & Walton. The "Register" is issued on each Monday and Thursday.

The "Salem Observer" was first issued Jan. 6, 1823, by William and Stephen B. Ives, as a weekly, appearing on each Monday evening. It was first published as the "Observer," next as the "Salem Observer," four years as the "Salem Literary and Commercial Observer," and last and now as the "Salem Observer" again. Its first two editors were B. Lynde Oliver, and Joseph G. Waters. George

W. Pease became a partner in 1837, and in 1839 Mr. Stephen B. Ives withdrew, leaving the firm, Ives & Pease. William Ives withdrew a few years ago, and Horace S. Traill became a partner. The "Observer" is now published by Pease, Traill & Fielden, Mr. Francis A. Fielden having been admitted Jan. 1, 1872. It is issued on Saturday mornings. Mr. Gilbert L. Streeter is its editor. Mr. Streeter wrote, in 1856, "an account of the newspapers and periodicals published in Salem," up to that year, and it contains much detailed information. The pamphlet is on file at the Essex Institute.

The "Salem Post" is the outgrowth of a free advertising sheet, published monthly by Charles H. Webber. On Jan. 1, 1873, it became a weekly, published by Mr. Webber and F. B. Browning, and was styled the "Salem City Post." For a time the publishing firm was Webber Bros., Mr. Putnam Webber being the junior partner. The "Post" is issued each Wednesday morning.

These four are the only newspapers now published in Salem, and, though neither of them is a daily, some one is issued on each morning of the week, except Sunday.

Many papers have been born in Salem only to die, most of them for want of support. Among them the "Salem Advertiser," published from 1832 to 1849; the "Salem Daily Chronicle," from March, 1848, to May 22, 1848; "Essex County Freeman," from Aug. 1, 1849, to June 14, 1854; the "Union Democrat," from July 31, 1852, to Oct. 6, 1852; the "People's Advocate," from Oct. 1854, to 1861; the "Salem Daily Journal," from July 24, 1854, to Nov. 24, 1855; the "Essex Statesman," from 1863 to 1868; the "Salem Enterprise," daily, from April 4, 1867, to Jan. 9, 1868; "Daily Evening News," a continuation of the "Enterprise," from March 4, 1868, to April 4, 1868. These were the most important. A host have been published during exciting political contests, for advertising purposes, or with a hope that they might gain a foothold in the community; but only the "Gazette," "Mercury," "Register," "Observer," and "Post," stand to-day as "news" papers. "The Pavilion" and "Fireside Favorite" are monthly advertising sheets that deserve mention, as they have been published regularly since 1869 and 1870 respectively. The latter is a successor of the "Hoop-Skirt," started in 1867.

Telegraph and Telephone. — The first communication between Salem and Boston by the magnetic telegraph was a dispatch sent by the

33

mayor of the former city to the mayor of the latter, Dec. 23, 1847. The first public exhibition of the telephone was made at Lyceum Hall, on the 12th of February, 1876, under the supervision of the inventor, A. Graham Bell. A despatch of a quarter of a column was sent by telephone the same evening to the "Boston Daily Globe," by Henry M. Batchelder, then connected with that paper. But three errors in receiving it were made, and it was the first despatch ever sent by telephone to a newspaper.

Salem Neck, like all other lands in this vicinity, was originally held in common and undivided. In 1714 the commoners granted the Neck lands and Winter Island, and from that date to 1728, the Neck was probably used for pasturage, and Winter Island for "the fishery"; that is, for drying fish. Who collected the rents cannot be determined; but, according to the vote of the commoners, the rents were to be paid into the town treasury. In 1729 the town let the lands on Winter Island to five shoremen. In 1735 it was voted to let so much as was sufficient to the shoremen, the remainder as a public pasture, and from 1738, up to 1824, the island was let for pasture lands. In March, 1756, the land on which the powder-house now stands, was let to Richard Derby for one shilling a year, and he built a wharf and warehouse. In 1859 the city authorities received $152 rent from Oliver M. Whipple (who had purchased the title of the Derby family) for the unexpired term of one thousand years. It is probable that, prior to 1714, the town owned a portion of the Neck, and the commoners the remainder. In 1765 the town treasurer was authorized to let Winter Island and the Neck together, for pasture lands. In 1679 there were so many people at Winter Island that John Clifford was licensed to keep a victualling house for their convenience.

The Neck has a long story in connection with the coast defences of the Colony and Commonwealth. Block-houses, stockades, and earthworks, almost innumerable, have been built there on various threatening occasions, ever since the first settlement. Their history is difficult to trace; but the notes which follow pertain to the most important defences. A ship which arrived in 1629 brought five cannon; but these were probably for the Darby Fort on the Marblehead shore, at Naugus Head, built about that year, as near as can be decided from the records.

A fort on the Salem shore (Winter Island) was commenced in 1643.

Felt says that in 1758 the Neck had "long been guarded" by two block-houses at the gate, and by another at Watch-house Point, familiarly called Hospital Point. Besides these defences, it had a fort on its heights, called "new," to distinguish it from the old one on Winter Island. In 1690 the Winter Island fort was repaired, and breastworks thrown up on the heights of the Neck. In 1699 the Winter Island fort was called Fort William, in honor of the king, and in 1704, Fort Ann, in honor of the queen. A new fort was built in 1742, on the heights of the Neck, the location fortified in 1690. In 1775 Fort Lee was built on the site of the fort of 1742. In 1787 there were three forts, known as William, Lee, and Juniper, the latter on the site of the present summer settlement at Juniper Point. In 1794 Fort William was ceded to the United States. In 1799 the name of Fort William was changed to Fort Pickering, by order of the secretary of war. In 1814 these forts were rebuilt, and Forts Pickering and Lee again in 1863, after the breaking out of the civil war. Both are now in a dilapidated condition.

The noted frigate "Essex," thirty-two guns, was built on the south side of Winter Island in 1799, and launched, September 30 of that year, from a spot not far from the lighthouse.

Old Mills.—Capt. William Trask, an original planter, erected one of the first mills in New England.* It was built on a small brook, running into the North River, near the Lowell Railroad station in Peabody. The first machinery was a "mortar mill" for pounding corn. Various changes were made at different times in the construction and uses of the building or buildings on this foundation. In 1692 it was rebuilt for a fulling mill. In 1640 Capt. Trask obtained permission, and, some years later, erected a mill a half mile further down the North River, and in a short time moved it another half mile down stream. This became known as Frye's Mill, being under the direction, the latter part of the century, of William Frye, father and son. In June, 1663, permission was granted to Walter Price, Henry Bartholomew, John Gardner, and Samuel Gardner, to build a mill on the South River, and it was completed in 1664. It was on the site of the grist-mill removed a few years ago by the Eastern Railroad, to build the engine-house, on Mill Street.†

* This was probably *the first* mill in New England.

† See "Bulletin of the Essex Institute," Vol. III.—an article on "Old Mills," by the Hon. James Kimball.

There was a windmill near "Burial Point," the present Charter Street Cemetery. The mill probably stood near Liberty Street, and the field became known as " Windmill Field." This was previous to 1660. Another windmill stood near Northey Street.

Glass Making. — For Salem is claimed the establishment of the first glass works in New England. The evidence is found in the early town records. In 1638 the following appears : — " 27th of the 11th. mo. 1638 — granted to Obadiah Hullme one acre of land for a house neere to the glasse house." Hence the manufacture of glass must have been established as early as 1638. This " glasse house " was located in a field now lying between Boston and Aborn streets, a part of which is owned by Gen. William Sutton. Glass slag has frequently been plowed up there.

Fire Clubs. — Associations known as " fire clubs " have existed in Salem since 1744. In the active days of these clubs, each member was required to have two substantial leather buckets, and they were usually painted with the name and device of the club. Many of these buckets may still be found hanging in the front or rear hall-ways of the old houses of Salem, usually under the stairs or on some projection or cornice. These buckets were kept thus handy, and when an alarm of fire was given, the owner was supposed to take his buckets and repair to the scene of the fire, to assist in passing water from the cisterns to the tubs of the engines, or to throw it on to the fire directly. This of course was before the introduction of the suction-hose. Each member of the clubs was also provided with a bag, in which to take property from buildings, and a bed-key to take down the old-fashioned bedsteads. Most of the clubs had ladders at convenient places about the town. In later years, these organizations having been mainly surpassed in usefulness by the introduction of improved fire apparatus, they have been maintained as social clubs, an annual meeting and supper being held, at which officers were chosen and reminiscences of former days related. The only clubs now in existence are the Enterprise, the Naumkeag, and Alert. The following clubs, with their dates of organization, were the most important of those that have existed in Salem : Old Fire Club, 1744; Union, 1770; Social, 1774; Number Five, 1783; Social (2), 1793; Amity, 1796; Relief, 1803; Washington, 1803; Adroit, 1806; Active, 1806; Hamilton, 1809; Enterprise, 1810; Union and Amity, 1812; Volant, 1816; Adroit (2), 1831;

Naumkeag, 1832; Boston Street; Sons of Temperance; Alert Social; Social (3).

These were active and useful organizations in their day. Some of them lived but a few months or years, while three, enumerated above, have come down to the present time.

The Post-Office. — The methods employed in carrying and distributing the mails have changed with the needs of the country, beginning in 1639, when the General Court ordered that all letters "from beyond the seas" should be deposited with Richard Fairbanks, of Boston, who was to receive one penny each for their delivery. In 1693 the postage from Salem to Boston was fourpence. Edward Norris was postmaster at Salem in 1768, and re-appointed by the Provincial Congress May 13, 1775. The post-office was then in a shop on Washington Street. In 1779 Mascoll Williams succeeded Mr. Norris, and the office was nearly opposite Mechanic Hall, on Essex Street. By 1792 there was a daily mail to Boston, transported by stage. The Marblehead mail was carried on foot, by a Mr. Fabens, who had lost one arm. John Dabney succeeded Mr. Williams, and after Aug. 21, 1792, kept the office at the corner of Essex and Washington streets. He removed in 1800 to the corner of Essex and Central streets, and afterwards to a new building at the foot of Central Street, on Concert Square. His last location was on the premises on Essex Street occupied by Bowker Place. Joseph E. Sprague succeeded Mr. Dabney in 1816. He moved the office to Franklin Building; to the corner of Court and Essex streets in 1817; to the corner of Essex and St. Peter's streets in 1818, and there it remained while he continued in office. Eben Putnam succeeded him in 1829, and the office remained for awhile in the last-named location, and was then removed to the East India Marine Hall Building, where it continued to be kept until Feb. 24, 1855, when it was removed to its present location in the Asiatic Building. Charles W. Woodbury succeeded Mr. Putnam as postmaster March 1, 1840, and held the office until Caleb Foote was appointed, in May, 1841. Benjamin F. Browne succeeded Mr. Foote in August, 1844, and was himself succeeded by George Russell in February, 1849. George B. Loring succeeded Mr. Russell in June, 1853, and was followed by Joseph S. Perkins in 1858. John Ryan was appointed in 1860, and continued in office until the appointment of John Chapman in 1861. Mr. Chapman was succeeded by

William W. Lander in 1867, and upon his removal from office, in 1869, George H. Pierson was appointed, and is the present postmaster of Salem.

Military Companies. — From the days of the first settlement, Salem has maintained organized bodies of soldiery. The earliest mention in the old records is only brief, but enough is found to prove that some organization existed. A Salem company saw service against the Dutch in Acadia at the capture of St. John and Port Royal, in 1654. In 1675 five Salem men were killed in an engagement with the Indians at Bloody Brook; and thirty-one Salem men were impressed for an expedition against the Narragansetts. During this campaign two Salem men were killed, and four wounded. Salem men were engaged in a battle with the Indians at Cocheco, in 1676. In 1707, "our soldiers, troop and foot," went to Haverhill to meet the French and Indians; two were killed and two wounded. Salem sent a quota in the Port Royal expedition, in 1710; and, in 1711, "twenty men of Col. Hathorn's Regiment" sailed in the English fleet for Canada. In 1745 a company of fifty was raised for the expedition against Louisburg. Timothy Pickering was chosen colonel of the 1st Regiment, Feb. 13, 1775, and his regiment marched to Lexington, April 19, 1775, but arrived too late to take part in the skirmish.

In April, 1776, the first uniformed infantry company appears under Capt. Joseph Sprague and Lieut. Joseph Hiller. A portion of Col. Pickering's regiment was at Bunker Hill, but does not appear to have fought there as an organization, though Lieut. Benjamin West is reported killed. The command fought through the war.

The present Second Corps of Cadets was organized July 10, 1786, with Stephen Abbott as its first commander. The uniform was red and white, and these colors have always been retained. The Cadets furnished a large proportion of the nucleus of the 24th Massachusetts Regiment in the civil war, and the corps was represented largely in the 2d and 19th Regiments and 1st Heavy Artillery. The corps is now a battalion of two companies, under Lieut. Col. Samuel Dalton.

In 1786 there was a volunteer company in Ward IV. The Salem Artillery made its first parade May 23, 1787, and continued with varying fortunes till the opening of the Rebellion, when it was merged with the 4th Massachusetts Battery. In 1798, a company of "exempts" was formed.

The present Salem Light Infantry was formed May 11, 1805, Capt. John Saunders commanding. It adopted the French Zouave drill at the opening of the Rebellion. It served in one of the "three months" regiments; in the "nine months" and "100 days" campaigns; furnished full companies in the 8th, 23d, and 50th regiments; and was represented in the 32d, 35th, and other Massachusetts organizations. The company is now attached to the 8th Regiment, and is under Capt. Jonathan Osborne.

The present Salem Mechanic Light Infantry was formed Feb. 26, 1807, and paraded for the first time July 4, 1807, under Capt. Perley Putnam. It served in the 5th Regiment during the civil war, as a "three months" organization. Its members afterwards saw service in several different regiments. The Essex Hussars existed for a short time, about 1808. In 1811, two new companies were organized, making eight in Salem at that time. The Essex Guards first paraded July 4, 1814, and became extinct at the close of the War of 1812. The Salem City Guards were formed Nov. 14, 1846, with Robert H. Farrant as captain, and made their first parade May 31, 1847. This organization was attached to the 5th Regiment at the opening of the civil war. It disbanded before the close of the war.

Ex-members of the Cadets and Salem Light Infantry have formed veteran associations, and have occasional parades, and elect officers annually. The Veteran Cadet Association was formed Oct. 11, 1866, with Gen. William Sutton as its first commander. The Salem Light Infantry Veteran Association was formed Nov. 11, 1862, with George Peabody as the first commander. The "veteran" members of the Mechanic Light Infantry have paraded several times, but have formed no definite organization.

Bands.— The first permanent military band in Salem was organized in June, 1837, and from this the present Salem Brass Band has descended. Prior to that year, it had been the custom for six or eight musicians to play together at parades. They were denominated "martial music." There had been an attempt to form a band at an earlier date, but after a very brief and feeble existence it dissolved. The first leader of the Salem Band was F. W. Moore. Jerome Smith succeeded him as leader, and at his death the now famous P. S. Gilmore became his successor. Under his direction the band soon acquired a high prestige, and became one of the first musical organizations in the Commonwealth. Gilmore was followed by Kerrahn, "the jolly trumpeter;" he, in turn, by J. H. Parsons, James Faxon, and the present energetic leader, Mr. John M. Flockton, Jr.

The Bay State Band was formed in 1852, and continued for several years a popular organization.

The Naumkeag Band, composed of members of the Naumkeag Boat Club, existed from 1870 to 1874.

The Salem Cadet Band, enlisted by the Second Corps of Cadets, M. V. M., was organized in the spring of 1878, by Mr. Jean M. Missud, a native of Nice, Sardinia, a musician of high reputation. Under his direction the band has attained high rank.

The Catholic Temperance Band is an excellent organization, composed of members of the Father Mathew Temperance Society. It has existed for several years.

Halls. — Salem is very well provided with halls suited for theatrical performances, concerts, dancing parties, and all description of public assemblies. Mechanic Hall is the largest and finest in the city. It is on the west corner of Essex and Crombie streets. It was built in 1839 by the Mechanic Hall Corporation, and in 1870 was enlarged and entirely remodelled. Its seating capacity is 1,093, and the stage is well adapted and furnished with good scenery for theatrical purposes. The interior of the hall is neat and beautiful, and its furnishings are in the most approved modern design. The hall has a very fine concert organ, built by J. H. Wilcox & Co., of Boston, and placed in the hall at the time of the remodelling, 1870. A company of seven gentleman, Messrs. Richard C. Manning, George M. Whipple, A. Aug. Smith, Jos. H. Webb, George Perkins, Thomas H. Johnson, and Parker L. Walker, associated themselves as a committee to ensure an organ for the hall, and this committee devised and executed the means which secured the instrument. The sum of $2,779.83 was raised by a general subscription; entertainments conducted by the organ committee netted $1,242.70; $330 was received for rent of the organ after it was placed in the hall, and the Mechanic Hall Corporation assumed the balance of the expense incurred by the committee, $1,839.90. Lyceum Hall, on Church Street, was built in 1830, and is the property of the Salem Lyceum. The hall was opened Jan. 19, 1831. The hall is semi-circular, amphitheatre form, and is well adapted for lectures. It seats about six hundred. Hamilton

VIEW ON CHESTNUT STREET.

VIEW ON LAFAYETTE STREET

Heliotype Printing Co., Boston.

Hall was built about 1810 by a company of gentlemen who intended it for assemblies, a use to which it has always been largely devoted. Many important events have been commemorated within its walls, including the fourth and fifth half centuries of the landing of Gov. Endicott. The hall has always been kept in excellent repair, and has been refitted within a half dozen years, and is to-day as ever a favorite gathering place for dancing and other parties. Central Hall, on Central Street, built in 1869, is well adapted for small parties and entertainments. It was for a number of years leased by Post 34, Grand Army. Each of the military companies occupies an armory sufficiently large for all gatherings of its own, and they are frequently let for public assemblies or dancing parties. The Young Men's Catholic Temperance Society has a good-sized hall, called Nonantum Hall, on Warren Street; and the Grand Army Post occupies a hall in Essex Block, St. Peter's Street. The Odd Fellows have nice halls in the Asiatic Building, Washington Street, and the Ancient Order of Hibernians in the Phœnix Block, Lafayette Street.

There has been no regular theatre in Salem since 1832, when the old Salem Theatre building on Crombie Street was sold to the Crombie Street Church Society. This building was erected for theatrical purposes in 1828, and was known as the Salem Theatre. Aaron J. Phillips was its manager and lessee. The first play performed there was the comedy, " Wives as They Were." The theatre was run to a losing business four years, and was then sold as above mentioned.

Cemeteries. — The Charter Street Cemetery is the oldest burying-ground in Salem, and was occupied before 1637. Among others interred there are Hilliard Veren, Martha Corey, Richard Derby, Warwick Palfray, Benjamin Lynde, William Browne, Simon Forester, and Deliverance Parkman. The Broad Street Cemetery was commenced about 1655. Capt. George Curwin, the sheriff of witchcraft days, is buried there. The Howard Street Cemetery was commenced about 1801. A part of it was originally reserved for colored people, and a part for strangers. The Orne Street Cemetery was originally laid out in 1807, and contained about two and a half acres. In 1864 about six acres were added to the former reservation. A soldiers' lot of eight thousand feet was set apart in 1872. Harmony Grove, near the Peabody line, is the largest and newest resting-place for the dead. It contains sixty-five acres, and is a beautiful spot, kept in the nicest

34

order. It was commenced in 1840. Many fine monuments and beautiful enclosures are here to be found. The Roman Catholic burying-ground, in North Salem, was laid out a few years since. The Quaker burying-ground, on Essex Street, occupies a lot of land adjoining the site of an old Quaker church.

"*The Willows*" is a portion of the north-eastern point of Salem Neck, and derived its name from the fact of there being there some large willow-trees. It was formerly known as "Hospital Point," and before that as "Watch-house Point." It has always been a favorite resort for picnic parties, and is now a public pleasure-park, controlled by the city. It is neatly laid out, and one large and several smaller pavilions have been erected. Its situation is a beautiful one, and the view of the harbor, the north shore toward Cape Ann, and the peninsula of Marblehead, is a rare bit of scenery. The tracks of the Naumkeag Street Railway extend to the Willows, conveying people thither in twenty minutes from the centre of the city.

Juniper Point, or "The Juniper," lies east of the Willows. Its historic features have been traced in an account of the early forts. It is now the locality of a large summer settlement of cottagers, mainly from Lowell and Nashua, but including some Salem people. The cottages extend all along the shore toward the Willows. Streets are laid out, and the little settlement is as regularly visited by the butcher, baker, and milkman as the city itself.

The Islands of Salem Harbor. — The principal islands of Salem Harbor are Baker's, Misery, and Lowell. The first-named was so denominated as early as 1630. It lies about four miles off the Salem shore, and contains about fifty-five acres. The United States government maintains two light-houses on this island. Misery Island was first called Moulton's Misery. It contains about sixty-four acres, and is connected by a bar with the "Little Misery." Lowell Island was granted, in 1655, to Gov. Endicott by the General Court. It was bequeathed in 1684, by Z. Endicott, to his daughters, under the name of Cotta Island. It was later known as Cat Island, and received the name Lowell when a party of Lowell people built a hotel there, a few years ago. In 1774, a small-pox hospital on the island, owned by the town of Marblehead, was burned by a mob. The chief of the smaller islands are Cony, Eagle, the Gooseberries, Ram, and Tinker, the three last owned by the city.

Distinguished Visitors. — Salem has entertained a large number of distinguished visitors. Lafayette was here Oct. 29, 1784, and attended a public dinner at Concert Hall, and a ball in the evening. He was in Salem again Aug. 31, 1824. On the 29th of October, 1789, George Washington visited Salem, and was entertained at the residence of Joshua Ward, on Washington Street. The house is now occupied by Dr. J. E. Fiske. James Monroe was in Salem July 8, 1817; Andrew Jackson, June 26, 1833; James K. Polk, July 5, 1847; and Ulysses S. Grant, Oct. 17, 1871. These comprise all the presidents of the United States who have been in Salem during their official term.

Historical Celebrations. — The landing of Gov. Endicott has twice been fitly celebrated in Salem. The 200th anniversary was observed Sept. 18, 1828. A procession, under the escort of the Cadets and Mechanic Light Infantry, marched to the North Meeting-House, and there were held commemorative exercises, the Hon. Joseph Story delivering the oration. The Rev. Dr. Prince and the Rev. Mr. Emerson offered prayers, and the Rev. Mr. Brazer read scriptural selections. At Hamilton Hall a dinner was spread, to which the company adjourned from the church. The venerable Dr. E. A. Holyoke presided, assisted by Judge Story, the vice-president of the Essex Historical Society, the Hon. William Reed, Willard Peele, Pickering Dodge, and the Hon. Gideon Barstow. Among the distinguished guests present were: Gov. Levi Lincoln, Lieut. Gov. Winthrop, the Hon. Daniel Webster, the Hon. Edward Everett, the Hon. B. W. Crowninshield, the Hon Josiah Quincy, Col. Aaron Ogden of New Jersey, Senor M. L. de la Vidaurre of Peru, William Shaler, consul at Algiers, Judge Davis, Gens. Sullivan and Dearborn, and Profs. Farrar and Ticknor.

The 250th anniversary of the landing of Gov. Endicott * was observed Sept. 18, 1878, under the auspices of the Essex Institute. At Mechanic Hall, at 11 A. M., there were appropriate exercises, and at 2 P. M. a lunch was served at Hamilton Hall, and this was followed by speeches from distinguished guests. The forenoon programme was as follows: Reading of Scripture, by the Rev. R. C. Mills, chaplain of the day; prayer, by the Rev. Dr. Mills; singing of an original hymn,

---

* A complete account of this noteworthy celebration may be found in a handsome volume published by the Essex Institute. It contains the oration, the poems, and a stenographic report of the speeches.

written by the Rev. Jones Very; poem, by the Rev. Charles T. Brooks, of Newport, R. I.; original ode, by the Rev. S. P. Hill; oration, by the Hon. W. C. Endicott, judge of the supreme court, and a lineal descendant of Gov. Endicott; singing of Mrs. Hemans's hymn, "The Breaking Waves Dashed High," by Mrs. J. H. West; poem written for the occasion by W. W. Story, and read by Prof. J. W. Churchill of Andover; singing of the 100th psalm; benediction, by the chaplain. At Hamilton Hall, Dr. Henry Wheatland, president of the Essex Institute, presided, and a distinguished company sat at the tables. After the lunch, which was one better entitled to the name of banquet, a number of toasts were offered by the Rev. E. C. Bolles, who was toast-master, and they were replied to by the following gentlemen: Gov. A. H. Rice, Mayor H. K. Oliver, the Hon. Robert C. Winthrop, president of the Massachusetts Historical Society; the Hon. Marshall P. Wilder, president of the New England Historic Genealogical Society; the Rt. Rev. Dean Stanley, of Westminister Abbey; the Hon. W. C. Endicott, orator of the day; the Hon. Leverett Saltonstall; Prof. Benjamin Peirce, of Harvard College; the Rev. Fielder Israel, pastor of the First Church; B. H. Silsbee, Esq., president of the East India Marine Society; and J. H. Choate, Esq., of New York.

The one hundredth anniversary of the destruction of tea in Boston Harbor was also observed under the auspices of the Essex Institute, Dec. 16, 1873. The principal feature was an address by the Hon. James Kimball.

On the 5th of October, 1874, there was celebrated in Salem, the Essex Institute again taking the honor of inaugurating and carrying out the observance, the centennial anniversary of the assembling here of the first Provincial Congress. Abner C. Goodell, Jr., Esq., one of the vice-presidents of the Institute, delivered an address on this occasion.

On Friday, Feb. 26, 1875, the city authorities duly commemorated the centennial anniversary of the expedition of Col. Leslie to Salem in search of Provincial cannon. A public assembly and addresses, with religious and patriotic services at the North Church, constituted the most prominent feature of the day's celebration. A salute of one hundred guns was fired at noon, the bells rung at morning, noon, and night, and the national flag displayed on the public buildings. The order of exercises at the church was as follows: Voluntary; prayer by the Rev. E. B. Willson, pastor of the church; original ode by Miss L. L. A. Very; address by Mayor Henry L. Williams; address by the Hon. George B. Loring; national song; address by the Rev. E. B. Willson; music — "America."

The Centennial Fourth of July (1876) was celebrated in Salem in a becoming manner. The chief part of the celebration consisted of a civic, military, floral, and trades procession, three miles or more in length. Salutes, fire-works, and other ordinary parts of a Fourth of July programme were in addition to the procession.

CHAPTER XII.

THE SALEM OF TO-DAY — HER PLACE AMONG THE CITIES OF THE
COMMONWEALTH.

The preceding chapters have given the readers a general insight into
the history of the good old city of Salem. Her progress has been
traced from the day on which Conant and his associates landed and
founded Naumkeag, through two centuries and a half — each one of
the two hundred and fifty years adding something to her fair name.
There have been dark passages in her annals; but no city
escapes some record that is not regretted when it has been engraven
by time on the page of history. More than any other place in the
county of Essex, Salem has attracted attention from the students of
local history. Within her borders was commenced the first permanent settlement of the county. In her early days she ranked with
Boston in importance, and had her location been as well adapted, she
would have been the capital of the State. Within the old town limits
centred the terrible witchcraft delusion of 1692 — the history of
which forms the one dark page in the chronicle of her progress. Her
commercial record is more brilliant than that of any other port in the
country. Here assembled the first Provincial Congress, and in Salem
was shed the first blood of the Revolution.

A quaint old city, Salem is often called; but she is not quaint to
that degree that she might be deemed a disagreeable place to those
who abide within her walls. Her antique features serve rather to
furnish a pleasing variation, and an added attraction to the general
modernness. Salem is no decrepit, tumble-down city. Modern
structures are the rule, not the exception. Her public buildings are
substantial and ornamental; her business blocks well built and of
pleasing architectural design, and fine houses adorn many streets in
the residence portion of the city. Salem is withal beautifully situated,
lying in a section of country which abounds in the loveliest natural

scenery, and bordered by a harbor that is one of the most picturesque on the Massachusetts coast. Her people are cultivated and social, and no pleasanter community could be desired for a home.

Salem has been a progressive place — progressive in that stronger sense, that means real advancement. Her growth has not been fabulous, or even rapid, but a steady pushing forward, till the Salem of to-day holds a high place among the cities of the Commonwealth. Though her commerce has fled, business of other and many sorts furnishes life to the municipality and employment to her citizens.

Purity and progress have always been her aim; and she has so nearly lived up to her aspirations that her record is almost an unblemished one. Her literary and scientific societies are numerous and prosperous, and her benevolent and charitable institutions are many; and all on the most liberal and stable basis. Salem has always afforded the best means of education for the young, and her school-system to-day is unsurpassed by that of any city of the Union. Salem's sons have won distinction and honor in all lands, and many who have made her the home of their adoption, have added to her already widespread honors. Few cities can point to such names in their annals, as those of Bowditch, and Hawthorne, and Prescott, and Story, and Choate. To do the city justice in chronicling the acts and deeds of her noted sons, would alone fill a volume. The list includes statesmen, merchants, scientists, and philanthropists; and to-day she can take just pride in men doing their full part in sustaining and perpetuating her good name. Her record in the councils of nation and State has been a worthy one; and she has to-day, for the fourteenth time, the honor of furnishing the representative of the Essex District in the National Congress. Of legal talent, Salem has always had the best of the time, and to-day, three judges of State courts reside within her borders, — Judges Lord and Endicott of the supreme bench, and Chief Justice Brigham, of the superior court, — each of them honored graduates from service at the bar. Eminent divines have filled her churches with their eloquence, and there always have been among her citizens, noted literary men, scholars, and orators. Salem has ever been deeply interested in scientific progress, and has attracted to her institutions many of the prominent men of their time. Not many cities can point to such literary institutions as Salem has; and in art, as well as literature and science, she takes high rank. Her artists have contributed worthy tributes to her honor, and the sculptors, Story and Rogers, revere her as their birthplace.

Of Salem, the old and the new, her citizens are alike proud; and their earnest desire for a bright and honorable future for their beloved city, is fully shared by her sons and daughters abroad, though they have long been dwellers without her gates.

APPENDIX.

LIST OF ILLUSTRATIONS.

Frontispiece:

EDWARD A. HOLYOKE.—Copied from a picture by James Frothingham, in the possession of the Essex Institute. The portrait was taken when Dr. Holyoke was about ninety years old. (See page 242.)

Facing page 14:

JOHN ENDICOTT.—Copied from an engraving. Gov. Endicott died March 15, 1665. He came from Dorchester in Dorsetshire, England. He moved to Boston a short time before his death, which occurred when he was seventy-seven years old.

SIMON BRADSTREET.—Copied from a painting in the possession of the Essex Institute. (See page 38.)

TIMOTHY PICKERING.—Copied from an engraving. Col. Pickering was "a clerk in the office of the registry of deeds" at the time of the death of Col. John Higginson, the register, and was appointed his successor, holding the office from September, 1774, to July, 1777, when he resigned to enter the army under Washington. (See page 240.)

LEVERETT SALTONSTALL.—From a portrait by Charles Osgood, now in the possession of the Essex Institute. The portrait is a copy from an original by Chester Harding. (See page 57.)

Facing page 30:

ROGER WILLIAMS HOUSE.—From a drawing in the possession of the Essex Institute. (See page 252.)

BRADSTREET HOUSE.—From a drawing in the possession of the Essex Institute. (See page 251.)

PICKMAN HOUSE.—From a lithograph in the possession of the Essex Institute. The house was built by Col. Benjamin Pickman in 1750. On its site once stood a house built by Henry Bartholomew, soon after the settlement of the town, and which was purchased in 1680 by Timothy Lindall, a prominent merchant of his day. Mr. Lindall died in 1699 and gave it to his widow, who, about the time of her death, in 1732, gave it to her daughter, Sarah Lindall. In 1749, Sarah Lindall (then Mrs. Morehead) gave the house and land to her nephew, Benjamin Pickman, who in 1750 pulled it down and built the house above alluded to. (See page 186.)

ELIAS HASKET DERBY HOUSE.—This picture is from a drawing. The house was built by Mr. Derby in 1799, at a cost of $80,000, and was completed a few months before his death. After his decease it became the property of his eldest son; but with the embargo and war there came a check to the prosperity of Salem, and although Mr. Derby left seven children in prosperous circumstances, and many merchants had risen to wealth in Salem, none of them were then willing to cope with the expense and style attendant in such a structure. The house was closed for years, and finally was taken down and gave place to the square and market which now bear the name of Derby. (See page 132.)

Facing page 46 :

Views on Essex and Washington streets, from photographs taken in the month of April, 1879.

Facing page 56 :

CITY HALL. (See page 55.)
CUSTOM HOUSE. (See page 203.)
COURT HOUSES. (See page 10.)
EASTERN RAILROAD STATION. (See page 254.)
Copied from photographs taken in the month of April, 1879.

Facing page 102 :

HIGH SCHOOL. (See page 102.)
NORMAL SCHOOL. (See page 108.)
PLUMMER HALL. (See page 111.)
PEABODY ACADEMY OF SCIENCE. (See page 115.)
Copied from photographs taken in the month of April, 1879.

Facing page 112 :

Two Interiors at Plummer Hall from photographs taken in the month of April, 1879. (See page 111.)

Facing page 116 :

Two Interiors at the Peabody Academy of Science, from photographs taken in the month of April, 1879. (See page 115.)

Facing page 130 :

ELIAS HASKET DERBY.—Copied from a portrait by James Frothingham, in the possession of the East India Marine Society. (See page 130.)
WILLIAM GRAY.—Copied from a portrait in the possession of the East India Marine Society. The original picture from which the portrait just mentioned was copied was painted by Gilbert Stuart. (See page 132.)
WILLIAM ORNE.—Taken from a portrait by Charles Osgood, now in the possession of the Essex Institute. The portrait is a copy from an original by Gilbert

Stuart. Mr. Orne was a prominent and successful East India merchant, who was born Feb. 4, 1751, and died Oct. 14, 1815.

JOSEPH PEABODY.—Copied from a portrait by James Frothingham, in the possession of his son, George Peabody, Esq. (See page 133.)

Facing page 146:

The ship " George." From a sketch in the possession of Capt. Charles H. Allen of Salem. The "George" made twenty voyages between Salem and Calcutta. (See page 146.)

Facing page 160:

NATHANIEL SILSBEE.—Copied from a portrait in the possession of the East India Marine Society. (See page 246.)

DUDLEY L. PICKMAN.—Copied from a portrait in the possession of the East India Marine Society. Mr. Pickman was born in Salem, in 1779, and died Nov. 4, 1846. He was an eminent and enterprising merchant, and was largely engaged in trade with the East Indies. He was a member of both branches of the State Legislature.

ROBERT UPTON.—Copied from a photograph. Mr. Upton was born in Salem, Feb. 16, 1788, and died there Sept. 9, 1863. He was a successful merchant, engaged principally in trade with South American ports. His sons continued the business for many years, and a large proportion of the Salem trade with the eastern ports of South America was in the hands of members of this family.

NATHANIEL L. ROGERS.—Taken from one of the earliest daguerreotypes, now in the possession of his family. Mr. Rogers was among the most enterprising and prominent merchants of Salem, and opened the American trade with Zanzibar and Australia. He was born in Ipswich, Aug. 6, 1785, and died July 31, 1858.

Facing page 182:

ROBERT BROOKHOUSE.—Copied from a photograph. Mr. Brookhouse was born Dec. 8, 1779, and died June 10, 1866. He was engaged in trade with Madagascar, Patagonia, the Feejee Islands, and largely with the west coast of Africa. He was very successful as a merchant, and accumulated a large property.

STEPHEN C. PHILLIPS.—Copied from a lithograph. (See page 57, and the account of the Manila trade.)

EDWARD D. KIMBALL.—Copied from a picture now in the possession of his widow. Mr. Kimball died in Paris, Sept. 22, 1867, aged 56 years. He was eminently successful as a merchant, amassing a large fortune. His vessels were found in the ports of the East Indies, and he was largely engaged in trade with the west coast of Africa.

JOHN BERTRAM.—Copied from a photograph in the possession of the trustees of the Old Men's Home in Salem. (See page 134.)

Facing page 240:

NATHANIEL BOWDITCH.—Copied from a portrait by Charles Osgood, painted for and now in the possession of the East India Marine Society. (See page 247.)

NATHANIEL HAWTHORNE.—Copied from a photograph. (See page 208.)

JOSEPH STORY.—Copied from a portrait by Charles Osgood, now in the possession of the Essex Institute. (See page 241.)

DANIEL A. WHITE.—Copied from an engraving. (See page 241.)

Facing page 250 :

PICKERING HOUSE.—This house stands on Broad Street, and was built about 1650, by John Pickering, whose descendants have ever since retained it in their possession. It is the birthplace of Col. Timothy Pickering, and is occupied to-day by one of his lineal descendants.

HAWTHORNE HOUSE.—The birthplace of Nathaniel Hawthorne. (See page 208.)

NARBONNE HOUSE.—This house, which stands on Essex Street, nearly opposite Pleasant Street, was built by Thomas Ives before 1680. It was owned and occupied by Capt. Simon Willard in the latter part of the seventeenth century. It is now owned and occupied by members of the Narbonne family.

OLD BAKE-HOUSE.—This house is situated on St. Peter Street, and is a good specimen of the style of architecture prior to the year 1700. But few houses were built, after that date, with the projecting second story. The house stands on land formerly owned by Christopher Waller, one of the early settlers of Salem.

The four pictures on this sheet are from photographs taken from the originals in April, 1879.

Facing page 264 :

Views on Chestnut and Lafayette streets, from photographs taken in April, 1879.

For the privilege of photographing pictures in their possession thanks are due to Mrs. Jonathan C. Perkins, Mrs. Edward D. Kimball, George Peabody, Francis H. Lee, Edward S. Rogers, George Upton, Charles H. Allen, and John Robinson, and to the officers of the Peabody Academy of Science, the Essex Institute, and the East India Marine Society. Thanks are also due to T. F. Hunt, of the Essex Institute, for assistance in the preparation of the illustrations.

The illustrations are by the heliotype process, and were made by the Heliotype Printing Company of Boston, from photographs taken expressly for this work.

NOTE. — In the preface to this work, the authors should have made their acknowledgments to the publishing firm of C. F. Jewett & Co., of Boston, for their kindness in permitting the use of material and standing type.

INDEX.

ImTheStory.com

Personalized Classic Books in many genre's

Unique gift for kids, partners, friends, colleagues

Customize:

- Character Names

- Upload your own front/back cover images (optional)

- Inscribe a personal message/dedication on the

  inside page (optional)

Customize many titles Including
- Alice in Wonderland
- Romeo and Juliet
- The Wizard of Oz
- A Christmas Carol
- Dracula
- Dr. Jekyll & Mr. Hyde
- And more...

Lightning Source UK Ltd.
Milton Keynes UK
UKOW01f0523181017
311192UK00009B/758/P